Practicing Organization Development

**The Change Agent Series
for Groups and Organizations**

MISSION STATEMENT

The books in this series are intended to be cutting-edge, state-of-the-art, and innovative approaches to participative change in organizational settings. They are written for, and written by, organization development (OD) practitioners interested in new approaches to facilitating participative change. They are geared to providing both theory and advice on practical application.

The Change Leader's Roadmap

The Change Leader's Roadmap

How to Navigate Your Organization's Transformation

Linda S. Ackerman Anderson
Dean Anderson

Foreword by Daryl R. Conner

JOSSEY-BASS/PFEIFFER
A Wiley Company
www.pfeiffer.com

Practicing
Organization
Development

Published by

JOSSEY-BASS/PFEIFFER

A Wiley Company
989 Market Street
San Francisco, CA 94103-1741
415.433.1740; Fax 415.433.0499
800.274.4434; Fax 800.569.0443

www.pfeiffer.com

Jossey-Bass/Pfeiffer is a registered trademark of John Wiley & Sons, Inc.

ISBN: 0-7879-5640-6
Library of Congress Catalog Card Number 00-011969

Copyright © 2001 byLinda Ackerman Anderson and Dean Anderson

Library of Congress Cataloging-in-Publication Data

Ackerman Anderson, Linda S., 1950-
  The change leader's roadmap : how to navigate your
organization's transformation / Linda S. Ackerman
Anderson, Dean Anderson.
      p. cm.—(The practicing organization development
series)
Includes bibliographical references and index.
  ISBN 0-7879-5640-6
  1. Leadership. 2. Organizational change. I.
Anderson, Dean, 1953- II. Title. III. Series.
  HD57.7 .D523 2001
  658.4′06—dc21

                              00-011969

Acquiring Editor: Matthew Holt   Senior Production Editor: Dawn Kilgore
Director of Development: Kathleen Dolan Davies   Manufacturing Manager: Becky Carreño
Developmental Editor: Susan Rachmeler   Interior and Cover Design: Bruce Lundquist
Editor: Rebecca Taff   Illustrations: Richard Sheppard

Printed in the United States of America

Printing 10 9 8 7 6 5 4 3

Contents

List of Tables, Figures, and Exhibits   xiii

Foreword to the Series   xv

Introduction to the Series   xvii

Statement of the Board   xxi

Foreword   xxvii

Dedication   xxx

Preface   xxxi

Acknowledgments   xxxv

Introduction   1

Section One
Upstream Change

1. Phase I: Prepare to Lead the Change: Start Up, Staff, and Create the Case for Change   **25**

Hearing the Wake-Up Call   26

Phase I: Prepare to Lead the Change   27

Activity I.A: Start Up and Staff the Change Effort   28

Activity I.B: Create the Case for Change and Determine Your
    Initial Desired Outcomes   39

Summary   50

Consulting Questions for Activity I.A   50

Consulting Questions for Activity I.B   52

2. Phase I: Prepare to Lead the Change: Assess the Organization's Readiness and Build Capacity for Change   55

Activity I.C: Assess the Organization's Readiness and Capacity
    to Succeed in the Change   55

Activity I.D: Build Leaders' Capacity to Lead the Change   59

Summary   71

Consulting Questions for Activity I.C   71

Consulting Questions for Activity I.D   71

3. Phase I: Prepare to Lead the Change: Identify and Build the Infrastructure and Conditions to Support the Change Effort   75

Activity I.E: Identify and Build the Infrastructure and Conditions
    to Support the Change Effort   76

Summary   106

Consulting Questions for Activity I.E   106

4. Phase I: Prepare to Lead the Change: Build the Change Strategy   113

Activity I.F: Clarify the Overall Change Strategy   114

Summary   124

Consulting Questions for Activity I.F   124

5. Phase II: Create Organizational Vision, Commitment, and Capacity   129

Activity II.A: Build Organizational Understanding of the
    Case for Change and the Change Strategy   130

Activity II.B: Create Shared Vision and Commitment   134

Activity II.C: Increase the Organization's Readiness and Capacity
    to Succeed in the Change   137

Activity II.D: Demonstrate that the Old Way of Operating Is Gone   141

Summary   143

Consulting Questions for Activity II.A   143

Consulting Questions for Activity II.B   143

Consulting Questions for Activity II.C   144

Consulting Questions for Activity II.D   145

6. Phase III: Assess the Situation to Determine Design Requirements   **147**

Activity III.A: Assess the Situation to Determine Design
   Requirements   148

Summary   153

Consulting Questions for Activity III.A   154

Section Two
Midstream Change

7. Phase IV: Design the Desired State   **159**

Activity IV.A: Design the Desired State   160

Summary   168

Consulting Questions for Activity IV.A   168

8. Phase V: Analyze the Impact   **171**

Activity V.A: Analyze the Impacts of the Desired State   173

Summary   177

Consulting Questions for Activity V.A   177

9. Phase VI: Plan and Organize for Implementation   **181**

Activity VI.A: Identify the Actions Required to Implement the
   Desired State and Develop the Implementation Master Plan   182

Activity VI.B: Prepare the Organization to Support
   Implementation   191

Summary   196

Consulting Questions for Activity VI.A   196

Consulting Questions for Activity VI.B   197

Section Three
Downstream Change

10. Phase VII: Implement the Change   **201**

Activity VII.A: Implement the Change   202

Summary   208

Consulting Questions for Activity VII.A   208

11. Phase VIII: Celebrate and Integrate the New State   **211**

Activity VIII.A: Declare, Celebrate, and Reward the Achievement
    of the Desired State   212

Activity VIII.B: Support Integration and Mastery
    of the New State   213

Summary   219

Consulting Questions for Activity VIII.A   219

Consulting Questions for Activity VIII.B   220

12. Phase IX: Learn and Course Correct   **223**

Activity IX.A: Build a System to Refine and Continuously
    Improve the New State   224

Activity IX.B: Learn from the Change Process and Establish
    Best Practices for Change   226

Activity IX.C: Dismantle the Temporary Change Support
    Structures, Management Systems, Policies, and Roles 228

Summary   231

Consulting Questions for Activity IX.A   231

Consulting Questions for Activity IX.B   232

Consulting Questions for Activity IX.C   232

Section Four
Leveraging the Change Process Model

13. Reactions to the Change Process Methodology   **235**

The Model as a Thinking Discipline   236

Developmental Stages for Learning the Change Process
    Methodology   236

Reactions to the Change Process Model 239

A Top-Down Versus a Multi-Directional Approach to Change 243

Summary 246

14. Opportunities for Leveraging the Change Process Methodology 247

Using the Change Process Model as an Operating System 248

Determining Who "Owns" the Change Process Model 251

Understanding the Just-in-Time Change Consulting Strategy 253

Accelerating the Change Process 258

Summary 259

15. Continuing the Journey to Conscious Transformation 261

Some Thoughts for Change Consultants 262

Some Thoughts for Leaders 263

Summary 265

Appendix: Phases, Activities, and Tasks of the
Change Process Model 267

Bibliography 275

About the Authors 285

About the Editors 289

Index 293

List of
Tables, Figures,
and Exhibits

Figure 0.1	The Drivers of Change Model	5
Figure 0.2	Twenty-One Dimensions of Conscious Transformation	7
Table 0.1	Comparison of the Industrial and Emerging Mindsets	9
Figure 0.3	The Fullstream Transformation Model	11
Figure 0.4	The Change Process Model for Leading Conscious Transformation	13
Figure 0.5	The Change Process Model As a Fullstream Process	15
Figure 0.6	The Change Process Model—Activity Level	17
Exhibit 1.1	Sample Project Community Map	35
Exhibit 1.2	Identifying the Project Community	37
Exhibit 1.3	Determining What Is Driving the Change	43
Exhibit 1.4	Initial Impact Analysis Audit	46
Figure 1.1	Three Types of Change	47

Exhibit 2.1	Team Effectiveness Assessment	68
Table 3.1	Five Levels of Communication	81
Figure 3.1	Course Correction Model	87
Exhibit 3.1	Checklist for Building Your Course Correction System	89
Figure 3.2	Seven Stages of Transition Model	91
Figure 3.3	Sample Temporary Change Structure and Sample Change Team Network Structure	94
Figure 4.1	Types of Participation	119
Exhibit 4.1	Template for Building Your Change Strategy	121
Exhibit 4.2	Highlights of a Sample Change Strategy	122
Exhibit 5.1	Vision for Your Transformation	135
Exhibit 6.1	Determining Your Design Requirements	149
Exhibit 7.1	How to Develop the Desired State Design	161
Figure 7.1	Levels of Design Model	165
Exhibit 8.1	Designing the Impact Analysis Process	174
Exhibit 8.2	Ways to Categorize Impact Issues	175
Exhibit 9.1	Questions for Resolving Impact Issues and Developing the Implementation Master Plan	183
Figure 9.1	Sample Flow Chart of an Implementation Master Plan	186
Exhibit 10.1	Change Process Topics to Monitor During Implementation	205
Exhibit 10.2	Desired State Topics to Monitor During Implementation	206
Exhibit 11.1	Integration and Mastery Strategies	216
Exhibit 12.1	Mechanisms to Continuously Improve the New State	225
Exhibit 12.2	Assessing the Change Process to Identify Best Practices	227
Exhibit 12.3	Designing Your Dismantling Strategy	230
Figure 13.1	Developmental Stages for Learning the Change Process Methodology	237
Exhibit 14.1	Determining the Value of Using a Change Process Operating System	250

Foreword
to the Series

ON **1967,** Warren Bennis, Ed Schein, and I were faculty members of the Sloan School of Management at MIT. We decided to produce a series of paperback books that collectively would describe the state of the field of organization development (OD). Organization development as a field had been named by myself and several others from our pioneer change effort at General Mills in Minneapolis, Minnesota, some ten years earlier.

Today I define OD as "a systemic and systematic change effort, using behavioral science knowledge and skill, to transform the organization to a new state."

In any case, several books and many articles had been written, but there was no consensus on whether OD was a field of practice, an area of study, or a profession. We had not even established OD as a theory or even as a practice.

We decided that there was a need for something that would describe the state of OD. Our intention was to each write a book and also to recruit three other authors. After some searching, we found a young editor who had just joined the small publishing house of Addison-Wesley. We made contact, and the series was born. Our audience was to be human resource professionals who spent their time consulting with managers in their development through various small-group activities, such as team building. More than thirty books have been published in that series, and the series has had a life of its own. We just celebrated its thirtieth anniversary.

At last year's National OD Network Conference, I said that it was time for the OD profession to change and transform itself. Is that not what we change agents tell our clients to do? This new Jossey-Bass/Pfeiffer series will do just that. It can be seen as:

- A documentation of the re-invention of OD;

- An effort that will take us to the next level; and

- A practical effort to transfer to the world the theory and practice of leading-edge practitioners and theorists.

The books in this new series will thus prove to be valuable resources for change agents to keep current with the new and leading-edge ideas and practices.

May this very exciting change agent series be most creative and innovative. May it give our field a renewed burst of energy and awareness.

Richard Beckhard
Written on Labor Day weekend 1999 from my summer cabin near Bethel, Maine

Introduction to the Series

"We must become the change we want to see."

—*Mahatma Gandhi*

"We live in a moment of history where change is so speeded up that we begin to see the present only when it is already disappearing."

—*R. D. Laing*

WE CAN EXPECT MORE CHANGE to occur in our lifetimes than has occurred since the beginning of civilization over ten thousand years ago. *Practicing Organization Development: The Change Agent Series for Groups and Organizations* is a new series of books being launched to help those who must cope with or create change in organizational settings. That includes almost everyone.

The Current State of Organization Development

Our view of OD in this series is an optimistic one. We believe that OD is gaining favor as decision makers realize that a balance *must* be struck between the drivers of change and the people involved in it and affected by it. Although OD does have

its disadvantages at a time characterized by quantum leap change, it remains prefer-able to such alternative approaches to change as coercion, persuasion, leadership change, and debate.[1] Organization development practitioners are reinventing their approaches, based on certain foundational roots of the field, in combination with emerging principles to ensure that OD will increasingly be recognized as a viable, important, and inherently participative approach to help people in organizations facilitate, anticipate, and manage change.

A Brief History of the Genesis of the OD Series

A few years ago, and as a direct result of the success of *Practicing Organization Development: A Guide for Practitioners* by Rothwell, Sullivan, and McLean, the publisher—feeling that OD was experiencing a rebirth of interest in the United States and in other nations—wanted to launch a new OD series. The goal of this new series was not to replace, or even compete directly with, the well-established Addison-Wesley OD Series (edited by Edgar Schein). Instead, as the editors saw it, this series would provide a means by which the most promising authors in OD whose voices had not previously been heard could share their ideas. The publisher enlisted the support of Bill Rothwell, Roland Sullivan, and Kristine Quade to turn the dream of a series into a reality.

This series was long in the making. After sharing many discussions with the publisher and circulating among themselves several draft descriptions of the series editorial guidelines, the editors were guests of Bob Tannenbaum, one of the field's founders, in Carmel, California, in February 1999 to discuss the series with a group of well-known OD practitioners interested in authoring books. Several especially supportive publisher representatives, including Matt Holt and Josh Blatter, were also present at that weekend-long meeting. It was an opportunity for diverse OD practitioners, representing many philosophical viewpoints, to come together to share their vision for a new book series. In a sense, this series represents an OD intervention in the OD field in that it is geared to bringing change to the field most closely associated with change management and facilitation.

---

[1]W. Rothwell, R. Sullivan, & G. McLean. (1995). Introduction (pp. 3–46). In W. Rothwell, R. Sullivan, & G. McLean, *Practicing Organization Development: A Guide for Consultants*. San Francisco, CA: Jossey-Bass/Pfeiffer.

What Distinguishes the Books in this Series

The books in this series are meant to be cutting-edge and state-of-the-art in their approach to OD. The goal of the series is to provide an outlet for proven authorities in OD who have not put their ideas into print or for up-and-coming writers in OD who have new, sometimes unorthodox, approaches that are stimulating and exciting. Some of the books in this series describe inspirational concepts that can lead to actionable change and purvey ideas so new that they are not fully developed.

Unique to this series is the cutting-edge emphasis, the immediate applicability, and the ease of transferability of the concepts. The aim of this series is nothing less than to reinvent, re-energize, and reinvigorate OD. In each book, we have also recommended that the author(s) provide:

- A research base of some kind, meaning new information derived from practice and/or systematic investigation and

- Practical tools, worksheets, case studies and other ready-to-go approaches that help the authors drag "theory" to "practice" to make these new, cutting-edge approaches more concrete.

Subject Matter That Will (and Will Not) Be Covered

The books in this series are varied in their approach, but they are united by their focus. All share an emphasis on organization development (OD). Hence, books in this series are about participative change efforts. They are not about such other popular topics as leadership, management development, consulting, group dynamics—unless those topics are treated in new, cutting-edge ways and are geared to OD practitioners.

This Book

The Change Leader's Roadmap equips leaders and consultants with what is often described as "the most forward-thinking, comprehensive change methodology available today." The featured nine-phase "Change Process Model" offers phase-by-phase guidance at both conceptual and operational levels. Used as a "thinking discipline," this roadmap gives the reader a way to build an integrated change strategy for transformation, as well as the detailed change plans necessary to design and implement it successfully. The model integrates organizational, cultural, behavioral, and mindset changes into one unified process. It informs critical change leadership decisions regarding speed and sequence of activities, and it provides guidance on how to design the infrastructure and conditions necessary for the change effort to deliver new organizational results successfully.

Series Website

For further information and resources about the books in this series and about the current and future practice of organization development, we encourage readers to visit the series website at *www.PracticingOD.Pfeiffer.com.*

William J. Rothwell
University Park, PA

Roland Sullivan
Deephaven, MN

Kristine Quade
Minnetonka, MN

Statement
of the Board

IT IS OUR PLEASURE TO PARTICIPATE in and influence the start up of *Practicing Organization Development: The Change Agent Series for Groups and Organizations.* The purpose of the series is to stimulate the profession and influence how OD is defined and practiced. This statement is intended to set the context for the series by addressing three important questions: (1) What is OD? (2) Is the OD profession at a crossroads? and (3) What is the purpose of this series?

What Is Organization Development?

We offer the following definition of OD to stimulate debate:

> Organization development is a system-wide and values-based collaborative process of applying behavioral science knowledge to the adaptive development, improvement, and reinforcement of such organizational features as the strategies, structures, processes, people, and cultures that lead to organization effectiveness.

The definition suggests that OD can be understood in terms of its several foci:

First, *OD is a system-wide process.* It works with whole systems. In the past, the bias has been toward working at the individual and group levels. More recently, the focus has shifted to organizations and multi-organization systems. We support that trend in general but honor and acknowledge the fact that the traditional focus on smaller systems is both legitimate and necessary.

Second, *OD is values-based.* Traditionally, OD has attempted to distinguish itself from other forms of planned change and applied behavioral science by promoting a set of humanistic values and by emphasizing the importance of personal growth as a key to its practice. Today, that focus is blurred and there is much debate about the value base underlying the practice of OD. We support a more formal and direct conversation about what these values are and how the field is related to them.

Third, *OD is collaborative.* Our first value commitment as OD practitioners is to bring about an inclusive, diverse workforce with a focus of integrating differences into a world-wide culture mentality.

Fourth, *OD is based on behavioral science knowledge.* Organization development should incorporate and apply knowledge from sociology, psychology, anthropology, technology, and economics toward the end of making systems more effective. We support the continued emphasis in OD on behavioral science knowledge and believe that OD practitioners should be widely read and comfortable with several of the disciplines.

Fifth, *OD is concerned with the adaptive development, improvement, and reinforcement of strategies, structures, processes, people, culture, and other features of organizational life.* This statement not only describes the organizational elements that are the target of change, but also describes the process by which effectiveness is increased. That is, OD works in a variety of areas, and it is focused on improving these areas. We believe that such a statement of process and content strongly implies that a key feature of OD is the transference of knowledge and skill to the system so that it is more able to handle and manage change in the future.

Sixth and finally, *OD is about improving organization effectiveness.* It is not just about making people happy; it is also concerned with meeting financial goals, improving productivity, and addressing stakeholder satisfaction. We believe that OD's future is closely tied to the incorporation of this value in its purpose and the demonstration of this objective in its practice.

Is the OD Profession at a Crossroads?

For years, OD professionals have said that OD is at a crossroads. From our perspective at the beginning of the new millennium, the field of organization development can be characterized by the following statements:

1. Practitioners today are torn. The professional organizations representing OD practitioners, including the OD Network, the OD Institute, the International OD Association, and the Academy of Management's OD and Change Division, are experiencing tremendous uncertainties in their purposes, practices, and relationships.

2. There are increasing calls for regulation/certification.

3. Many respected practitioners have suggested that people who profess to manage change are behind those who are creating it. Organization development practitioners should lead through influence rather than follow the lead of those who are sometimes coercive in their approach to change.

4. The field is defined by techniques.

5. The values that guide the field are unclear and ill-defined.

6. Too many people are practicing OD without any training in the field.

7. Practitioners are having difficulty figuring out how to market their services.

The situation suggests the following provocative questions:

- How can OD practitioners help formulate strategy, shape the strategy development process, contribute to the content of strategy, and drive how strategy will be implemented?

- How can OD practitioners encourage an open examination of the ways organizations are conceived and managed?

- How can OD focus on the drivers of change external to individuals, such as the external environment, business strategy, organization change, and culture change, as well as on the drivers of change internal to individuals, such as individual interpretations of culture, behavior, style, and mindset?

- How much should OD be part of the competencies of all leaders and how much should it be the sole domain of professionally trained, career-oriented OD practitioners?

What Is the Purpose of This Series?

This series is intended to provide current thinking about OD as a field and to provide practical approaches based on sound theory and research. It is targeted for full-time external or internal OD practitioners; top executives in charge of enterprise-wide change; and managers, HR practitioners, training and development professionals, and others who have responsibility for change in organizational and trans-organizational settings. At the same time, these books will be directed toward cutting-edge thinking and state-of-the-art approaches. In some cases, the ideas, approaches, or techniques described are still evolving, so the books are intended to open up dialogue.

We know that the books in this series will provide a leading forum for thought-provoking dialogue within the OD field.

About the Board Members

David Bradford is senior lecturer in organizational behavior at the Graduate School of Business, Stanford University, Palo Alto, California. He is co-author (with Allan R. Cohen) of *Managing for Excellence, Influence Without Authority,* and *POWER UP: Transforming Organizations Through Shared Leadership.*

W. Warner Burke is professor of psychology and education and chair of the Department of Organization and Leadership at Teachers College, Columbia University, New York, New York. His most recent publication is *Business Profiles of Climate Shifts: Profiles of Change Makers,* (with William Trahant and Richard Koonce).

Edith Whitfield Seashore is organization consultant and co-founder (with Morley Segal) of AUNTL Masters Program in Organization Development. She is co-author of *What Did You Say?* and *The Art of Giving and Receiving Feedback* and co-editor of *The Promise of Diversity.*

Robert Tannenbaum is emeritus professor of development of human systems, Graduate School of Management, University of California, Los Angeles; recipient of Lifetime Achievement Award by the National OD Network. He has published numerous books, including *Human Systems Development* with Newton Margulies and Fred Massarik.

Christopher G. Worley is director, MSOD Program, Pepperdine University, Malibu, California. He is co-author of *Organization Development and Change* (7th ed.), with Tom Cummings, and of *Integrated Strategic Change,* with David Hitchin and Walter Ross.

Shaolin Zhang is senior manager of organization development for Motorola (China) Electronics Ltd. He received his master's degree in American Studies from Beijing Foreign Studies University, Beijing, China, and holds a Ph.D. in sociology from York University, Toronto, Canada.

Foreword

THIS BOOK IS ABOUT CHANGE LEADERSHIP, specifically how to
lead transformational change. It builds on and expands the use of a powerful
business solution called "change management"—a set of principles, techniques,
and prescriptions applied to the human aspects of executing major change initiatives in organizational settings. Its focus is not on "what" is driving change (technology, reorganization plans, mergers/acquisitions, globalization, etc.), but on
"how" to orchestrate the human infrastructure that surrounds key projects so that
people are better prepared to absorb the implications affecting them.

Compared with other disciplines, the field of change management is a relative
newcomer. As a discrete field of practice, its theoretical roots can be traced back to
the late 1940s/early 1950s. Among management ranks, widespread knowledge of
its existence didn't come about, however, until the 1960s—and even then, it was
considered an obscure specialty for human resource or organization development
types. It wasn't until the 1980s that it developed any real degree of acceptance from
the line side of business, and it wasn't until the 1990s that it became an accepted
strategic tool for senior officers. Today, change management has come into its own

and is considered a must for most organizations engaged in critically important change efforts.

As is true with any business tool that obtains widespread notoriety over a relatively short period of time, the field of change management has become populated with more than its share of academicians who write about organization change but don't live the experience on a daily basis. There are many well-meaning, but inexperienced, novice practitioners and, unfortunately, even some who are willing to peddle smoke-and-mirror "snake oil" that produces little real value. Thankfully, the field has also produced many excellent practitioners who work from the inside to provide genuine value to their organizations or from the outside as they assist the clients they serve. Within this population is a smaller number of individuals who have immersed themselves in both the study and application of organization change to a point where their understanding of the phenomenon far surpasses what others are able to see or do. What you have in your hands is the result of two such people committing their experience to print.

You are about to read the lessons learned from two individuals who have both practiced and contributed to the change management craft as few others have. For over twenty-five years, the experience base Linda Ackerman Anderson and Dean Anderson have acquired in this field is such that they have forgotten more about this art form than most who claim expertise in it ever learned. In this book, they are stretching us from the boundaries of change management to the new terrain of change leadership. This is a book about mastery of leading the transformational change process written by masters of the craft. As such, I recommend you approach its contents with the proper balance of excitement and caution.

The exciting news: Masters of a discipline don't just know more than most people about the conceptual frameworks and practical application of a subject; they are eager to share their wisdom in order to aid others in their journey toward excellence. Linda and Dean do just that in this outpouring of insights, guidelines, and specific action steps. By articulating their hard-won lessons from decades of successes and failures, they allow you the opportunity to stand on their shoulders and reach even higher.

The cautionary news: You will see in the pages to follow that, like all true masters, Dean and Linda respect their students too much to mask the truth about what it takes to truly succeed. This book is not for the casual browser or for those looking for bandages and aspirin. It's a serious read for corporate leaders and consultants who consider themselves committed students of the process of organization change. It covers the subject by going deep, broad, comprehensive, and thorough rather than trying to seduce the reader with superficial, simplistic explanations and gimmicks. The authors choose to reflect the true complexity organization change imposes, instead of placating the reader with the veneer so often applied in the name of change management.

Nothing of *real* value comes without a significant investment. The challenge this book presents doesn't stop with the time and effort you will find necessary to fully absorb what is offered here. The more substantial investment opportunity is the chance to dive deeply into your soul in search of whether change leadership is really a path for you. With the release of this manuscript, Linda and Dean have done their part in paving the path. The ball is now in your court.

Daryl R. Conner
CEO, ODR, Inc.,
Author, *Leading at the*
Edge of Chaos and
Managing At the
Speed of Change
January 2001

To Terra—for being the loving
inspiration in both of our lives

Preface

OUR LIFE'S WORK HAS ALWAYS BEEN ABOUT CHANGE, Linda's about organization change and Dean's about personal change. In 1986, when we met, it became clear that our two professional specialties were meant to be merged into one unified approach to transforming organizations.

Linda was one of the founding leaders of the Organization Transformation movement, focusing on teaching the process of organization change and transformational leadership to executives and consultants worldwide. Dean was one of the first people doing personal mastery work in organizations, having created the Optimal Performance Institute to bring his approach to breakthrough performance, originally developed for world-class athletes, to people in business. At the time of our meeting, Linda had recognized that her work required more overt emphasis on personal and cultural change to fortify her large systems work, while Dean concurrently had realized that his personal and team performance models needed to align with the complexities of larger organizational systems.

In 1988, we brought our specialties, insights, and theories together to create our approach to leading conscious transformation and to form Being First, Inc.

For fourteen years we have mentored and coached one another in our individual specialties, and we now stand as peers in both arenas—personal and organizational change.

Individually, and then collectively at Being First, we have always considered ourselves thought leaders in the field of organization change. We have helped define the field of Organization Transformation and are committed to pushing the envelope of thinking and practice for accomplishing tangible transformational results. We created Being First—appropriately named for our bias toward the personal work required to transform individuals and organizations—to offer our thinking and advice to people and large systems around the world.

Today, Being First, Inc., is a full-service change education, consulting, and change leadership development firm assisting organizations to design and accomplish their transformations while building their internal capacity for continuous change. We provide enterprise-wide breakthrough training for culture and mindset change, personal transformation training, change strategy consulting, change leadership skill development for leaders and consultants, licensing of our Change Process Methodology, coaching, and transformational team development. We offer consulting guidance, consultant support, and application tools to design and implement transformational change consciously. We are also developing a curriculum for women executives called "Women As Leaders of Change."

Our style, based on our commitment to walk our own talk, is to co-create a personalized strategy for each client with the appropriate balance of consulting and training, combining both change for the individual employee and change for the system as a whole. We are devoted to our own continuous learning through true partnership with our clients. We hope this way of working is evident in what we offer in this book.

Our work in organizations continues to provide us the opportunity to develop, field test, and write about what we believe is required to transform human systems successfully and consciously. Through our practice, as well as in the current management literature, it has become clear that several essential messages and competencies are missing from the field. These need to be given voice. Some are about how leaders lead profound change in their organizations. Some concern consultants and their approaches or ability to influence their clients as change leaders. We deeply believe that leaders and consultants need to hear these messages and develop these competencies in order to transform their organizations to stay in sync with their rapidly changing environments. We have attempted to articulate clearly both the messages and the competencies in this book and its companion, *Beyond Change Management.*

Through writing these books, we have attempted to capture what is true for us in this moment in time in the evolution of change and leadership. This has been a challenging effort—a bit like trying to capture a river that keeps on flowing. The insights we explore here will continue to evolve—and have done so even as we have written them. We explore ideas and theory at the conceptual level, offer strategies, actions, and tools at the pragmatic level, and attempt to bridge the two in the clearest and most useful way possible for you, our reader.

For two decades, we have thoroughly danced the debate of personal change versus organization change, change the people or change the structures, plan versus unfold, process versus outcome. The dances continue, and we offer you where we currently stand. In our writing, we have attempted to be forthright about what we see as true about how change and leadership are evolving. We have also attempted to denote what we think is factual, what we believe due to our own experiences, and what we are still learning or questioning.

We are very much on the continuing journey of inquiry, discovery, and adaptation of what we think and feel about what we have written here. We invite you, our reader, into this exploration with us—into the inquiry—into our attempt to give language, guidance, and incentive to growing the field of transformational change leadership. We hope you will participate in the conversation about the issues and propositions in these books, as well as put them into practice to reap their value.

Please read with the spirit of inquiry. Read with your concern for the state of today's organizations. Read to contribute to our collective ability to transform organizations into places in which people love to work and feel regenerated, as well as adding value to their customers or constituents. Read on while honoring how far the field of organization development has come from its first attempts to infuse the notions and values of planned change and human development into organizations. And please read with yourself in mind as a leader or consultant of change. Our message is written for you, and we hope it benefits you personally and professionally.

Linda S. Ackerman Anderson
Dean Anderson
Durango, Colorado
Summer, 2000

Acknowledgments

WE EXPRESS OUR DEEP APPRECIATION for all of the people who helped us write and produce both *Beyond Change Management* and *The Change Leader's Roadmap.* Completing these books was very much a group effort. We received tremendous support from our families and friends, while we took on the challenge of writing two books simultaneously—and completing them.

Above all, we appreciate our young daughter, Terra, whose heartfelt understanding and patience for the time and focus these books required of us was essential to our process. Her smiles and gentle offerings of help and support provided food for our souls, and her reminders that there was more to life than writing created humbling perspective for our prolonged effort. And we appreciate one another for being such a full partner in co-creating our relationship, lives and work. We are in awe of the process we are living—consciously listening to Spirit, accepting our humanness, and surrendering ourselves and our relationship to the fire of transformation.

We received direct help from our trusty readers, friends and colleagues all, including insightful input from John Adams, Carol Tisson, Jean Redfield, and, of course, our series editors, Kristine Quade, Roland Sullivan, and William Rothwell. Their feedback and encouragement was invaluable to us, as was that of our Pfeiffer editors.

Our staff was untiring in their assistance with editing and production. We sincerely appreciate Cindy Lancaster, Orion Lukasik, Marilyn Leftwich, Steve Elfrink, Lisa Liljedahl, Kevin Smith, and Cindy Marquardt for their dedication and patience.

In addition, we appreciate all of our Being First, Inc., consulting and training associates for being the road warriors who kept our clients happy while we wrote for so many months. For this, we are deeply grateful.

And finally, we appreciate Martin Marquardt for his partnership, friendship, and positive influence on our thinking over the last seven years.

The Change
Leader's
Roadmap

Introduction

ON OUR EARLY YEARS AS CHANGE CONSULTANTS, in the mid-1970s, the change game was very different than it is today. Organizations were changing, but leaders considered change to be a momentary blip on the screen, something to be delegated, a problem to be solved and put to rest. Most changes were considered "improvement efforts," such as productivity improvement, implementing new performance appraisal systems, management development, and human interaction skills training.

Although the field of organization development (OD) was growing, its application, at least for us, was more on people development, survey feedback, team building, and running effective meetings. Little pragmatic attention was given to organization-wide change, despite "planned change" being one of the field's theoretical claims to fame. Organization development was buried someplace in the organization. Leaders never thought to ask OD consultants to help them create an enterprise-wide strategy for transforming the corporation. And the practice of change management wasn't even a twinkle in their eye!

The most exciting dynamic of those days and the decade of the 1980s was that we had free reign to invent a lot of new approaches to our consulting work; we made up models and activities on the spot and used them successfully. Senior leaders didn't yet know what to ask for or expect from us, so we had a lot of leeway; in fact, as much leeway as we had "chutzpah" to fly these new approaches and produce results! Yes, those were the good old days.

Today, organization change is fast, pressured, constant, and competitive. Leaders are confronted with change that is much more complex and dynamic. They have little choice but to pay attention, get involved, and spend untold dollars on consultants who promise answers, help, and relief. If the changes required today were as simple as they were in the 1970s, leaders' and consultants' lives would be a good deal less tumultuous.

Unfortunately, not only are leaders responsible for more complex changes, but the social, technological, economic, and political terrains they have to navigate during change are themselves shifting faster than leaders can keep up with. The name of today's game is: "Change as fast as you can, certainly as fast as the marketplace demands!" And the marketplace is operating in hyper-speed. Leaders of today's organizations have their hands full, to say nothing of their heads, hearts, and minds. Do they long for the good old days? Perhaps some do, but those committed to succeeding in this crazily changing world are so focused on today's and tomorrow's challenges that they hardly have time to think about the past.

Without question, the nature of change has evolved over the past twenty-five years. The most prevalent type of change in organizations today is *transformation*, which is vastly different from the dominant types of the 1970s, 1980s, and early 1990s, which were developmental and transitional in nature. Developmental and transitional change can be managed. Transformation cannot. The challenge of transformation is that leaders and consultants are applying the old change management approaches for developmental and transitional change to transformation, and they just don't work.

It is time to move beyond change management and learn advanced strategies for transformational change. Transformation requires entirely new approaches, strategies, leadership mindsets, and behaviors. Both leaders and consultants must learn how to master transformational change—in style, behavior, and strategy. Both must evolve to become competent transformational *change leaders*—a new caliber of leader for a new type of change.

We have written this book to support the evolution of leaders and consultants to become successful transformational change leaders—conscious of what transformation requires and capable of providing it. Both this book and its companion, *Beyond Change Management* (Anderson & Ackerman Anderson, 2001), are designed to explore the foundational concepts of transformational change, how leaders and consultants must develop to be successful at leading it, and pragmatic approaches to guide organizations realistically through the dynamic river of today's ever-changing business environment.

We believe that leaders and consultants are in need of a comprehensive approach for leading transformation: (a) a meaningful context for transformational action; (b) guidelines for thinking through how to plan and respond to transformation; and (c) a methodology for doing so. The context and guidelines for thinking are featured in *Beyond Change Management*. This book provides the methodology.

Beyond Change Management describes the conceptual underpinnings of transformation and what it takes to lead it consciously to become more than a leader—a change leader. This book delivers a specific change process model to put these concepts into practice. *Beyond Change Management* explores the theory, and this book offers the pragmatics. We have written both books simultaneously to blend conceptual understanding with tangible guidance. Together, they provide an integrated and balanced approach to this essential evolution in the fields of OD and change leadership. We offer these books to compel leaders and consultants to step into the role of *consciously* shaping the transformation of their organizations and to provide a primary tool for doing so, a comprehensive change process methodology.

The cornerstone of a transformational change methodology needs to be a change process model that is designed to handle the many dynamics occurring throughout the entire process of transformation. Our model is called the *Change Process Model for Leading Conscious Transformation*. We will describe both the change process methodology and our model shortly and then explore them in depth in the remainder of this book. But first, we will provide an overview of the key points covered in *Beyond Change Management*.

Key Points from *Beyond Change Management*

1. Change has evolved over the last thirty years. The most prevalent type of change occurring in today's organizations is transformation.

The three types of change occurring in organizations are *developmental* change, *transitional* change, and *transformational* change. It is essential to know which type you are leading, because the type dictates the strategies and leadership approach required for the change to succeed.

Briefly, developmental change is an improvement on an organization's existing way of operating—increasing skills, improving the performance of a business process, or learning how to sell more products. Transitional change, rather than simply "developing" the current state, replaces it with a *known* new state that is intentionally formulated to resolve the inadequacies of the old state. Transitional change entails the design and implementation of something different from what exists, requiring the leaders to dismantle the current way of operating and systematically put in place the newly designed desired state. The process of transitioning from the old to the new can be planned, paced, and *managed.* Reorganizations, the installation of new computer hardware, and the creation of new products or services are most often transitional changes.

Transformation occurs when the organization recognizes that its old way of operating, even if it were to be "improved," cannot achieve the business strategies required to succeed in its radically different business environment. Transformation, then, is the fundamental shift from one state of being (its old state) to another (its transformed state), a change so significant that it requires the organization to shift its culture and people's behavior and mindsets to implement it successfully and to sustain it over time. In addition, the new state that results from the transformation is largely uncertain at the beginning of the change process and emerges as a product of the change effort itself. Unpredictable, uncontrollable, and often messy, the change process must be crafted, shaped, and adapted *as it unfolds.* Some significant examples of transformation today include old economy organizations moving into e-businesses, the deregulation of utilities, and major information technology overhauls.

2. Leaders create new business strategies to respond to the profound changes in the environment and marketplace. These business strategies drive the organization's need to transform, which requires the leaders to build a transformation strategy to achieve their desired results. Although most leaders attend to their business strategy diligently, they place minimal attention on their change strategy.

A comprehensive change strategy is composed of three key elements: content, people, and process. The *content* component refers to *what* must change in the formal organization—structure, business processes, management systems, technology, etc. The *people* component refers to the human dynamics that either influence the change or are a product of it—dealing with people's emotional reactions, learning new behaviors, changing mindset, and addressing cultural implications. The *process* component is *how* the organization will transform. The process denotes the flow of activity that will produce the content changes while simultaneously transforming the people and culture as required to operate the new organization successfully. Change strategy is the change leaders' high-level approach to an integrated, organization-wide transformation.

3. Change leaders must more accurately scope the organization's transformation by determining what is driving the transformation and how those drivers impact what has to change.

The mammoth changes in today's business environment and marketplace, fueled by information technology, deregulation and the speed of product and service innovation, require a wider scope of change in organizations. Scope is the breadth and depth of what is included in the organization's transformation. It is determined, in part, by assessing the seven drivers of change shown in Figure 0.1.

Figure 0.1. The Drivers of Change Model

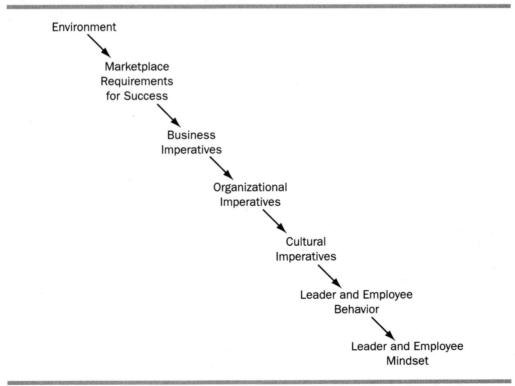

Notice the direction of impact among the drivers. The larger, external forces (environment, marketplace requirements, business and organizational imperatives) drive the need to change in the more internal forces (culture, behavior, and mindset). Leaders are most accustomed to focusing on the external drivers and the content of change. Now they must attend to the internal drivers and the people dynamics. Transformation requires conscious attention both to the external drivers *and* to the internal drivers of change.

4. Leading transformational change requires leaders and consultants to expand their conscious awareness so they can see and respond to the unique dynamics of transformation.

Leaders and consultants approach transformation either consciously or reactively. With a conscious approach, leaders are more aware and reflective about the dynamics they encounter—both internal and external—as the transformation proceeds. They inquire about those dynamics to expand their awareness of them and learn how to deal with them effectively. A reactive approach means limited awareness, as leaders and consultants respond automatically and unconsciously to the change based on conditioning, habits, and current skill sets. They are largely at the mercy of the forces at play.

There are twenty-one dimensions of focus required for change leaders to design and navigate the transformational journey successfully. Conscious leaders attend to all of these dynamics, while reactive leaders attend only to the external dynamics. These twenty-one dimensions are represented in a model (see Figure 0.2) that outlines five levels of organizational reality—individual (self), relationship, team, the organizational system as a whole, and the marketplace. Four domains of human experience exist within each of these levels of reality—physical (structure or body), emotional (feelings), mental (assumptions, beliefs, mental models), and spiritual (purpose, vision, values). The addition of the environment makes twenty-one dimensions.

Typically, leaders are more comfortable with the external or physical dimensions and OD consultants are more attuned to the internal, more personal dimensions. For successful transformation, the change process must adequately address all twenty-one dimensions, which requires a partnership of leadership and consulting competencies and a focus on both internal and external realities.

5. Transformational change requires that leaders and employees transform *themselves*—changing their mindsets and fundamental assumptions about

Figure 0.2. Twenty-One Dimensions of Conscious Transformation

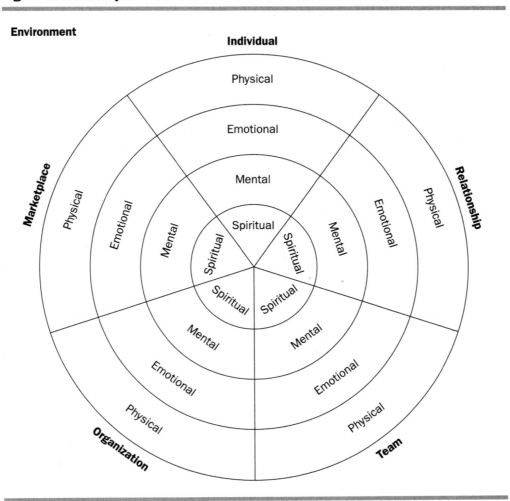

reality, their behavior, their ways of relating to others, and their ways of causing or supporting things to happen in the organization. Personal transformation is a nonnegotiable requirement of organizational transformation. If the
change leaders don't overtly model this personal change themselves, they cannot ask it of the people in the organization. Both are essential to the success of
transformation, and both must be built into the change strategy. For consultants, this level of personal transformation is equally important. Otherwise,
they cannot model this type of change nor coach their clients through it.

6. Leading transformation requires a process orientation. By "process," we mean the natural or intentional unfolding of continuous events, at all levels of reality, toward a desired outcome. The key word is "continuous."

Transformation cannot be achieved solely through isolated, disconnected, or random events. Change leaders must ensure that all change-related activity is purposeful and integrated. Each action or event must build toward the next. In this way, momentum is created and the change process rolls out toward its desired result.

A process orientation is especially critical in transformation, more than any other type of change, for two reasons. First, because the future state of the organization is unknown at the beginning of the process, it has to emerge as the transformation unfolds. This requires designing a process that supports this "re-invention" to occur. Second, the transformation requires significant personal and cultural change, which only occur over time.

7. Transformational change leadership must be based on *conscious process thinking,* which is used to design and implement the transformation with the process orientation described above.

Conscious process thinking is a reflection of a new set of fundamental assumptions about reality, which we call the "Emerging Mindset." Much of the current "new science" literature speaks to the same assumptions. The Emerging Mindset is replacing the long-standing Industrial Mindset that has shaped traditional command-and-control leadership approaches for the last two centuries. The Industrial Mindset sufficed for driving the strategies for managing current operations, developmental and transitional change, but is sorely insufficient for leading transformation. Designing and facilitating transformation requires the Emerging Mindset worldview. A comparison of the Industrial and the Emerging Mindsets is shown in Table 0.1.

8. We observe three primary styles of change leadership—controlling, facilitating, and self-organizing. The *controlling* style is a direct reflection of the Industrial Mindset. Given how unpredictable and uncontrollable transformation is, this style is not appropriate or adequate, as it squelches the emergent nature of transformation. The *self-organizing* style reflects the opposite

Table 0.1. Comparison of the Industrial and Emerging Mindsets

The Industrial Mindset "Reality As a Great Machine"	The Emerging Mindset "Reality As a Living System"
Separate Parts	Wholeness/Relationship
Power and Control	Co-Create and Participate
Certainty/Predictability	Uncertainty/Probability
Objective/Knowable	Subjective/Mysterious
Discrete Events	Continuous Process
Entropy	Self-Organization
Order into Chaos	Order out of Chaos
External Causation	Internal Causation
Scarcity	Abundance

extreme; it is organic and unstructured. It can be used successfully for transformational change, but only when the leaders using it have mastered the dynamic nature of transformation and when their organization possesses adequate change capacity to "self-organize" in a productive manner.

Facilitative change leaders engage in conscious process design and conscious process facilitation. They intentionally design the change process and strategy up-front, then facilitate it based on *both* their process and the dynamics that emerge in real time. They don't force the process to go as designed, and they don't just allow the plan to evolve on its own. In facilitating the transformation process, the change leaders create the best conditions for their plan to roll out effectively, observe how well it is going with an eye to emergent information, and course correct the process as circumstances dictate.

We believe that the facilitative style is the most appropriate for leading transformational change in *today's* business environment for three reasons: (1) It reflects the Emerging Mindset and can readily use the operating principles of conscious transformation (listed below); (2) while a stretch, it can be learned by most of today's leaders; and (3) it fits with the level of readiness and capabilities of most organizations. Throughout this book, we assume the leadership style applied to the Change Process Model to be facilitative.

9. Ten operating principles of conscious transformation are used to govern conscious process design and facilitation. They reflect the fundamental assumptions of the Emerging Mindset as well as conscious process thinking. The ten principles are:

   • Wholeness;

   • Interconnectedness;

   • Multi-dimensionality;

   • Continuous process;

   • Learning and course correcting;

   • Abundance;

   • Balancing planning with attending to emerging dynamics;

   • Leading as if the future is now;

   • Optimizing human dynamics; and

   • Evolving mindset.

These principles enable change leaders to integrate content changes with people's needs and account for the twenty-one dimensions to which change leaders must attend as the process unfolds. The Change Process Model presented in this book embodies these ten principles.

10. Change leaders and consultants must consciously design and facilitate the change process as a "fullstream" process. The Fullstream Transformation Model (Figure 0.3) shows that transformation has an upstream component, a midstream component, and a downstream component, all of which need to be designed and led for the transformation to succeed. The *upstream* stage sets up the foundations for success. The *midstream* stage focuses on designing the desired state, while the *downstream* stage is implementation.

Traditionally, most leaders have thought of "planning for change" as "planning for implementation." If leaders think only of implementation, it is no wonder that

Figure 0.3. The Fullstream Transformation Model

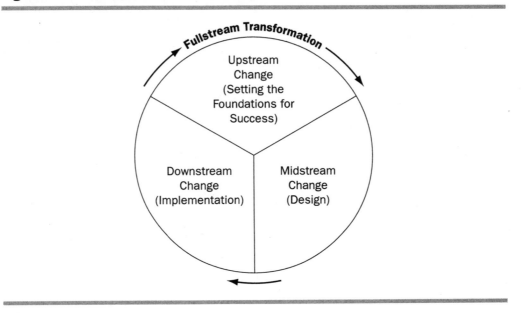

their well-intentioned efforts flounder! When they neglect critical upstream activities such as creating a clear case for change, building an integrated change strategy, and preparing the organization to receive and participate in the transformation, their change efforts struggle. When they rush through the midstream stage and design the desired state with little or no organizational involvement, people do not understand the new reality they are being held accountable to create.

The seeds and roots of successful transformation are sewn in the design of the upstream and midstream stages. Implementation is essential, yet it is the last of three stages of the change process.

11. The major tool of the facilitative change leadership style of conscious transformation is a change process model. Change *process models* are very different from change *frameworks*. Frameworks are static depictions of types of change activity requiring attention. Process models demonstrate the flow of the activity itself or what has to occur to get from point A to point B, which is the intention of transformation.

12. Any change process model fit for transformation must be a *thinking discipline*, not a cookbook of prescriptive action. It should guide action, not mandate it. It should inform process design decisions, not dictate them. It should organize the plan, not rigidify it. In short, it can be structured, but it must accommodate the evolving, multi-dimensional *process* nature of transformation.

The Change Process Model described in this book is such a thinking discipline. As we mentioned earlier, it is the heart of a change process methodology fit for transformation.

What a Change Process Methodology Is

An effective transformational change methodology must accomplish the outcomes of transformation while building essential and lasting change competencies. A sample list of what is entailed includes:

- The understanding of transformation as a multi-dimensional process;
- Conscious process design: The knowledge and skills for designing a transformational change strategy and a change process roadmap that integrates content and people changes;
- Conscious process facilitation: The ability to nurture, learn from, and course correct the change strategy and change process over the full lifecycle of the transformation;
- Breakthrough in the mindset and behaviors of the leaders, the workforce, and all relevant stakeholders;
- Infrastructures, roles, and conditions for success required to increase the likelihood of achieving desired outcomes;
- Strategies to deal effectively with the people dynamics of change, individually and collectively, including changing the existing mindset and culture and helping people through their natural reactions to the change; and
- Strategies to manage and permeate the boundaries between the organization's ongoing operation and the rollout of the change.

This book presents what is required in a transformational change process methodology. Our model for delivering it is the Change Process Model, shown in Figure 0.4. Let's describe it further.

Figure 0.4. The Change Process Model for Leading Conscious Transformation

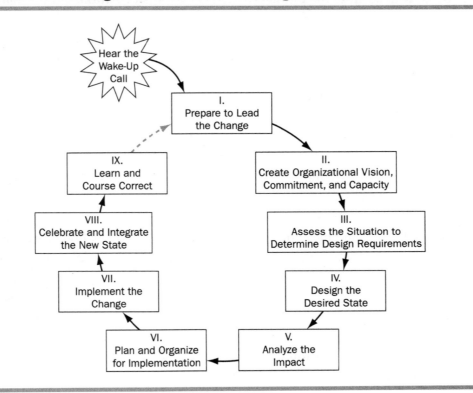

The Change Process Model for Leading Conscious Transformation

The model outlines a fullstream roadmap for getting an organization from where it is to where it wants to be. The model portrays nine phases of activity that represent generically how transformation takes place in organizations. As a roadmap, it can't tell you which destination to pursue or which turns to make to get there, but it does provide guidance regarding what lies ahead. It outlines the general process you will take to discover your destination and how to arrive there as expediently as possible.

We have been developing the Change Process Model for twenty years. As we learned more about transformational change and the Emerging Mindset, we evolved it to address the unique dynamics of transformation and the conscious approach to leading it. We have officially named the model The Change Process Model for Leading Conscious Transformation. However, for the purposes of brevity, we will refer to the model only as the Change Process Model throughout this book.

Although designed for transformational change, the Change Process Model can be tailored for all types of change, as well as for any magnitude of change effort. Smaller, less complex changes will require selective tailoring of the activities in the model. Remember that the model is just a model until you tailor it to fit your particular situation. Then, the model comes to life and becomes your particular transformational change.

As we describe the model, we refer frequently to "the transformation of your *organization*." It is important to note that not every transformation is organization-wide. Transformation can occur in a business unit, plant, group, or any intact segment of the organization. Any of these segments of the whole organization is a system in and of itself. The model still pertains to its transformation, just at the smaller boundary of that system. The transformation, even in these smaller systems, must attend to the *whole* system. Thus, when we refer to the "organization," it means whatever is within the boundary of the system that is undergoing the transformation.

The depiction of the nine phases of the model is designed to represent the inherent logic and flow of the activities of transformation. You may, however, interpret the model's sequential nature to mean that you must complete one phase before you proceed to the next. In reality, you may be in two, three, or even four phases simultaneously. You may do the work of some phases in parallel with the work of other phases, as your situation allows. Different levels of the organization may be in different phases at the same time, and you may need to cycle through all nine phases many times until all aspects of your transformation conclude.

In organization-wide transformation, the enterprise is going through an overarching nine-phase process as individual change initiatives within the larger effort engage in their own change processes. Therefore, different change initiatives, business units, or areas of the enterprise may be in different phases and will likely need integration so that all initiatives support the overarching transformation. When each change effort is using the same process model, integration becomes much easier. We offer strategies for integrating various initiatives in Chapter Three.

Structure of the Change Process Model

Each of the nine phases of the model accomplishes a specific body of work. Together, they generate the activities required to complete a full life cycle of transformation. In the Fullstream Transformation Model, each of its three stages covers three of the nine phases of the Change Process Model: Phases I to III are the *upstream* stage (setting the foundations for success), Phases IV to VI comprise the *midstream* stage (design), and Phases VII through IX denote the *downstream* stage (implementation). Figure 0.5 shows this graphically.

Figure 0.5. The Change Process Model As a Fullstream Process

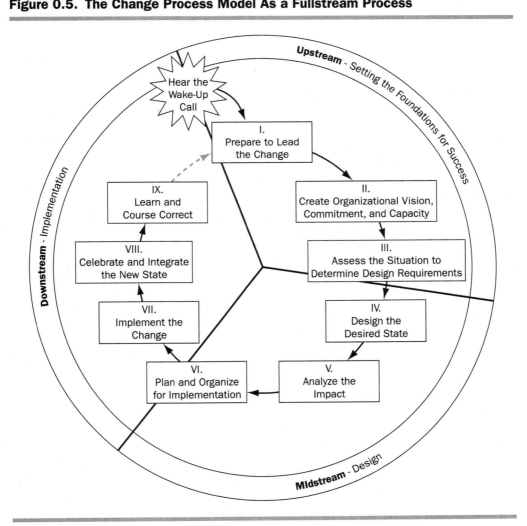

Depending on your need, you can customize the model to any level of detail. The most conceptual level is the general description of the nine phases as outlined in Figure 0.4. Each phase is divided into major activities, as shown in Figure 0.6. The activities are achieved through focused tasks, all of which have deliverables. The deliverables of each task, at the most operational level, are accomplished through a series of suggested work steps.

We have structured the material in this way—phase, activity, task, work steps—for ease of use for line managers who are familiar with similarly structured project management methods. The structure also provides the greatest versatility for the various people who use it, be they executives who need only the conceptual phase level or change process leaders, project managers, or consultants who benefit from the greater detail of the activities, tasks, and work steps.

In this book, we present the purpose of each phase, its major activities, and its tasks. A listing of the task deliverables for each phase is included at the beginning of each chapter. In the overview of each phase, we point out several of its predictable underlying dynamics so that change leaders and consultants will become conscious of these forces at play and attend to their causes or resolutions when planning their change process.

A complete outline of the phases, activities, and tasks is included in the Appendix. The work steps are not included because this book is not intended to serve as an operational manual. More in-depth information about the work steps within each task, additional consulting guidelines, and detailed application tools are available from Being First, Inc.

We have designed the Change Process Model to be as comprehensive as possible, including all that we have found necessary to support transformation. This does not mean you will have to do all of the activities the model suggests. In all of its comprehensiveness, the model is designed to support you to ask which of its many activities are critical for *your* transformation's success. The application of the model must be tailored, *always,* to the outcomes, magnitude, style, pacing requirements, and resource constraints of your situation. Remember, the model is a thinking discipline, not a prescription for action.

We recommend that you be selective about the work you include in your change strategy and plans. In any given change effort, we suggest that you consider all of what is offered here and then select *only* the work that is appropriate to your transformation and only what will help you guide and accelerate your effort. You should

Figure 0.6. The Change Process Model—Activity Level

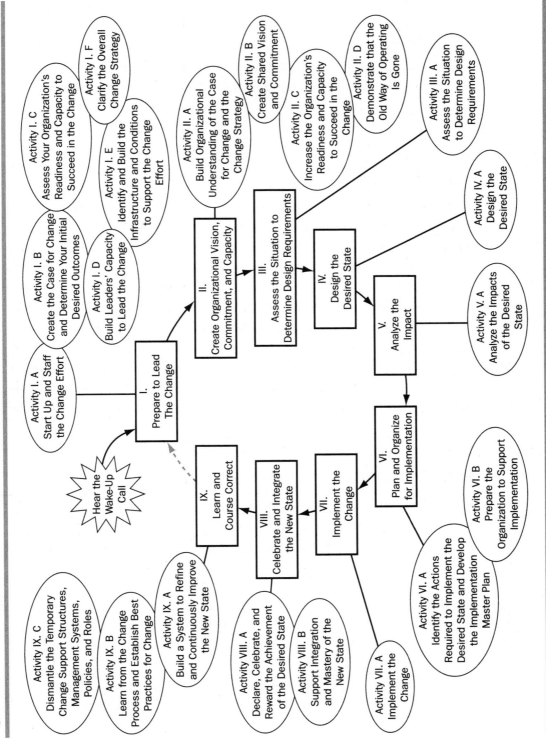

skip activities that have been completed already or are irrelevant. You will likely combine tasks to achieve multiple deliverables, and you will certainly need to design the process consciously to accomplish each chosen task. We hope that the information presented here will help you see the implications of omitting or skimming through important work in your change process.

Our Audience

We write for both change leaders and change consultants. Our intention is to provide useful information about what it takes to both *lead* transformation and *consult* to it. Separating the two audiences is, in our opinion, one of the conditions that can impair the success of transformation. Leaders must understand more about the nature of transformational change and all of the dynamics—external as well as internal—that are required to guide it effectively. Change process consultants must understand more about the business realities of the organizations they are supporting. It is our hope that consultants will have their line clients read both this book and its companion, *Beyond Change Management,* and discuss their learnings and impressions of both as they relate to leading their actual transformations more successfully. It is also our hope that leaders who read these books will share them with their consultants or will hire consultants who aspire to this level of work.

How This Book Is Organized

The book is organized into four sections. The first three reflect the three stages of the Fullstream Transformation Model—upstream, midstream, and downstream. The chapters in each of these sections present the three phases of the Change Process Model within that stage, as described earlier. Each chapter begins with an overview and a list of task deliverables. At the end of each chapter are high-leverage consulting questions to help you to apply and tailor the work of that phase. The questions can be used to help you determine whether your transformation requires the actions included in the phase. Worksheets and tools are also included to assist you.

The fourth section in the book, "Leveraging the Change Process Model," consists of three chapters—the first describing the most common reactions leaders and consultants have to the Change Process Model, the second discussing the opportunities for gaining the greatest value from the methodology, and the last giving personal guidelines and questions for you to make the most of the insights and motivation you have gained from your reading.

Using This Book to Your Advantage

Before you begin exploring the model, we have a few suggestions. The most appropriate way to grasp and use the material is to read the chapters in their entirety for general understanding and reaction, the 30,000-foot level, first. Compare the content and structure of this model with other models or approaches to change with which you are familiar.

Then review the model again with a real transformational change in mind, now at the 5,000-foot level. Identify which activities or tasks you need to perform and how you will tailor them to fit the change effort. Consider the consulting questions as they relate to the initiative and fill out the worksheets. Review the phases and activities periodically as the transformation proceeds. Then apply the model on other change efforts to broaden your use of it.

No matter how great or comprehensive a change model is, it is only valuable when it is put into use. Imagine how many good change plans lie gathering dust on the shelf! Your thinking and skill in tailoring and applying this model to a real transformation brings it to life. Theory is one thing; pragmatic application is another. Remember, the map is not the territory, especially for transformational change!

Our Challenge to You

Learning to master the leadership of transformational change is a monumental challenge. We have spent our careers building and testing approaches, strategies, and tools for supporting leaders to lead transformation consciously and proactively. Our body of evidence for the success of these approaches is in some cases twenty years deep and, in other cases, still in its infancy. The more we learn, the more we realize there is to learn.

Both this book and *Beyond Change Management* are products of our consulting and training experience. Writing these books has been a major step in our continual process of learning about transformational change. Putting our ideas into words makes them appear so permanent! But, because we understand the transformational process, we know that we will continue to evolve ourselves and the ideas and approaches captured in these pages.

We want to share this challenge with you. We challenge you to deepen your learning about transformation. We challenge you to create a breakthrough in your ability to lead transformational change. We challenge you to design and develop your organization to be change-ready, change-capable, and change-healthy. And we challenge you to take on the personal development required to master transformational change leadership.

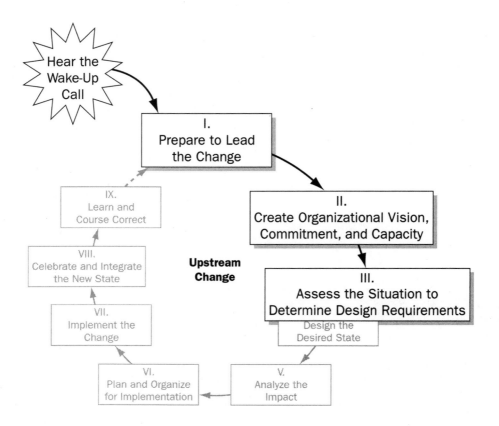

Upstream Change

Section One
Upstream Change

Phase I: Prepare to Lead the Change

Chapter 1: Start Up, Staff, and Create the Case for Change   25

Chapter 2: Assess the Organization's Readiness and Build Capacity
    for Change   55

Chapter 3: Identify and Build the Infrastructure and Conditions to
    Support the Change Effort   75

Chapter 4: Build the Change Strategy   113

Phase II

Chapter 5: Create Organizational Vision, Commitment, and Capacity   129

Phase III

Chapter 6: Assess the Situation to Determine Design Requirements   147

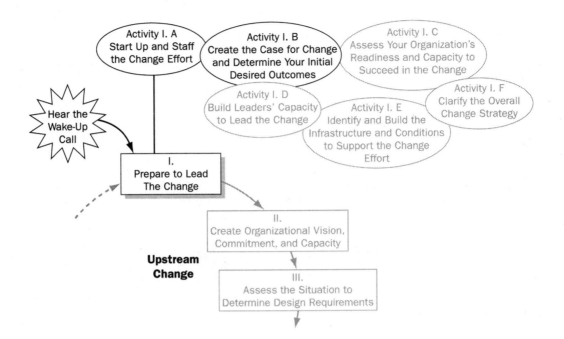

Activity 1.A and 1.B Task Deliverables

I.A.1: A project briefing has been obtained, shared, and agreed on by all key leaders.

I.A.2: Change leadership roles have been defined, and the change effort is staffed with qualified people.

I.A.3: Optimal working relationships among all change leaders have been established.

I.A.4: The project community has been identified and mobilized to support the change.

I.B.1: The process for creating the case for change is clear and has been staffed appropriately.

I.B.2: The drivers of the change have been determined.

I.B.3: The organization's systems dynamics have been mapped, and the leverage points for making the change have been identified.

I.B.4: An initial analysis of the organizational and human impacts of the transformation has been done.

I.B.5: The primary type of change is known, the scope of the change is clear, and the targets of the change have been identified.

I.B.6: The degree of urgency for making the change has been assessed.

I.B.7: The complete case for change has been prepared for communication, and the initial desired outcomes for the change have been determined.

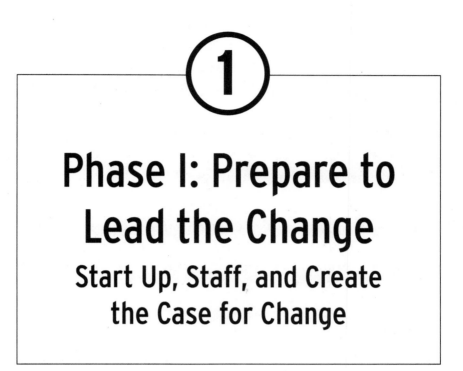

Phase I: Prepare to Lead the Change

Start Up, Staff, and Create the Case for Change

MOST OFTEN, WHEN LEADERS DECIDE to mobilize a change effort, events are already underway and information has already been surfaced that affect what the leaders must do. Consequently, they need to figure out what has been happening, what is known, and who is doing what. Phase I has been designed for the leaders to discover where they are in their effort's start-up and what additional clarity and action are needed.

The overall purpose of Phase I, which is covered in Chapters 1 through 4, is to establish the shared intention and strategy for a successful transformation and to prepare the leaders to lead the effort through:

- Clarifying their roles and the status of the change effort, and staffing the effort with the right people;

- Determining initial desired outcomes and creating a clear case for change that will be used to inform and compel the people of the organization to support and succeed in this change;

- Assessing the organization's capacity to take on and succeed in the effort;

- Strengthening leaders' capacity, individually and collectively, to understand, commit to, and model the behaviors and approaches required to lead this change successfully;

- Designing the optimal approach, process, conditions, and structures for facilitating this change successfully; and

- Clarifying the overall change strategy.

These efforts represent the six activities of Phase I. This chapter covers the first two activities, *Start Up and Staff Your Change Effort,* and *Create the Case for Change and Determine Your Initial Desired Outcomes.* Before we address the work of these two activities, let's start the action where it actually begins, with the first notion of the need for change.

Hearing the Wake-Up Call

The actual process of change begins the moment a person or a group hears the wake-up call and recognizes that there is a reason to change—an opportunity to be pursued or a threat to be removed. The wake-up call can be heard anywhere in the organization, at any level. At times, there is grass-roots awareness of the need long before the executives take notice. However, for an organization-wide transformation to mobilize, the leaders of the organization affected must ultimately hear the signal clearly enough to warrant attention and discussion, if not action. In change-resistant organizations, executives typically do not get or heed wake-up calls until the signals become so painful and dangerous that they threaten the organization's very survival.

The wake-up call may come in the form of a dramatic event, such as the competition beating you to market with a similar or better product than you have under development; or it may be the accumulation of many small indicators that finally culminate in a loud and meaningful message. Examples of the latter include loss of market share, new technological advancements in your industry, mergers of your key competitors, the required closure of a once valuable factory, the initiation of a hostile unionization effort, or an increase in turnover of critical employees.

At this very early stage in the transformation, it is important to identify and understand what wake-up calls exist, what they mean, and what is being done with them by those in positions to initiate a change effort. The mindset of the leaders has a major impact on the meaning made of the information in the wake-up call. If the leaders are conscious and open to learning and changing, they will deal with the wake-up call differently than if they are not. However, let's assume that, at some point, the signal is received, the insight about the need for change is registered, and the change process is set in motion.

In *Beyond Change Management,* we introduce four levels of wake-up calls that set the stage for a transformation to be led in a conscious manner. They include recognition that: (1) a change is needed; (2) the change is transformational; (3) transformation demands new approaches, strategies, mindsets, and behavior; and (4) transformation requires the leaders to personally change their mindset, behavior, and style.

The change strategy the leaders ultimately design will be determined by their depth of understanding of these four wake-up calls. If you are consulting to the change, your initial responsibility is to assist leaders to acknowledge and respond to these wake-up calls in depth. This is the first moment of truth in the change effort; it can mean the difference between a reactive, superficial change and one that is conscious, purposeful, and profound for everyone involved.

Those who hear these wake-up calls will automatically create an initial or informal case for change in their minds. This initiates the formal change process. These informal impressions about the meaning of the wake-up calls will be used later as the starting point for designing the official case for change. After the wake-up calls have been heard by enough people to mobilize action, the change process is underway, officially beginning Phase I.

Phase I: Prepare to Lead the Change

Identifying and establishing clear foundations for a successful change effort from the beginning increase the organization's likelihood of success. Phase I accomplishes the majority of this work.

Phase I is *critical* for the leaders and for the success of the effort. Phase I covers 50 to 60 percent of the decisions made in your change strategy and plan. It does not take that same percentage of time, but it requires that amount of up-front decision making. This work cannot be delegated, although other people can be involved and supportive of the effort and help lay the groundwork for the change leaders. Remember the television commercial where a car repairman removes himself from under the hood of a car and says to the viewer, "Well, you can pay me now, or you can pay me later." He is referring to the fact that work *must* be done. You can do it now, or you can do it later; but you cannot skip it. Doing this required work up-front will undoubtedly be easier and less costly than neglecting it and dealing with the problems downstream. In our experience, attention to the work of Phase I is the most powerful of all change acceleration strategies. It models the principle "Go slow to go fast" and is well worth the time and effort.

Activity I.A: Start Up and Staff the Change Effort

This first activity organizes the start-up of the change effort. Although the change may already be underway, you will have to obtain a realistic picture of the status of the effort, clarify leadership roles, and ensure that everyone initially working on the effort is aligned.

Task I.A.1: Obtain a Project Briefing

After the leaders decide formally to initiate a change process to orchestrate the transformation, it is imperative to gather and coalesce all of the existing information and opinion about the effort. Without a clear picture of what is known, who has been doing what, and what the current reactions are, attempting to lead the change will be like herding cats.

You may find it useful to interview the various people or groups that know about the change and are going to be impacted by it to assess how they view the effort. Questions to these people usually address their knowledge about the drivers of the change, the history of the effort, perceptions of the current change events and activities underway, key issues that have arisen, and future plans. Once gathered, this information is prepared as a briefing for everyone who needs to know the status of the change effort at this early stage, including all consultants in the effort.

Briefing data usually reveals whether key stakeholders see the change effort through the same set of lenses or whether there are potentially confusing or conflicting discrepancies in people's perceptions. How people are talking about the change effort at this early date can be a significant predictor of how well it will be received once it gets underway.

For change consultants, a very powerful intervention at this point is feeding back the survey data to the senior leaders, pointing out where they are aligned and where they are not. This often initiates the first intervention to raise their awareness about how they are viewing the change and, if successful, can save tremendous time and confusion and expedite early alignment among the leaders.

Task I.A.2: Clarify Required Change Leadership Roles and Staff the Change Effort

The second task in this activity is to determine how the transformation will be led—who is sponsoring the effort, who is designing and leading the change strategy and process design, and who is involved in various other ways. Clear roles and responsibilities are needed for all of the change leaders to minimize redundancy and ensure full coverage of change leadership responsibilities.

Because taking on change leadership responsibility is usually considered an addition to one's existing duties, frequently these roles are assigned to people who are the most available. Caution! Roles should be given to the people who are the most *competent* and *best positioned to successfully lead the effort.* These selections must be very strategic, as your effort will either be enhanced or encumbered by these staffing selections. If your best people are busy, then you must ask yourself whether their current activities are more important than the successful transformation of your organization.

The following boxed copy presents a list of six typical change leadership roles. You can use all of them as described, or you may want to tailor them to fit the magnitude of your change effort and the available resources for it. To tailor the roles, you can use different titles and determine expanded, reduced, or different responsibilities for each role.

Change Leadership Roles

Sponsor	Individual with highest line authority over the transformation; "owner"; primary influencer of values and culture; sets parameters, allocates resources, often has veto power over decisions; appoints the change process leader and provides him or her support; keeps the transformation in alignment with overall business strategy, redirecting the change process or outcome when information surfaces to do so; handles major communications; undergoes required personal change in mindset and behavior and models the transformation in word and action; celebrates and acknowledges benchmark successes; and maintains ongoing link with key stakeholders.

Executive Team

The executive leadership team of the organization within which the transformation is occurring (may be the entire company or a segment); responsible for supporting and modeling the desired outcomes of the transformation (usually at a vision, strategy, and behavioral level); runs the business and buffers the change effort from organizational constraints; makes strategic decisions for the transformation as negotiated with the sponsor (however, the sponsor and/or executive team in a large organization-wide transformation may delegate all or part of this responsibility to a change leadership team.); participates in designing the change strategy and design of the desired state, as needed.

Change Leadership Team

The group of leaders or cross-functional or key stakeholder representatives from the entire system being transformed with delegated authority to shape both the desired outcomes and the change process; usually focuses on the vision, strategy, and managerial level design and planning of change activities; assures adequate resources; actively involved in directing and guiding communications and course correcting the transformation. Depending on the scope of the change, this team may be the same as the executive team, in which case it would have responsibilities for the combined functions of both teams.

Change Process Leader

A line manager or executive as high in the organization as possible who has been delegated the authority by the sponsor to lead the change process; facilitates the process of defining, planning, and course correcting the change strategy and change process; responsible for clarifying the scope, outcomes, pace, conditions for success, constraints, and infrastructure; provides advocacy for and integration of change initiatives; secures resources for the transformation; oversees communication, information generation, and course correction; engages in mindset and behavioral changes along with the other leaders; provides feedback and coaching to all change leaders and stakeholders; leads the change leadership team and the change project team.

Change Project Team

Cross-functional representatives, subproject/process leaders, and/or specially skilled individuals, who assist the change process leader in the day-to-day activities of facilitating the change effort, doing the work required to complete the various activities of the change process (for example, design and impact analysis); pursue feedback and information for course correcting; and communicate as appropriate.

Change Consultant

Change process expert and coach; acts as a sounding board and third party; educates about transformation and strategies for how to proceed; helps plan change strategy and major events, communications, training sessions, and meetings; assesses progress, problems, concerns, political and cultural issues; helps facilitate change in mindset and behavior; facilitates course corrections to the change strategy and change process; coaches, provides feedback, and acts as a conscience for the sponsor, change process leader, executive team, change leadership team, and change project team; advocates for conditions for success; interfaces and coordinates with other consultants working on the transformation.

We have labeled the role of the person in charge of planning the change effort as the change process leader, rather than change project manager. This title conveys the required shift in the organization from project-oriented thinking to process thinking, as described in *Beyond Change Management,* and emphasizes that the person in this role is responsible for designing and overseeing the transformational change strategy and the transformational change *process.* This person may become involved in the content of the change, but the priority of this role is to shape *how* the change is led, designed, implemented, and course corrected.

The person selected as the change process leader will represent the degree of importance the transformation has for the organization. The more well-respected the person is, the more important the change will be perceived as being. In most cases, our bias is that a high-level line executive should fill the role of change process leader. This role should not be filled by a consultant or a staff person, unless the change is occurring primarily in a specific staff organization or the staff person is well-respected by the leaders and the organization. It is critical that the entire workforce respond positively to the leaders of the change. The person selected to fill this role is one of the first clear signals leaders send about the magnitude and priority of what is to follow.

The change process leader should be selected not only for the respect he or she commands from the line organizations, but also for his or her ability to demonstrate conscious process thinking and design skills and a facilitative change leadership style. In addition, the more dedicated he or she is to personal development, the better, for all the reasons discussed in *Beyond Change Management.* Change process leaders stuck in the reactive, controlling, or project thinking modes will severely limit the probability of a successful transformation.

Once change leadership roles have been defined and staffed, a common dynamic that surfaces is the confusion or tension created when leaders are asked to wear two very distinct hats—a functional executive hat and a change leadership hat. Most often, the functional hat takes precedence because it is most familiar and immediate. Plus, leaders' compensation is often tied only to their functional performance. Without support to balance leaders' drive to keep the business running *and* the need to change it, this conflict can sandbag the change effort before it gets off the ground.

Under normal circumstances, leaders' tendency to take care of daily crises in their functional organizations first is a good thing. However, when an organization is undergoing major transformation, the functional leader mindset is not sufficient.

Change leaders must focus on *doing what is good for the overall organization as it transforms* while keeping it operational, especially at start-up. There is no formula for the percentage of time a leader will spend wearing each hat. We do know, however, that keeping full-time functional responsibilities without making real space for change leadership duties is a formula for failure. Therefore, you will need to set clear priorities and expectations for how and when the leaders should be wearing each hat. The resolution requires a shift of both mindset and behavior because there is only so much time available for both roles.

We have seen many creative ways of identifying and tailoring the change process leader role. One way is to create a "project/process" partnership between an individual who has the technical or business content expertise required for the change and a consultant with process design and organization development expertise. The benefit of this scenario is that the technical leader learns how to design a complex change process and the consultant learns about how to make the process relevant and timely to the business. This design requires that the two leads have clearly defined "decision rights" and work in true partnership.

Ensuring that the right people are in key change leadership roles and that core responsibilities are fully covered is essential to mobilizing the quality of leadership required for conscious transformation. Our definition of "right people" here means the best match of mindset, behavior, expertise, and leadership style with the magnitude and type of change you are facing.

An exploration of your change leadership roles may reveal that the wrong people are in key roles. This task is an opportunity to correct your change leader selection and role expectations. Although this can be politically ticklish, making these changes now is far less costly than doing it later.

Task I.A.3: Create Optimal Working Relationships

Building and sustaining effective working relationships is an important condition for success. When people take on special change leadership roles, it is essential to clarify the working relationships among them and with their peers who retain existing functional roles. Too often, old political struggles will surface and hinder the change leaders from doing what the change effort requires. By addressing and clearing up past history, conflicts, or political dynamics, the leaders ensure the cleanest, clearest leadership thinking and behavior to support the overall transformation. Having the leaders model the healing of broken relationships and the creation of effective partnerships is a powerful cultural intervention, one that is absolutely required to make your change effort successful and expedient.

When key change leadership roles, such as the change process leader or the top change consultants, are filled by people from lower levels in the organization, you must re-establish effective working relationships among all of the change leaders and the executives. Everyone who has a key role must be clear about who has responsibility and authority to do what so that everyone can pull in the same direction. It is especially critical that people from lower in the hierarchy be given the authority they need to succeed in their new roles.

The relationship between the executive team running the business and the change leadership team changing it has to be crystal clear. The business must continue to operate effectively during the transformation, and it must also be enabled to change so that it can better serve its customers' new needs. This requires negotiating clear decision authority and responsibilities between these two teams. Make the predictable tension between these teams overt and clarify how both teams can best serve the overall good of the organization. Organization development consultants can assist with this work, which should begin when the change leadership team is established and be re-visited periodically throughout the transformation.

Task I.A.4: Identify the Project Community

How clear are you about who is or should be involved in this transformation? Who has a vested interest in its success? Who is going to be seriously impacted by it? Whose voice has to be heard as the transformation is being planned? It is essential at start-up to identify everyone, internally and externally, who has a stake in the change effort and is involved in or affected by it. This identification will provide you an easy reference for thinking through various stakeholder needs as you shape your change strategy and process plan. It will also help identify the critical mass of support required for the transformation to succeed.

Some change management approaches refer to this exercise as building a "stakeholder map." We call this group the "project community," preferring this language to convey the intention of this group to share a common vision of the change and to work together for the collective good of the organization. Exhibit 1.1 shows a sample project community map.

Exhibit 1.1. Sample Project Community Map

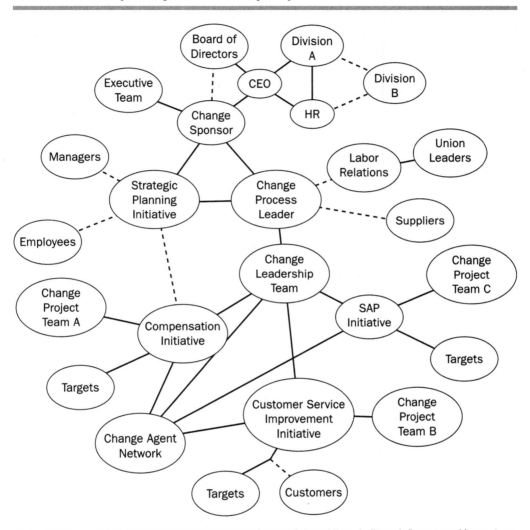

Note: Solid lines represent direct reporting relationships and dotted lines indicate influence and/or partnership or cross-boundary relationships.

When you map your project community in detail, specify the various roles of each member. For example, in Exhibit 1.1, the CEO is the sponsor, leads the executive team, and is a member of the change leadership team as well. Be sure to specify all roles for any individual or group.

Your project community map should graphically reveal the relationships among its members. This will enable you to leverage these relationships strategically throughout the change process. You may also want to identify any relationships within the community that need improvement, because you will be counting on these relationships to function effectively to support the overall transformation. Use this information as input to Task I.A.3, Create Optional Working Relationships.

You can work with your project community in many ways—in person, by memo, or electronically. Your primary intention for the community is to create the conditions among all of the members to support the transformation actively as it unfolds. We are not advocating that you make this group into a formal structure. You will likely have greater impact by allowing it to operate organically, working with parts of it as your change process requires. Your strategies for this group may include:

- Publishing who these people are as key players in the transformation;

- Keeping them informed of the status of the change effort;

- Interviewing them to gather pertinent input or using them as sounding board advisors on various strategic or operational choice points during the transformation;

- Assigning them key roles in major change activities or events;

- Establishing shared expectations for how they can add value to the effort;

- Working with them to create a critical mass of support for the vision and desired state; and

- Positioning them as change advocates, models of the new mindset and behavior, information generators, and so on.

Exhibit 1.2 presents a worksheet to assist with identifying your project community.

Exhibit 1.2. Identifying the Project Community

Identify the members of your project community for your project. Name the key players from the following groups:

Change Leadership:

- Sponsor

- Change process leader

- Executive team

- Change leadership team

- Change project team

- Change consultants (internal and external)

Stakeholder Groups or Individuals:

- Board of Directors

- Executives

- Upper management

- Mid-management

Exhibit 1.2. Identifying the Project Community, Cont'd

- Employees

- Stockholders

- Unions

Customers:

- Internal

- External

Suppliers:

Areas of the Organization (Functions/Processes):

Locations Within the Organization:

Other Important Change or Improvement Initiatives:

Related Change Process Leaders or Project Managers:

Others:

Now that you are clear about who is doing what and what the current status of the change effort is, you can proceed with the important work of creating your official case for change.

Activity I.B: Create the Case for Change and Determine Your Initial Desired Outcomes

No one, leader or employee, will give heart and soul to such a complex and challenging effort as transformation unless he or she understands why the change is necessary and what benefit it promises—personally and organizationally. This activity answers the basic questions: "Why transform?" "What needs to transform?" and "What outcomes do we want from this transformation?" Frequently, people have many different views of why change is needed, what is driving it, and how big it is. Until your desired outcomes are clear, people will not know why they should invest the effort it will take. Creating the case for change and your initial objectives for it creates a common view for the change leaders and gives their efforts meaning, direction, and energy for aligned action. Without a clear case for change, the transformation will lack relevance for employees, causing resistance, confusion, and insecurity.

The case for change includes the following:

- Why the transformation is needed;
- What needs to transform about the organization;
- Leverage points for changing the systems dynamics of the organization in support of the transformation;
- Initial impacts on the organization and its people;
- Type of change;
- Scope of change;
- Targets of change;
- Urgency for the change; and
- Initial desired outcomes for the change.

Although we have positioned this work as a part of leader preparation for the transformation, many other people may be involved in shaping the case for change and its outcomes. The marketplace, as the primary driver of the transformation, dictates the content of the case for change. Marketplace requirements for success can be sought by anyone who has a perspective on what your customers and competitors are doing. When front-line employees and middle managers participate in creating the case for change, they add credibility to the assessment of need, leverage points for transformation, and impacts. Their participation is an enormous catalyst for their understanding and commitment. No matter who generates the data for the case, we believe the leaders are responsible to put all of this information into a clear picture that they agree with and will communicate to the organization during Phase II.

The information for your case for change may already have been generated through the organization's business strategy efforts. If so, take the exploration of the business strategy to the next level of specificity: How does the strategy require the organization to change? Use the business strategy as input to the tasks of this activity to ensure that you have a complete picture and that your case for change and your business strategy are aligned.

Task I.B.1: Identify Who Will Do This Work and the Process for How It Will Be Accomplished

Who builds the case for change and how is it best accomplished? Your decision criteria for both answers should include: (1) People who have a big-picture understanding of the systemic and environmental dynamics creating the need for the transformation; (2) people who model your desired mindset and culture; (3) the level of urgency you face; (4) the degree to which your case has already been formulated by your business strategy; and (5) people's expertise in the areas defined by the predicted scope of your transformation.

Design your process for creating the case by reviewing all of the tasks of this activity and then determining how to accomplish them in a way that reflects your desired culture.

Task I.B.2: Assess the Drivers of Change

At this point, you must assess what is driving the transformation. *Beyond Change Management* introduces the drivers of change as the essential triggers for the scope of change facing the organization. The Drivers of Change Model is shown in Figure 0.1 in the Introduction to this book. The following boxed copy briefly defines each driver. Each provides essential data for the determination of what must change in the organization and why.

The Drivers of Change

Environmental Forces	The dynamics of the larger context within which organizations and people operate. These forces include social, business and economic, political, governmental, technological, demographic, legal, and natural environment.
Marketplace Requirements for Success	The aggregate set of customer requirements that determine what it takes for a business to succeed in its marketplace. This includes not only the actual product or service needs, but also requirements such as speed of delivery, customization capability, level of quality, need for innovation, level of customer service, and so forth. Changes in marketplace requirements are the result of changes in environmental forces.
Business Imperatives	Business imperatives outline what the company must do *strategically* to be successful, given its customers' changing requirements. This can require systematic rethinking and change to the company's mission, strategy, goals, products and services, e-commerce position, pricing, or branding. Business imperatives are usually identified through the organization's strategic planning process.
Organizational Imperatives	Organizational imperatives specify what must change in the organization's structure, systems, processes, technology, resources, skill base, or staffing to realize its strategic business imperatives. Examples include reengineering, restructuring, or work redesign.
Cultural Imperatives	Cultural imperatives denote how the norms, or collective way of being, working, and relating in the company, must change to support and drive the organization's new design, strategy, and operations.

Leader and Employee Behavior	Collective behavior creates and expresses an organization's culture. Behavior speaks to more than just overt actions; it describes the style, tone, or character that permeates what people do and how their way of being must change to create the new culture. Leaders and employees must choose to behave differently to transform the organization's culture.
Leader and Employee Mindset	Mindset encompasses people's worldview, assumptions, beliefs, and mental models. Mindset causes people to behave in the ways in which they do; it underlies behavior. Becoming aware that each of us has a mindset and that it directly impacts our feelings, decisions, actions, and results is often the critical first step in building individual and organizational capacity to change. Mindset change is often required to catalyze and sustain new behaviors in both leaders and employees. A shift of mindset is usually required for organizational leaders to recognize changes in the environmental forces and marketplace requirements, thereby being able to determine the best new strategic business direction, structure, or operation for the organization. Mindset change in employees is often required for them to understand the rationale for the changes being asked of them.

Exhibit 1.3 provides a worksheet to assist you with an assessment of what is driving your change.

Exhibit 1.3. Determining What Is Driving the Change

Environmental Forces	
Marketplace Requirements for Success	
Business Imperatives	
Organizational Imperatives	
Cultural Imperatives	
Leader/Employee Behavior	
Leader/Employee Mindset	

Task I.B.3: Assess the Organization's System Dynamics to Identify the Leverage Points for Change

Organizations are extremely complex. They are multi-dimensional systems comprised of an enormous number of variables. For example, organizations have strategies, structure, management systems, and business processes. They have cultural expectations and people who are all unique. They are affected by marketplace dynamics, competitive pressures, and employee morale. They may have excellent teamwork or hostile internal role conflicts. The list of elements within organizations is virtually endless. All of these variables are interdependent. Change in one factor may have either immediate or distant impacts on other variables. The dynamic interactions of all of these variables comprise the organization's "system dynamics."

For those of you knowledgeable about the principles and tools of systems thinking, this is familiar territory. Systems thinking describes that, within every organization's system dynamics, there exist underlying patterns of interaction between variables. These patterns are referred to as the organization's "underlying dynamic structure." This structure, or set of interactive patterns, causes the organization's current behavior and performance—both what is working well and what is not.

Systems thinking approaches use "systems diagrams" to map an organization's underlying structure. Systems diagrams can be incredibly revealing as they graphically portray, in clear and simple terms, not only the dynamic "causes" of current behavior but "leverage points" for change. Leverage points are places in the organization where small, focused action can produce larger positive changes. In other words, by altering the dynamic interactions between certain variables, positive results occur across larger domains of the overall organization.

The objective of this task is to map the organization's systems dynamics that are relevant to the change to reveal the underlying structures that are causing its current behavior and performance. Using this information, you can gain insight about what needs to change in your organization and where the leverage points are for producing that change.

Once you have identified the underlying structure and leverage points, they become inputs to your case for change. Both are central forces for *why* you need to change and *what* needs to change. Unless you understand them, your effort may never affect the kinds of shifts required for your organization to achieve its desired outcomes.

System dynamics, underlying structures, and systems diagrams deserve a thorough description and exploration, which we cannot do justice to here. We refer you to *The Fifth Discipline* (Senge, 1990) and *The Fifth Discipline Fieldbook* (Senge, Kleiner, Roberts, Ross, & Smith, 1994) for a further introduction to these concepts and tools and guidance on how to use them to support the identification of your organization's underlying structure and leverage points for change.

Task I.B.4: Perform an Initial Impact Analysis

As you become clearer about what this change effort entails, it is important to clarify the types of impacts it will create throughout the organization. At this point in the process, an assessment of impacts can only be done at a generalized level. When you have designed the actual future state, you will be able to do a more thorough analysis. That is the focus of Phase V. For now, this general assessment focuses the leaders' attention on both the business/organizational elements and the personal/cultural impacts.

A helpful tool to perform this assessment, the Initial Impact Analysis Audit, is provided in Exhibit 1.4. This tool lists many typical impact areas affected by change in the organization. These areas will tell you, at a high level, how broad and how deep the impact of making the transformation will go. This information, in addition to the assessment of the drivers of change and your system dynamics and leverage points, is critical to understanding what your change strategy needs to include for the transformation to succeed. This information will be used as input to determining the scope of the change.

To fill in the Impact Analysis Audit, consider the change effort as you currently understand it. Review each item in the tool, marking it if your change effort will impact it directly (D) or indirectly (I) when it is successfully completed. Each item with a "D" or "I" requires more detailed planning and attention as a part of Phases V and VI in your change process plan. For now, noting the areas requiring more focus will help you to clarify your scope of change.

The initial impact analysis is a powerful way to expand the change leaders' view of the amount of attention, planning, and resources the change will require. It is designed to create a systems view of the organization and the transformation.

Exhibit 1.4. Initial Impact Analysis Audit

What aspects of your organization will be impacted by the change? How will the organization be affected? Mark the following areas that apply to your case by writing a "D" on the line for *direct* impact and an "I" on the line for *indirect* impact.

BUSINESS/ORGANIZATIONAL IMPACTS:

___ Purpose/Vision/Mission

___ Business Strategy

___ Market Posture

___ Organizational Structure

___ Management Systems and Processes

___ Technology/Equipment

___ Tasks/Job Definition/Job Levels

___ Products and Services

___ People: Numbers/Skills/Systems

___ Policies/Procedures

___ Resources Needed/Resources Available

___ Space Requirements/Layout/Moves

___ Image (How we are perceived by others)

___ Identity (Who we are; how we see ourselves)

___ Customer Service

___ Union Activity

___ Response to Government Regulations

___ Merger or Acquisition

___ Splits/Divestitures

___ Downsizing

___ Growth/Expansion/Start Ups

___ Management Succession

___ Work Flow

___ Governance and Decision Making

___ Team Structures

___ Technical Skills

___ Current Skills Training

___ Communication Systems

PERSONAL/CULTURAL IMPACTS:

___ Resistance and Anxiety

___ Sadness at Letting Go of Old Ways

___ Motivation and Commitment

___ What People Are Recognized for

___ Inclusion/Exclusion Issues

___ Politics and Power Plays

___ Perceptions of Fairness

___ Values

___ Expectations

___ Employee Mindset, Attitude

___ Norms

___ Need for Learning and Course Correction

___ People Skills

___ Changes in Relationships

___ Leadership Style/Executive Behavior

___ Employee Behavior

___ Team Effectiveness

___ Leader Mindset, Attitude

___ Management Development/People Effectiveness Skills Training

Task I.B.5: Identify the Type, Scope, and Targets of the Change
Determining the Type of Change

The drivers of your change tell you the primary type of change you are leading—*developmental, transitional,* or *transformational.* The type of change has direct implications for the change strategy the effort requires. The consequences of not defining the type of change accurately can create costly havoc or failure for the effort. Figure 1.1 graphically portrays the three types, discussed in depth in *Beyond Change Management.*

Figure 1.1. Three Types of Change

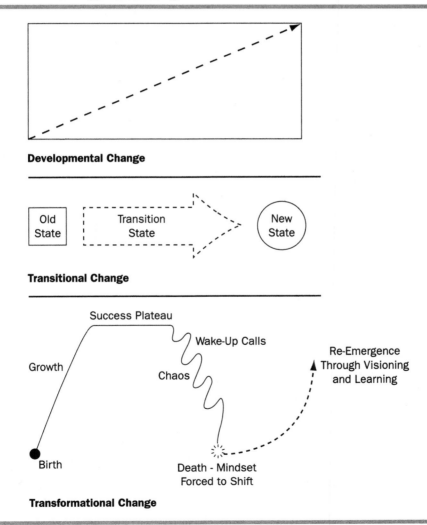

Developmental Change

Transitional Change

Transformational Change

Although you may have multiple types of change present within your overall effort or your composite initiatives, one type is always primary. That is the one that will most influence the design of the change strategy. For instance, you may need to develop better marketing skills and systems (developmental change), and you may need to consolidate several functions to improve efficiencies (transitional change), but the primary change is a radical transformation of your business model to e-commerce. Such a change is transformational because it calls for a significant shift in direction and requires major behavior and mindset change in your people.

Identifying the Scope and Targets of the Change

One of the most common mistakes leaders make in change is to misdiagnose its scope, typically making it too narrow. Scope determines what you will pay attention to and plan for. If it is too limited, repercussions will be occurring outside of your view of things, creating all kinds of unpleasant surprises. If your scope is not accurate, you may be missing key leverage points for getting the change to happen or expending energy on the wrong things.

Inaccurate identification of scope is one of the leading causes of failure in reengineering efforts. The classic reengineering effort's scope has focused on changing business processes, structure, and job definition. These are all organizational imperatives for change in the Drivers of Change Model. However, reengineering efforts typically have overlooked the internal system dynamics of people's behavior, communications, and working relationships, which are cultural, behavioral, and mindset drivers. For successful transformation, scope must attend to all of the drivers, both external and internal.

Your case for change must accurately identify the scope of change required in the organization, as well as the targets of the transformation. Scope is the breadth and depth of the change effort. Targets are the groups and people who will be directly impacted by the change or who are essential in carrying it out. The three assessments performed in Tasks I.B.2, 3, and 4 are all inputs to the identification of scope. Review this information and determine the breadth and depth of your change.

Task I.B.6: Determine the Degree of Urgency

Another output of your assessment of the drivers of change is the determination of the degree of urgency for making the transformation. A common error in leading transformation is the automatic assumption that the change needs to occur faster than is humanly possible. Our society assumes urgency; we live in the face of the tidal wave of speed. Urgency, in and of itself, is not a bad thing. It is an important motivator for focused action. However, when leading transformation, a *realistic* sense of urgency is essential. It is one of the key determinants of how well the organization will respond to the change.

Wanting speed is not the same as the marketplace absolutely dictating it. Employees will understand a true need for speed, but will disregard fabricated urgency and label it one more reason executives cannot be trusted to tell the truth. Don't make this mistake. Executives who push transformation into unrealistic timetables, without thinking through their internal motivations or the state of their people, usually cost the organization in damaged morale, lost productivity, or impaired quality, all of which inevitably take more time to repair.

Phase VI of the Change Process Model, *Plan and Organize for Implementation*, provides a more informed determination of the timeline required for the change process based on a more detailed impact analysis of both external factors (environment, marketplace, and organization) and internal factors (culture and people's capacity). At that point, the real work of the change, outlined in the Implementation Master Plan, better indicates how long the effort will take if done well. At this early stage, however, the change leaders can only guess, using their initial assessment of its scope and their impression of people's ability to do what is required. Therefore, in communicating timelines at this early stage, present them only as general estimates.

Task I.B.7: Determine Your Initial Desired Outcomes and Compile the Case for Change

The results of the six tasks of this activity provide information for your initial take on what you want this transformation to produce. You may have outcomes for any of the drivers of change as well as one central objective for the overall organization. This determination begins to shape the vision for this transformation. It is used to provide motivation, rationale, and inspiration for the organization to take on this effort. The change leaders can use the desired outcomes they identify here to craft their vision for the transformation or provide them as input to members of the organization engaging in the visioning process. (Task I.E.5 is to shape the change leaders' visioning strategy and establish whether it will be primarily leader-driven or participatory.)

All of the information generated in this activity forms the basis of the case for change. The introduction at the beginning of the chapter lists all of the elements of your case for change. Review them, refine the results of all of the tasks of this activity, and write your case for change.

The case for change is critical input for your change strategy, which is compiled as the last activity of Phase I. Both the case for change and your change strategy will be communicated to the organization at the beginning of Phase II. With this in mind, tailor your case for ease of communication, making it concise, informative, and inspirational.

Summary

You have now formed a realistic picture of the current status of the change effort and staffed its leadership. You understand who all of the stakeholders are and have begun to align all of these key players to support the transformation. In addition, you have clarified your initial assumptions about your case for change, desired outcomes, scope, and pace of the transformation. The next chapter continues with more Phase I work, addressing the organization's level of readiness and capacity to proceed with what you are currently planning.

Consulting Questions for Activity I.A: Start Up and Staff the Change Effort

Task I.A.1: Obtain a Project Briefing

- Who has to be briefed about the status of the transformation (leaders, key stakeholders of the change effort, consultants)?

- What information will you gather about the history, current reality, and future plans of the effort?

- What methods will you use to gather briefing information, and whom will you interview?

- What will you do if you surface conflicting data about what has been happening and how it is perceived? How will you secure leadership alignment with the current reality?

Task I.A.2: Clarify Required Change Leadership Roles and Staff the Change Effort

- Who is currently in charge of the change effort?
- What roles are needed for this effort to be led and facilitated effectively?
- How will you select the best people to staff each of the change leadership roles? Who will fill each role?
- How will these people be informed and introduced to the expectations and deliverables of their roles?
- How will you address the conflict or time pressures for individuals who are asked to wear both a functional leadership hat and a change leadership hat?
- What will you do if someone currently in a change leadership role is not the best person for the job?
- What is your role in this change? Is it what you think it needs to be to make your greatest contribution? If not, what will you do to reposition it?
- What consultants are being used in the transformation and for what purposes? How will you interface with the consultants involved, integrate their activities, and bring them up to speed regarding current plans?

Task I.A.3: Create Optimal Working Relationships

- What is the current condition of the relationships among all of the people filling change leadership roles? Between those in change leadership roles and those in functional leadership roles? Do any of these relationships need to improve? In what way? How can you help?
- How can the relationship between the executive team and the change leadership team be clarified and strengthened between the sponsor and the change process leader?

Task I.A.4: Identify the Project Community

- Who are all of the stakeholders of this change effort? Is everybody who must have a voice in this transformation identified and able to be heard as the change is being planned?
- How does this change effort interface with other groups or projects underway in the organization?

- What are all of the connections and organizational relationships among the change stakeholders? Are the relationships that will be called on for change tasks working well? If not, how can they be strengthened?

- How will you inform the stakeholders that they are an important part of this effort's project community?

- What will the various members of the project community be asked to do? How will the project community be used to support the overall good of the transformation?

Consulting Questions for Activity I.B: Create the Case for Change and Determine Your Initial Desired Outcome

Task I.B.1: Identify Who Will Do This Work and the Process for How It Will Be Accomplished

- Who are the best people to determine the transformation's desired outcomes and create the case for change? Should the people who created the organization's business strategy be included? How?

- What process will be used to accomplish this work? How will you ensure that the process reflects the organization's desired culture? How will you use your business strategy to inform your case for change?

Task I.B.2: Assess the Drivers of Change

- How will you go about assessing the drivers of this transformation?

- What is driving this change? (Consider environmental forces, marketplace and customer requirements for success, strategic business imperatives, organizational imperatives, cultural imperatives, leader and employee behavior changes needed, and leader and employee mindset changes needed.)

Task I.B.3: Assess the Organization's System Dynamics to Identify the Leverage Points for Change

- Who are the best people to accomplish this task?

- Who should champion it and who should provide input?

- What tools will you use to map the organization's system dynamics and underlying structures?

- What underlying patterns of interaction among organizational variables are revealed?

- What are the leverage points within them for the transformation?

Task I.B.4: Perform an Initial Impact Analysis

- What is the change leaders' initial assessment of the business and organizational impacts of this transformation?

- What is the change leaders' initial assessment of the personal and cultural impacts of this transformation?

Task I.B.5: Identify the Type, Scope, and Targets of the Change

- What is the primary type of change happening in this effort?

- What other types of change are also involved in it?

- How will you integrate the drivers of change, leverage points for change, and the initial impact analysis data to determine an accurate scope for this transformation?

- What is the scope of the effort?

- Who are the targets of this transformation?

Task I.B.6: Determine the Degree of Urgency

- What is the realistic degree of urgency of this transformation?

- What are the operational and people implications of this degree of urgency? What implications do you see for the organization's readiness, morale, and stamina?

Task I.B.7: Determine Your Initial Desired Outcomes and Compile the Case for Change

- What are your initial desired outcomes for this transformation?

- How would you summarize the case for change in a way that can be effectively communicated to the organization?

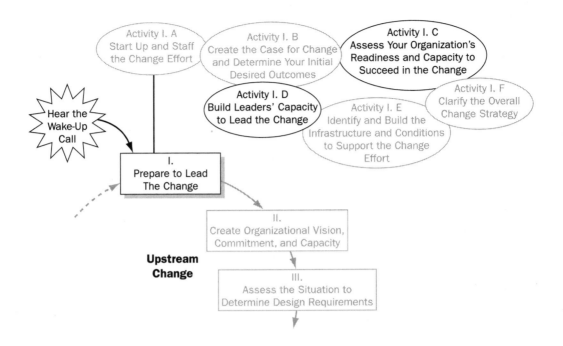

Activity I.C and I.D Task Deliverables

I.C.1: The organization's level of readiness and capacity for making the transformation has been determined.

I.C.2: The strategy for building the organization's level of readiness and capacity for transformation has been prepared.

I.D.1: A plan to engage the executives in their own development and transformation has been established.

I.D.2: Leaders understand how their mindset, style, and behavior must change to lead the organization's transformation successfully and are beginning the process to achieve this.

I.D.3: Leader commitment and alignment to the transformation have been established.

I.D.4: The executive team and change leaders better understand how organization transformation happens and what is required to lead conscious transformational change.

I.D.5: The executive team and change leadership team are able to lead the transformation effectively and work well together.

I.D.6: Individual leaders of the change are being trained and/or coached to increase their ability to lead and walk the talk of change.

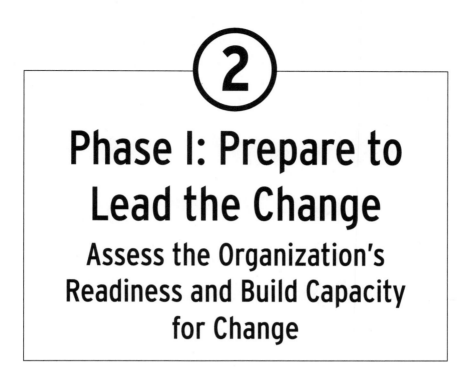

Phase I: Prepare to Lead the Change

Assess the Organization's Readiness and Build Capacity for Change

BY NOW YOU HAVE A FAIRLY CLEAR IDEA of what the transformation is going to require of both the organization and the leaders. Are people ready? Are they willing to change? Are they able to carry out the transformation and deliver its intended outcomes? Are the leaders prepared and capable of leading the transformation, individually and collectively? The accurate answers to these questions are essential to formulating a change strategy consciously. Activity I.C assesses the organization's readiness and capacity to take on the transformation. Activity I.D builds the leader's capacity to lead the effort.

Activity I.C: Assess the Organization's Readiness and Capacity to Succeed in the Change

One of the most tragic mistakes made in leading transformation is to impose it on an organization that is not ready, able, or willing to proceed. Many executives, so focused on what the organization needs to do differently, overlook the requirement to determine whether their people are capable of the changes required. This is a pattern we see in leaders who do not understand the human or process dynamics of leading transformation. Not many athletes would consider running two marathons without sufficient time in between to recuperate. However, leaders frequently ask their organizations to make change after change after change. When most of these efforts are transformational, the pressure of the emotional and operating demands can overwhelm even the most hardy and committed employees. All too often, employees become demoralized, skeptical, or burned out. Worse yet, they leave the organization.

Rather than foisting the transformation on the organization without concern for people's current work levels or residual emotions from past changes, you must become aware of the organization's current state of receptivity and ability to make this change. This activity assesses where the workforce is in relation to what you currently assume is required for success. It demands that you listen to the data generated and respond to it responsibly.

Task I.C.1: Assess the Organization's Readiness and Capacity to Succeed in the Change

In this task, the executives examine the readiness and capacity of their organization to do what is required to change. Readiness and capacity are influenced by many factors, both internal and external. People need to be ready physically, emotionally, mentally, spiritually, and behaviorally. A deficiency in any one of these capacities may slow the transformation, especially if the deficiency is widely shared.

▶ CASE IN POINT

In one utility organization, we assisted the leadership team to develop a major change strategy affecting the organization's overall structure and culture. Before completing the strategy, we encouraged the change leaders to assess the readiness and capacity of their primary targets of the change. Although they were pleased with the support and enthusiasm in their middle management ranks, they were shocked to uncover serious problems with their first-line supervisors.

Apparently, the supervisors were still infuriated about the last change effort, which had affected their role authority, performance measures, and compensation. They felt angry and distrustful, wary of any hint of more change.

We convinced the leaders of the need to address this emotional residue before rolling out the new changes. The leaders worked with the supervisors to express the concerns, explore various points of view, and clear the air. This healthy process enabled the leaders to build even greater readiness in the organization. Had they not assessed the true emotional state of the supervisors, they would have had to struggle with inordinate resistance, with failure an almost certain result. As it turned out, the supervisors got on board and championed much of the change. ◀

A thorough assessment of readiness and capacity includes a variety of topics critical to planning a conscious change strategy, such as those we have been discussing. We have identified five categories that affect readiness and capacity to change:

1. *The organization's history and track record with past change.* This category focuses on the degree to which past efforts used effective change leadership strategies such as those we have been discussing. If past change efforts did not, for example, provide sufficient time, attention, and resources to the change, people will likely be wary of the burden of new changes.

2. *Felt need for the current change.* This category assesses the effectiveness of the case for change in articulating compelling reasons for the change, its desired outcomes, and its benefits. It also looks at the degree of realism in the prescribed urgency and timetable.

3. *Leadership's capacity to lead this transformation.* Transformation requires change leadership knowledge and skills that are very different from those required to run current operations or lead developmental or transitional change. Most leaders automatically assume they already possess these transformational leadership competencies. We challenge this assumption. Do the leaders already know everything they need to know about transformation and how to lead it? Are they as comfortable and adept at attending to people and process as they are to content? Are they prime examples of the behavior the future requires? Are they fully capable of building an integrated change strategy? Are they masters of mobilizing their organizations to deliver their intended *transformational* outcomes on time?

   It is useful to evaluate the answers to these questions in advance of obtaining the leaders' commitment to build their own capacity to lead the transformation. If the leaders are not willing to transform personally and become models of the change, or if they do not possess sufficient mental and physical stamina to lead this transformation, their capacity will be inadequate. Activity I.D focuses on building the leaders' capacity in areas in which this assessment indicates it is necessary.

4. *Employees' capacity to engage successfully in the transformation.* It is valuable to know whether employees affected by this transformation are able to let go of the status quo or past and are willing to pursue the outcomes of this change. If their current workload is too much to accommodate the requirements of this transformation, or if their emotions, mindset, skills, or physical state is not adequate for dealing with it, the leaders will have serious human dynamics issues to address, as the previous case illustrated. It is also helpful to know whether employees have the knowledge, skills, mindset, and behavior that will be required in the new state.

5. *The organization's capacity to transform while it continues its day-to-day operations.* It is valuable to know whether there is sufficient stability in the organization for making the change within the desired timeframe. If there are too many other major change initiatives underway, the organization's capacity to accept this one is going to be adversely affected.

Consider the various audiences whose readiness and capacity you will study. Audiences might be any of the groups in your project community, especially people involved in designing or implementing the transformation and all groups to be impacted directly by the change.

Most leaders have never addressed these topics in preparation for a major change effort. Some may resist delving into such matters. Inquiring into these subjects will likely surface information that, although it may be uncomfortable for the leaders to acknowledge, is key to aligning their change strategy with the true condition in the organization. At the very least, raising these topics will start many conversations among leaders and employees that would never otherwise have occurred, all in the name of building awareness for leading conscious transformation.

Use this assessment data as input to your strategy to build the organization's readiness and capacity for transformation, which occurs in Task I.C.2. You will roll out this strategy in Phase II.

Task I.C.2: Identify the Strategy for Building Organizational Readiness and Capacity for the Change

Based on the results of the readiness and capacity assessment, this task creates a plan to raise the organization's level of readiness and capacity to carry out the transformation. For instance, if your data show that groups within the organization are not clear about or aligned with the need for this change, you would create ways to further communicate and explore the drivers of this change, its importance, and the degree of urgency. This would enable the workforce to more readily take it on. Or if the managers or employees were fully focused on imminent production pressures and did not have any time or attention to give to the start-up of this transformation, you would want to consider your timing requirements or provide extra help to make space for the added burden of this change. These strategies will be initiated in Phase II and continue as long as they are necessary to establish people's capacity to make this transformation successful.

Activity I.D: Build Leaders' Capacity to Lead the Change

Few leaders possess the complete capacity to lead transformation successfully. In fact, learning transformational change leadership is an ongoing process. By definition, transformational change is radically different from any other leadership activity. It is fraught with uncertainties and surprises, and leaders cannot possibly know what to do from the beginning. Yet they so often dive into transformational change full steam ahead, calling for action and decisions without strategically understanding the dynamics they are facing.

Leaders are most comfortable in "do mode," focusing on external action and circumstances. Transformational change calls for equal parts of self-reflection, personal change, and continuous course correction of the change process. Because transformation calls for an essential shift in mindset, style, and behavior, leaders must look first at themselves rather than automatically ask the workforce to make all of the changes. Leaders must model what they are asking of the organization to be able to compel the workforce to take on the challenge of transformation. There is no worse condition when initiating change than to have the leaders of the organization espouse one set of norms for the organization and then behave according to an obviously different set of norms.

This activity requires leaders to acknowledge that they have to change personally and collectively. This is not comfortable work, and in many organizations it has been forbidden from executive development agendas. As yet, it is rare to see leaders actively pursuing their own personal change and expanding their transformational change leadership knowledge and skills. However, because this is so essential, this activity is designed to crack the barrier that keeps these topics "undiscussable." It makes explicit the subject of personal transformation and positions it as a nonnegotiable part of the organization's overall transformational change strategy. *Leaders must engage in their own development as a core part of the transformation.*

A conscientious assessment of the leaders' mindsets, skills, knowledge, and approach to change, either done in the previous task or here, is essential for shaping a focused change leadership development strategy. Ultimately, this strategy should enable the leaders to model the change, as well as capably guide the organization through it. Some of this development can be done in real time on actual change work while the effort is being planned and carried out.

Task I.D.1: Create an Overall Strategy for Building Leadership's Capacity to Lead the Change

The first task in this activity is to create a plan for how to engage the executives in committing to their own development. This may take some careful marketing. The change readiness and capacity assessment work performed earlier in Activity I.C provides much of the data to make your case for this activity. This task requires leaders to agree that they need development to become more effective change leaders and that they are willing to undergo this development.

There are five potential areas of change leadership development addressed in this activity. These are represented by the tasks that follow. The first task determines which of these five areas should be included in the leaders' development process and how it will be addressed. Be sure to incorporate those you deem pertinent into one *integrated* development strategy. Dealing with each task as a discrete, piecemeal intervention will weaken the overall impact of the required development.

Task I.D.2: Initiate the Strategy for Addressing Leadership Mindset, Style, and Behavior

If the change effort is truly transformational, you must address whether the leaders' mindsets, style, and behavior fit the future requirements of the organization and, if they do not, you must decide how to change them. The leaders must first explore what mindset is, how it impacts results, and how it is a central driver of the organization's transformation. We discuss all of this in depth in *Beyond Change Management* and we emphasize that, unless leaders address these aspects directly, these factors will continue to impact their ability to lead the organization and the transformation. *We cannot underscore the importance of this task enough! It is the source of making your organization's transformation conscious.*

Once the definition and power of mindset, style, and behavior are understood and accepted, the leaders should explore any or all of the following areas:

- Their leadership and behavioral styles;

- Their underlying assumptions about the nature of people, organizations, and change;

- How their mindset, style, and behavior may contribute or help to resolve challenges the organization is facing;

- How their current mindset, style, and behavior may have to change to support the organization's transformation and successful future;

- Their interpersonal skills; how they relate to one another and the workforce;

- Their communication style and the underlying assumptions they hold about information sharing;

- Their personal issues surrounding topics such as power and control, competence, inclusion, wanting to be liked, or justice and fairness.

This exploration will assist the leaders to determine how they must be different to be more successful. They must commit to undergo the personal development required of them and demonstrate the importance of this kind of personal change to the rest of the organization.

How do you change mindset, style, and behavior? Discussing the concept of mindset and behavior as an agenda item in an executive meeting does nothing to actually change them. In fact, doing so often creates the trap of executives thinking they have "handled" the issue. Even if the leaders agree that shifts in mindset, style, and behavior are needed, these changes cannot be forced on them or mandated. Both leaders and employees have to *experience* the benefit of shifts in mindset and then choose to change themselves. This is accomplished through personal transformation training, tools, and techniques. Competent facilitators are required to teach them how to apply personal change approaches.

There are many strategies for addressing leadership mindset, style, and behavior. In our own consulting, we begin all transformation efforts with a strategy that we have found to be very powerful—a system-wide intervention we call the "leadership breakthrough" process. Briefly, the leadership breakthrough process is comprised of a four-day training session preceded by pre-session interviews and reinforced with follow-up sessions and ongoing coaching. In the main training session, participants experientially come to understand what mindset is and the power it has over their performance and results. They explore if and how their own mindset, style, and behavior fit the world in which they are striving to succeed. They address the topics listed above and learn a systematic personal transformation process, complete with tools, techniques, and daily practice.

Transformational experiences like the leadership breakthrough process provide leaders with a mirror in which to see both the positive and negative effects of their current mindset, style, and behavior. The sessions create a safe environment for leaders to explore and commit to the personal change required of them to be more effective in the new reality they face, and they build sustainable teamwork. To be effective, leadership breakthrough trainings must address the leaders as individuals, the quality of their relationships with others, and the level of their team performance and learning ability.

We can best describe the "leadership breakthrough" strategy by sharing how one company used it.

▶ CASE ɪɴ POINT

The transformation of DTE Energy from a regulated to a "fiercely competitive" deregulated business was mindset driven. When we began supporting this effort, both the CEO and president realized that even though they could not yet specify all the changes required in their business strategy and organization, they could and must begin shifting their culture from entitlement to an entrepreneurial, service-oriented style. Early on, they realized that this responsibility began with them.

The strategy for dealing with the leaders' mindsets was developed in partnership with DTE Energy's internal change leaders. We agreed to provide the top executives with a four-day breakthrough experience aimed at "walking the talk of change." This session was designed to wake the leaders up to the limitations of their old mindset and style of leading and introduce them to new ways to see themselves, one another, their role in the organization, and the opportunities in deregulation. Motivated by the results and power of this experience, the executives decided to provide the same session to all three hundred of their top leaders over the next six months. The impact of these sessions then motivated the executives to offer this session to their remaining twelve hundred leaders over the next two years. In the following year, the remaining seven thousand employees were also introduced to the principles of the training through an abbreviated program.

The overall strategy went far beyond the four-day workshop. Our experience of delivering breakthrough training has demonstrated to us that, although the multi-day workshop is a central component, the tangible results required to support the organization's transformation comes from a much larger, integrated process. For DTE, this included pre-session interviews of each of the participants by the facilitators to establish clear personal objectives, follow-up sessions, pre- and post-session meetings between bosses and subordinates, large group meetings, executive coaching, on-the-job feedback, and team development. Each of these reinforced and extended the insights from the initial program.

Every follow-up session included the executives, who shared with their managers their own personal development experiences from the program. The executives modeled telling the truth, being vulnerable and openly correcting their relationships with one another, various management groups, and the unions.

During these sessions, vital information was shared in a safe environment, the healing of old wounds began, and movement toward greater collaboration was established. Over time, a number of leaders began to see the importance of operating openly and "consciously" with one another. Both the CEO and the president felt strongly that the values and principles "taught" in the breakthrough training were to be modeled overtly in the organization. As feedback among the leaders increased in real time, they set better conditions for the overall organization to become faster acting and more entrepreneurial—and to be a healthier place to work. This established a valuable foundation for the organization's transformation. ◄

Transformational change strategy must attend to changing mindset, style, and behavior across the entire system. Beyond the leadership breakthrough training rollout, examples of interventions that catalyze and reinforce mindset and behavioral change include:

- Sharing the case for change featuring mindset and behavioral change as primary drivers;

- Determining the desired culture as a reflection of the new mindset and style;

- Creating high participation in re-visioning the organization's future;

- Employing whole-systems meeting technologies to design the future state;

- Building the teams required to implement the future state in ways that address mindset, style, behavior, and relationships; and

- Performing an impact analysis comparing the desired state scenario and the current organization using the new mindset and culture criteria.

Each of these can be delivered through a cascade or large group approach.

We have outlined a five-step process for designing an organization-wide mindset change strategy, which is summarized in the following boxed copy. It can be fully integrated into your change strategy and will likely occur throughout the entire transformation.

The Process for Changing Organizational Mindset

1. *Set the Foundation and Motivation for Changing Leaders' Mindsets.* This step creates the case for changing the mindsets of the leaders and secures their commitment to do so in the most positive and unified way. The results of your exploration of the drivers of change and your change readiness and capacity assessment can provide helpful input, as can the findings from benchmarking admired or visionary companies. Your goal here is to establish that changing leaders' mindsets is critical to their ability to lead the organization's transformation consciously.

2. *Get the Attention of Individuals and the Organization.* This step establishes the non-negotiable reality of changing the organization's collective mindset as the key to transforming the organization successfully and begins to demonstrate what the change will mean for people and the system as a whole. Highly

visible executive decisions about business strategy and personnel changes, communications, and other bold actions can help accomplish this.

3. *Build Organizational Momentum for the Change in Mindset.* This step creates a critical mass of support, activity, and energy for the personal and organizational mindset shifts needed. It usually includes breakthrough training to accelerate personal growth for a critical mass of the organization's influential leaders and employees.

4. *Reinforce and Sustain the Change in Thinking and Behavior.* This step deepens and further establishes the changes happening in people and the organization. Executive coaching, 360-degree feedback, continuous communications, and focused large group meetings and celebrations are common strategies.

5. *Align and Integrate the Changes in the Organization with the New Mindset.* This step ensures that the organization can effectively operate from the new mindset and sustain its performance throughout the transformation. Changes in business processes, culture, decision making, structure, policy, and systems, all aligned to the new mindset, support this work.

Task I.D.3: Build Leader Commitment and Alignment

The principle underlying this task must be made explicit: The leaders of the organization must act as a unified team, modeling their collective commitment to the future in both words and action. Examples abound of executive groups not being aligned behind the major changes they face. The majority of these cases occur because the change leaders or the change consultants do not think to assess or require leadership alignment. It is, perhaps, too politically sensitive to make this internal dynamic overt. The executives proceed anyway, and the change inevitably falters or self-destructs. Lack of alignment is one of the biggest slow-down factors in the speed of change.

The first step in this task is to assess the current degree of common understanding, alignment, and commitment to the transformation. Alignment does not mean that everyone has to be in lockstep before proceeding. Diverse views can be highly beneficial as long as they do not counteract forward progress or set up the conditions for political battling or outright sabotage. If the change leaders have engaged in the earlier activities of Phase I, there will likely be significant alignment and commitment already. If not, a strategy for dealing with disparate levels of alignment and commitment must be created and carried out.

Strategies vary widely. Examples include directly addressing the issue and exploring people's reasons for withholding their commitment, creating face-saving but sideline positions for those opposed to the change, mediating diverse positions, and direct removal of an individual who refuses to get on board.

The best strategy, we believe, is dialogue. Dialogue is a communication tool that we use heavily in our leadership breakthrough strategy. Dialogue is a simple communication structure and process through which executives discover and tell their truth to each other about any relevant issue. The participants in dialogue reflect on their own feelings and thoughts, including their hopes and fears, and listen deeply to one another. This process usually uncovers and helps resolve what has previously blocked alignment.

We must note that squelching a resistor's or naysayer's voice is the worst strategy and almost always generates negative repercussions. The only time such heavy-handed approaches should be used to build alignment is after dialogue and other exploratory strategies have proven unsuccessful. Then, it simply is time to say, "Get on board or be left behind!"

A major advantage of offering breakthrough training early in the change process is that it builds leaders' ability to understand and share what is true for them. They learn to really listen to each other. Often, this in itself produces most of the commitment and alignment needed for the transformation.

Task I.D.4: Initiate the Plan to Educate the Executive and Change Leadership Teams About Change

There is much to learn about leading transformation consciously and successfully. Anyone who has led or directed a sports team or a project team knows the importance of ensuring competent players before the action begins. The worst condition is when team members *think* they know what to do when they really don't! The best scenario is to have players who are open to learning and then developing their understanding and skills as they proceed with the task at hand.

Essential change education topics that we feel must be understood by leaders are listed below. *Mastery of these subjects means the difference between traditional leadership and conscious change leadership.* The first five are covered in our companion book and represent the foundation of conscious transformational leadership. The remaining topics constitute what change leaders *do* to lead transformational change successfully.

1. The Drivers of Change (that is, environmental forces, marketplace requirements for success, business imperatives, organizational imperatives, cultural

imperatives, leader and employee behavior changes, and leader and employee mindset changes);

2. The three types of change (development, transition, transformation);

3. The two approaches to leading transformation (reactive and conscious) and the facilitative style of leading change;

4. The importance of changing mindset, style, and behavior and of modeling this personal change;

5. Project thinking, systems thinking, and conscious process thinking; conscious process design and facilitation;

6. Knowing how to create a comprehensive change strategy that integrates content, people, and process issues;

7. Recognizing the difference between change frameworks and change process models and selecting those that are required for successful transformation;

8. Being able to use and customize a change process model and a complete change methodology that serves the organization; and

9. Knowing how to determine and create a comprehensive change infrastructure and conditions for success.

You can use the information in both books as a template to assess your leaders' understanding, knowledge, and skills and to create development plans to build their capacity to lead transformational change. Development plans will likely be long-term processes and will require the full commitment of the leaders they are designed for. These plans should be integrated into the executive, management, and supervisory level development curricula offered in the company. Section IV of *Beyond Change Management* explores how to develop conscious transformational change leaders and its Appendix includes a checklist of knowledge areas, skills, and behaviors to support these efforts.

Task I.D.5: Initiate the Process to Develop the Executive and Change Leadership Teams into Teams Capable of Successfully Leading the Change

The goal of this task is to develop the executive and change leadership teams so that they are collectively capable of leading both the current organization and the transformation to deliver intended business results. Leaders' inability to work well together can be one of the earliest and most costly factors in their capacity to lead transformation. Until the leaders are able to perform as a unified team, politics notwithstanding, their chances of planning and overseeing a complex transformation are painfully low. If the team has participated in a leadership breakthrough program, the core issues blocking the team's success have usually surfaced and have begun to be resolved. This task can then enable their development to continue as the change proceeds. We often provide executive and change leadership team development in the follow-up sessions as a part of the leadership breakthrough strategy.

Exhibit 2.1, the Team Effectiveness Assessment, covers important topics for high-performing teams. Each individual on a team can fill it out, and the entire team can then discuss the results to focus its developmental needs. If the change leadership team is just beginning, the topics in the assessment can be used to guide its start-up goals.

Exhibit 2.1. Team Effectiveness Assessment

1. The team charter is understood and agreed on by all team members.

1	2	3	4	5
Agree	Tend to Agree	Don't Know	Tend to Disagree	Disagree

2. Conditions for success for high performance are developed and agreed to by all team members.

1	2	3	4	5
Agree	Tend to Agree	Don't Know	Tend to Disagree	Disagree

3. Team member roles are clearly defined and accepted.

1	2	3	4	5
Agree	Tend to Agree	Don't Know	Tend to Disagree	Disagree

4. Task processes (goal or outcome oriented) for the team are in place and effective.

1	2	3	4	5
Agree	Tend to Agree	Don't Know	Tend to Disagree	Disagree

5. Group processes (interaction oriented) for the team are in place and effective.

1	2	3	4	5
Agree	Tend to Agree	Don't Know	Tend to Disagree	Disagree

Exhibit 2.1. Team Effectiveness Assessment, Cont'd

6. The team has the time and resources it needs to function optimally.

1	2	3	4	5
Agree	Tend to Agree	Don't Know	Tend to Disagree	Disagree

7. The team has a high degree of diversity and uses it well.

1	2	3	4	5
Agree	Tend to Agree	Don't Know	Tend to Disagree	Disagree

8. The team has a clearly defined decision making process and uses it effectively.

1	2	3	4	5
Agree	Tend to Agree	Don't Know	Tend to Disagree	Disagree

9. All team members are highly committed to the success of the team and its charter.

1	2	3	4	5
Agree	Tend to Agree	Don't Know	Tend to Disagree	Disagree

10. All team members are skilled in two-way coaching and facilitating others' learning.

1	2	3	4	5
Agree	Tend to Agree	Don't Know	Tend to Disagree	Disagree

11. All team members are skilled at giving and receiving feedback.

1	2	3	4	5
Agree	Tend to Agree	Don't Know	Tend to Disagree	Disagree

12. The team is able to identify and resolve conflicts well.

1	2	3	4	5
Agree	Tend to Agree	Don't Know	Tend to Disagree	Disagree

13. The team has and uses a well-defined course correction process for both behavior and results.

1	2	3	4	5
Agree	Tend to Agree	Don't Know	Tend to Disagree	Disagree

14. The team is able to change directions or practices quickly once it recognizes the need to do so.

1	2	3	4	5
Agree	Tend to Agree	Don't Know	Tend to Disagree	Disagree

Exhibit 2.1. Team Effectiveness Assessment, Cont'd

15. The team has a clear accountability process and actively uses it to hold team members accountable for behavior and results.

1	2	3	4	5
Agree	Tend to Agree	Don't Know	Tend to Disagree	Disagree

16. The relationship between this team and other teams supporting the organization and the change is effective.

1	2	3	4	5
Agree	Tend to Agree	Don't Know	Tend to Disagree	Disagree

17. Team members have a high degree of trust in each other.

1	2	3	4	5
Agree	Tend to Agree	Don't Know	Tend to Disagree	Disagree

18. The team has good spirit and energy.

1	2	3	4	5
Agree	Tend to Agree	Don't Know	Tend to Disagree	Disagree

Task I.D.6: Initiate Development Plans for Individual Executives and Change Leaders to Increase Their Ability to Lead and Walk the Talk of the Change

This task develops personal mastery in the individual change leaders and reinforces the desired personal changes begun in Task I.D.2: Initiate Your Strategy for Changing Leadership Mindset, Style, and Behavior. It provides for individualized training and coaching of leaders. In some cases, this task is fulfilled through one-on-one executive coaching. In other cases, the leaders actually form two-way coaching partnerships with each other to support one another's development. The two-way coaching partnerships are often formed as a part of the leadership breakthrough strategy. The partners can focus on the mindset, behavior, language, knowledge, and/or skills required by the change effort. The tools learned in the breakthrough training can be employed in partnership coaching. This work continues as long as it adds value to the individuals involved and benefits their participation in the change effort.

Summary

Through these Phase I activities, you have assessed the organization's readiness and capacity to succeed in the transformation being planned. You have also designed your strategy for building the leaders' capacity to lead the change, individually and collectively. As accelerators of the change, readiness and ability are high-return investments in the creation of your desired outcomes and are well worth the time and energy. Now your attention turns to the many decisions that enable the organization to carry out the transformation effectively. The next chapter covers the identification and building of the organizational infrastructure and conditions to support the change effort.

Consulting Questions for Activity I.C: Assess the Organization's Readiness and Capacity to Succeed in the Change

Task I.C.1: Assess the Organization's Readiness and Capacity to Succeed in the Change

- How will the organization's readiness and capacity for making this transformation be assessed?

- What aspects of readiness and capacity will be assessed?

- Are the change leaders prepared to hear the results of the assessment and incorporate them in their plans for rolling out the change?

Task I.C.2: Identify the Strategy for Building Organizational Readiness and Capacity for the Change

- How will you build readiness and capacity in the various audiences that need it?

- How will you know when you have succeeded?

Consulting Questions for Activity I.D: Build Leaders' Capacity to Lead the Change

Task I.D.1: Create an Overall Strategy for Building Leadership's Capacity to Lead the Change

- How will you position the leadership development requirement with the change leaders and executives in the organization?

- How will you obtain both their understanding and commitment to proceed with this work?

- How will you assess the need for leadership development in each of the areas in this activity?

Task I.D.2: Initiate the Strategy for Addressing Leadership Mindset, Style, and Behavior

- What strategy will you use to initiate the process for addressing leadership mindset, style, and behavior?

- Will you use a leadership breakthrough process? Will you design and deliver it yourself or bring in specialists in this type of work?

- How will you reinforce and sustain this personal change work throughout the change process?

- How will you model the changes in mindset, style, and behavior yourself?

Task I.D.3: Build Leader Commitment and Alignment

- How will you address the issue of commitment and alignment among the change leaders and the executives?

- What is the current level of commitment among the change leaders and the executives for making this transformation successful?

- What meaning do you make of the current insufficient commitment and/or alignment?

- How will you increase commitment to where it needs to be?

Task I.D.4: Initiate the Plan to Educate the Executive and Change Leadership Teams About Change

- What additional information do the executives and the change leadership team need to know about change, transformation, the Change Process Model?

- Do the leaders understand and buy into the new standard of conscious transformational leadership?

- How will you provide them what they need to develop into more capable leaders of change?

- How can you tie this education to your content changes to make it relevant and results oriented?

Task I.D.5: Initiate the Process to Develop the Executive and Change Leadership Teams into Teams Capable of Successfully Leading the Change

- What is the status of team effectiveness in the executive team and the change leadership team?

- How will you strengthen each team's functioning and the relationship between them so that they can lead this transformation in the most conscious and effective way?

Task I.D.6: Initiate Development Plans for Individual Executives and Change Leaders to Increase Their Ability to Lead and Walk the Talk of the Change

- Which individuals on the executive team and the change leadership team need personal coaching or development to ensure that they are able to contribute their best to this change effort?

- Does each of these people recognize his or her need? Is each open to receiving support?

- How will you engage these people in a personal development process? Does a senior leader have to request that they pursue this development? Should their development be attached to their incentive program? Should it be voluntary?

- Who is best to provide this support to each individual?

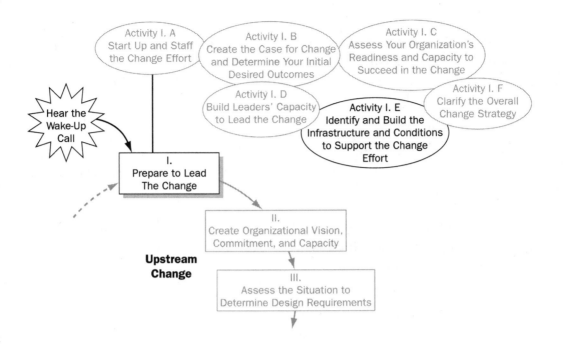

Activity I.E: Task Deliverables

I.E.1: The political dynamics within the change effort and among the change leaders have been identified, and strategies for dealing with them have been established.

I.E.2: The process and style for making all major change-related decisions are clear.

I.E.3: Conditions for success have been identified, committed to, and initiated.

I.E.4: A communication plan has been created for the transformation, and the change leaders are clear about how they will kick off the effort in the organization.

I.E.5: A strategy to create shared vision in the organization has been developed.

I.E.6: Formal strategies for generating and using new information related to the transformation have been developed.

I.E.7: A course correction strategy and system have been designed to ensure that the change process remains on the best possible track.

I.E.8: Current change plans have been assessed for their likely impact on people, and a strategy to address people's reactions to these impacts has been developed.

I.E.9: Temporary change support structures, systems, policies, and roles have been designed and initiated.

I.E.10: The resources required to make the transformation have been estimated, and the leaders are committed to providing adequate resources throughout the change process.

I.E.11: Measurements for the change process and outcome have been determined, and the strategy for how these measurements will be obtained and used is clear.

I.E.12: Temporary rewards for supporting the change process have been designed and are aligned with the organization's existing rewards.

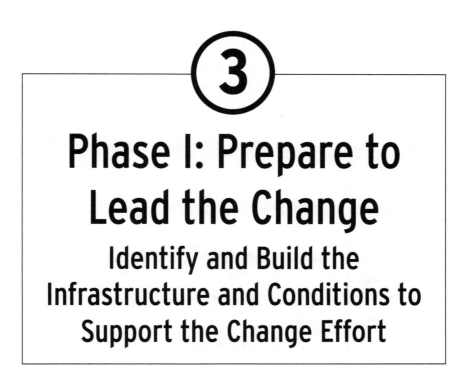

Phase I: Prepare to Lead the Change
Identify and Build the Infrastructure and Conditions to Support the Change Effort

LEADERS OFTEN ASSUME THAT THEY CAN MANDATE TRANS-FORMATION, which means they expect it to happen without thinking through the need for adequate infrastructures and conditions for its success. Transformation requires both a strong infrastructure and consciously created conditions that support its start-up and ongoing process. This activity addresses twelve key support mechanisms that, like spokes of a wheel, are essential to the smooth rollout of the transformation. If one or more spokes are weak or missing, the wheel will not turn smoothly or for very long before shattering under the weight of the transformational "load."

The spokes, or tasks in this case, deal with both process facilitation and people dynamics. Each task is included because it focuses leaders' and consultants' attention on an aspect that supports the overall change effort, especially its beginning. If addressed well, the tasks collectively add viability, speed, and energy for the entire transformational journey. They also provide a tangible opportunity to design the change effort in ways that model the transformation's intended mindset, style, and behavior.

The needs of the transformation and the state of the organization will determine which of these tasks are critical to your particular effort. Remember, the Change Process Model is intended to be a thinking discipline, not a mandatory checklist. You will not need to attend to every task, at least not with the same level of thoroughness. Every task in this activity is included because it has been shown to be a factor in leading transformation successfully. Consider them all before determining which you will attend to and which you can afford to skip or address minimally. Time, resources, and a quick assessment of each task's costs and benefits should be considered in your decisions.

Activity I.E: Identify and Build the Infrastructure and Conditions to Support the Change Effort

Task I.E.1: Develop and Initiate Strategies for Dealing with the Politics of Change

Some of the most powerful forces occurring in change are the political dynamics created by the introduction of a new direction. People naturally want things to go their own way, to be viewed as "winners" in the change, and they act to benefit their own interests. However, political maneuvering is rarely focused solely on what is good for the larger organization. Long before a major change is announced, personally motivated political behavior escalates. Individuals and factions exert influence over others for their own agendas. Uncertainty, risk, and opportunity for power suddenly increase, especially when decision making and authority may not be clear. In some cases, both covert and explicit power dynamics mushroom, leading to chaos, competition, and even malicious behavior.

An intriguing aspect of politics is that most people assume their efforts to influence others are invisible, with most political maneuvering occurring behind closed doors. Yet in reality, people see it clearly, discuss it actively, and can even predict it. Political behavior is far more obvious than its perpetrators would like to believe. As long as people collude with the unconscious norm of never discussing negative political realities overtly with the main players, they are allowing its consequences to run rampant, which does not support the overall transformation.

Depending on the organization's culture and the breadth of the transformation, politics can have a damaging effect on the success. It is our bias that political dynamics be addressed and dealt with openly, *consciously.* Unless they are worked out through open dialogue, they can derail even the best of changes. As uncomfortable as it may be to unravel political behavior, leaders need to deal with their own power struggles impacting the transformation, as well as those within the project community and across the organization. Therefore, staying on top of the political terrain is critical to shaping a sound and conscious change strategy.

It is essential to create a positive climate within the change leadership team—and across the organization—for addressing difficult political realities. The relationship, team, and personal development work initiated in Activity I.D are invaluable in supporting the constructive resolution of potentially damaging politics and for preventing further political disruptions. In particular, building commitment and alignment to the larger business outcomes of the transformation and creating a solid case for change and shared vision help immensely.

This task ensures that you create specific ground rules for how to deal with negative political behavior when it arises. At this early stage of the change process, it is helpful to scan the existing political dynamics to identify the patterns currently at play, assess their impact on the transformation, and then devise positive strategies for how to deal with them.

Another powerful influence strategy is to create a "critical mass of support" for the change by identifying top executives, special experts, opinion leaders, important customers, and grassroots representatives throughout the organization and mobilizing their advocacy for the new directions. Project community members can serve as the basis for your critical mass. They can be tasked with influencing others, including resistors and "fence-sitters," to back the effort and spread the word. Eventually, when enough people support the transformation, critical mass will actually be attained, and the change will take on a life of its own. When this occurs, leaders can guide the process toward the desired outcome and let go of any notion of forcing it forward through political manipulation.

Task I.E.2: Clarify the Process and Style for Making All Major Change Decisions

Architects say that building a house requires approximately twenty thousand decisions; major transformational change efforts certainly require as many. Some of the decisions are strategic and conceptual, some operational. Imagine the chaos and in-fighting that occur when the decision-making process and authority are unclear! Who makes which of these change decisions, and what happens if key people disagree? How are the decisions to be made and when? Which are to be made unilaterally, and which require majority vote or consensus? At this point in the change process, it is essential for the change leaders to clarify how to handle this critical function.

This task identifies the early strategic-level change decisions that set the precedent for all key decisions to follow and consciously determines *how* these decisions will be made. This is especially important if you are intentionally changing your leadership style and culture. Clarifying the decision-making style and processes *before* heated issues surface expedites decisions tremendously and prevents change leaders from falling back into habitual or positional behavioral patterns that don't support the culture change. Decision-making processes are agreed on here, in advance, at least at the macro level.

This task can be used as a cultural change strategy. It is always extremely revealing to ask leaders: "How are decisions made around here?" The question typically surfaces a range of important data—about culture, politics, behavior, emotional states, and team practices. This discussion helps to further the executive team development begun earlier and highlights how the leaders function together and whether they are truly walking their talk.

Furthermore, clarity of decision making has major ramifications for employees. Building participative, self-directed cultures is impossible when employees don't know who owns what decisions or how they will be made. Accountability starts with *both* clarity of responsibility and authority for decision making.

The change leaders may need some education about the various decision-making styles available to them. Most OD consultants are familiar with the traditional styles of decision making—authoritarian, majority vote, consensus, alignment, and consultative input. Consider adapting a style that fits your desired culture and the capability of the organization.

Task I.E.3: Create Conditions for Success

It is safe to assume that all change leaders *want* their transformations to be successful. However, to increase the probability of success, they must establish practices, circumstances, and resources that will enable it to flourish. This task identifies the factors and conditions that change leaders believe are required for their particular transformation to succeed. We call these factors *conditions for success.*

Conditions for success are requirements essential to the achievement of your desired outcome, such as adequate resources, sufficient time to do a top-notch job, or quality communications that keep everyone engaged. Conditions for success may also refer to a particular state of being that enables the transformation to occur more smoothly, such as the leaders taking a conscious approach, the executives presenting a unified front in support of the transformation, and people realizing that their needs are actually being considered as the transformation is planned and implemented. Conditions for success can also support the personal transformation work required by the change, such as creating a safe environment for truth-telling, supporting personal breakthrough, and encouraging cross-boundary conflict resolution, communication, and collaboration.

Imagine your conditions for success as gas pedals for accelerating the transformation. They set the stage for an expedient journey and a positive outcome from the beginning. Once agreed to, they influence leadership, management, and employee behavior to support the entire transformational process. An added advantage is to use them periodically as a template to measure how the transformation is going and whether the change leaders are walking their talk. This review can trigger immediate course corrections when the conditions are not being lived up to. Conditions for success are also great inputs to Task I.E.ll: Determine and Initiate Appropriate Measurements of Change.

The following boxed copy provides a sample list of conditions for success. Change leaders should reflect on their own experience and the situation they face and identify their unique list of conditions. They must agree on how to establish them in the organization, identify who will oversee and monitor them, and determine how the conditions will be used to have the greatest impact on the transformational experience. Notice that the statements are written in the present tense. This is intentional to model the conscious transformational principle, "Lead as if the future is now" (Anderson & Ackerman Anderson, 2001). We have found that doing this with conditions for success, as well as with vision statements, helps people experience the future they want to create as an existing reality, thereby accelerating its actual creation.

Sample Conditions for Success

- Total organization (management and workforce) shares a common vision for what the desired state has to be and how to get there.
- Leadership presents a unified front in support of the desired state.
- A learning-oriented, feedback-seeking climate is encouraged.
- A collaborative relationship exists between those who are running the ongoing business and those who are changing it.
- Sufficient time and resources are allocated to the change effort.
- The reward system directly reinforces support for the change process and the desired state.
- People impacted by the change have timely input to the design, impact analysis, and course corrections affecting them.
- Communication is frequent, accurate, and complete.

- Leaders consistently and visibly support efforts to achieve the desired state. They are models of the mindset and behavioral changes required by the desired outcomes.

- Change leaders and consultants are sufficiently trained to be able to succeed in the transformation.

- Mindset and behavior change are supported and expected from all stakeholders in the transformation.

Task I.E.4: Design and Initiate the Overall Communication Plan for the Change and Decide How to First Inform the Organization

Communication is the life force of the organization, especially in times of change. In these early days of the effort, as soon as people catch wind of the transformation, their needs for information and attention escalate significantly. They want to know what will happen to them and whether their position in the organization is secure. In the worst case, leaders keep people in the dark or only inform them of decisions without any opportunity to influence or respond—just when people's need to do both is the highest.

Even if change leaders give the workforce a briefing, the stress of the transformation can severely limit people's ability to retain and understand the leaders' communication. Thinking that they weren't given clear answers, people's anxiety grows. How are leaders going to address these very real human dynamics? In large part, they will attend to them through the conscious design of a competent communication plan and by developing understanding of how best to communicate with people during change.

Communication must be an early and lasting priority in the leaders' change plans. They must pay careful attention not only to what is communicated and how much, but when and how it is done. Communication timeliness and leader credibility go hand in hand at this stage. When change is in the air, employees tend to be extra sensitive to tone, candor, and concern.

This task builds the communication plan and the kickoff communication strategy. It ensures that relevant information about the transformation will be shared, understood, and used to support the effort. This means more than giving the organization information. Table 3.1 provides a model for planning communications beyond the typical "talking head" strategy. The model is called the Five Levels of Communication. The concept of the five levels was originated by ARC Worldwide and expanded by Being First, Inc., for this change methodology.

Table 3.1. Five Levels of Communication

Level & Outcome	Style	Media, Vehicles	Reaction When Received
1. Information Sharing	Telling; one way	Lecture, presentation, memo, video	"Thank you for telling me this information."
2. Building Understanding	Dialogue; two-way; exploring and answering listener-generated questions	Small group meetings; breakouts to develop questions; facilitated Q&A	"Having explored my concerns and tested this, now I under-stand the focus of the change and why it is needed."
3. Identifying Implications	Introspection; discussing with co-workers what the message means to you and to the organization; multidirectional	Group interactive discussions ranging from multilevel, large or small group discussions to work team discussions; most important exploration done with work team and immediate supervisor	"This change means X for my department and Z for me and my job."
4. Gaining Commitment	Sorting out inner feelings and choices; may require time and multiple returns to the discussion with peers, immediate supervisor, or senior leaders	Alone time for personal introspec-tion; opportunity to readdress issues with co-workers, direct supervisor, and/or leaders of the change	"I personally want this change to succeed and am willing to contribute fully so that it does."
5. Altering Behavior	Demonstrating new behavior; may require training, feedback mechanisms, and coaching over time to ensure that the behaviors stick	Training, coaching relationships; opportunities for practice and learning; can be supported with policy or systems changes to reinforce desired behavior	"I am learning the new behaviors required for this change to succeed and I am open to receiving your feed-back and coaching to keep improving."

Based on original model developed by ARC Worldwide.

Applying this model has profound impact on communication planning. The model begins where most people end their communication efforts—sharing information. It goes on to four subsequent levels in the communication process: building understanding, identifying implications, gaining commitment, and altering behavior.

Each of the five levels describes its own outcome. The culmination of all five outcomes defines excellent communication—behavior change or behavior reinforcement. In scanning the model, notice that each level requires a different style and medium to achieve its outcome. You may need only some of the levels of communication at any point in time. Again, your knowledge of all of the levels will assist you in choosing how and when to use them and their strategies. Keep in mind that if you want true commitment and behavioral change as the result of your communication process, you must include strategies that produce both. You cannot expect to use only information sharing strategies to produce behavior change. Once designed, support your communication plan with the appropriate resources, meeting planning, facilitators, logistics, and follow-up. Here is an example of a unique communication strategy.

▶ CASE ɪɴ POINT

One of the major telephone companies created an informal network to assist with a major change it was undergoing. The group liked the idea of remaining informal and grass roots in its support of the transformation and operated only in "behind the scenes" ways.

The network was comprised of over one hundred employees from all levels in the organization, including the union ranks. The group was designed to serve many roles, including communication, sounding board for change decisions, two-way linkage to leadership, organization problem solvers, and as support to help individuals work through their emotional reactions to the change. They ensured that all five levels of communication were carried out.

Created to be a part of the fabric of the transforming organization rather than to have a formal role, the group was able to listen to the real needs of all groups impacted by the transformation. To support this ability, the network was acknowledged by the change leadership team, and a relationship was built between the two groups. The network was trained in the skills required for their "informal" roles. They met quarterly to give input to or resolve critical issues about the change, working directly with appropriate senior leaders.

A key strategy of the network was to communicate a message *informally* to the organization in less than three collective rounds of interactions. For each message delivered to the organization, each member would have at least ten conversations, and in turn, it was assumed that these ten people would have ten more conversations, and so on (100 people × 10 × 10 × 10 = 100,000 conversations).

The network lasted for four years before being dismantled. It made a lasting impression on the direction and energy of the transformational process, helping to move the behavior of people and the culture of the organization in very significant ways. ◄

Planning Your Kickoff Communication

The second requirement of this task is planning how you will communicate the initiation of the transformation. Your kickoff communication may include any of the following content:

- Who is leading the change and in what capacity; who the sponsors are;
- Your case for change, including all of the drivers of the change;
- Your overall change strategy (to be designed in the next activity);
- Scope of the change and why it is transformational;
- Conditions for success;
- Expectations for the quality of experience intended by the change process; and
- Other decisions to be made in the remaining Phase I tasks, such as temporary change support structures, systems, policies, and roles; the organization-wide visioning plan; participation strategies; resources; measurements; and rewards.

It is very important that the style and tone of your kickoff communication be carefully planned. This communication will be the first time the change leaders will be "officially" communicating with the stakeholders of the change, and the impression the leaders make here will affect the entire start-up. We will have more to say about this when we discuss Phase II, when the plan is carried out.

This task also focuses on clarifying the best communication role for change leaders. The change leaders have to be visible spokespeople, helping to prepare information, making presentations, and responding to employee feedback and input. They need to quell rumors, overtly model the new mindset and behavior, be vulnerable, and reveal their own personal experience and challenges in making this transformation successful.

Task I.E.5: Identify the Process for Creating Shared Vision Throughout the Organization

This task is designed based on two assumptions we make about leading change: (1) Transformation has more vitality and purpose when it is inspired by a desired future state—a vision—that compels unified action throughout the organization and (2) the vision for the change is most powerful when co-created by the whole organization rather than handed down by the leaders. When people participate in the formation of a shared vision, they are far more likely to achieve it. We must also say that we have seen examples where a vision, created only by the top leaders or executive team, produced sufficient energy and motivation to mobilize an organization-wide transformation. These particular leaders were well-respected and charismatic in their own right. Whereas either strategy can work, we prefer a shared visioning strategy because we believe it has a higher probability of building shared commitment and responsibility for success.

This task reflects these assumptions. The change leaders now design the *process* for creating shared vision for the overall organization and/or the transformation itself. They can develop the vision themselves and then devise a compelling roll-out strategy, or they can create a more participative approach. This strategy will then be carried out in Phase II after the case for change and the change strategy are communicated to the organization.

Designing a participative visioning process, if they elect to do so, is an important exercise for leaders. It tests their commitment to employee involvement, their change leadership style, and their process design skills. There are many options for creating shared vision. The process chosen by the change leaders will be a function of their mindset and style. Conscious change leadership teams typically decide to involve all or a significant part of the organization in the visioning process itself. Options for participative visioning processes include:

- A cross-organizational visioning committee that produces the vision statement;

- An iterative cascade of the vision draft, inviting input and improvement;

- The tailoring of the vision for and by each segment of the organization; and

- Large group visioning sessions during which participants collectively work on different aspects of the vision in unison.

Some organizations use large group meeting approaches such as Future Search (Weisbord & Janoff, 1995), Real Time Strategic Change (Jacobs, 1994), or Visioning Conferences (Axelrod, 1992). These innovative processes are well worth the effort because this type of participation can save months, if not years, of implementation time once people are on board with the change. They are powerful strategies for generating a critical mass of commitment to the outcome of the transformation. Ideally, the visioning process leaves people chomping at the bit for making their transformation a reality.

Task I.E.6: Design Information Generation Strategies

At this point in the change process, there is a whirlwind of activity. Imagine the change leaders striving to plan the best strategy for the transformation while the marketplace is jumping around like a toad on hot pavement. Perhaps rumors are stirring up the organization, and your peers are lobbying for the very resources you need for this transformation. People are likely tossing about potential solutions and predicting insurmountable roadblocks. All the while, you are doing your best to orchestrate the magnitude of information swirling about, searching for the confidence that what is being planned will work.

In the face of such chaos, some executives react by exerting control and demanding that the change be managed exactly as planned, as if their plan will act like a wall of protection against the complexity and volatility. However, transformational change demands that leaders work *with* the chaos, staying tuned to the continuous stream of new information it surfaces around them. Nothing is static in the marketplace or in the organization; new information is everywhere. It cannot be stopped, and it is not the enemy. In fact, transformational change leaders *need* this information to generate required course corrections in their desired outcomes or their current plans. The challenge is to sort out what information is actually relevant. This is the purpose of having an information generation strategy.

Information generation is a central theme of the conscious approach: *Increase your awareness about what is needed for the transformation process and use this information as guidance for course correcting where you are going and how you are getting there.*

What do we mean by new information and information generation? Old information is what you already know. New information is what you are currently discovering or learning that has the potential to alter your understanding or perception of reality, or, in this application, the outcomes or process of the transformation. Information generation is proactively seeking new information to help drive decisions about the change.

You never know where and when new information will surface. Being open to new information enabled 3M's discovery of its wildly successful Post-it® Notes. Microsoft's eventual awakening to the potential of the Internet changed the face of the company, and with it, Internet accessibility.

Although uncovering new information may prove disruptive or disconcerting to people, it is an essential condition for success for long-term transformation. This task formalizes your strategies for generating new information throughout the transformation and identifies the sources and methods for its discovery. As sources of information, be sure to consider people both internal and external to the organization, other organizations inside and outside of your industry, and other disciplines or bodies of knowledge. Also consider how you can use technology to improve information generation and how you will screen for information that is most relevant to the transformation.

Task I.E.7: Design and Initiate the Course Correction Strategy and System

The greatest enemy of new information is the leadership attitude that "I already know this" or "That isn't important to what we are trying to do here." Leaders who assume they already have all of the information and insight required to transform their organizations successfully, or who don't have the openness to look at things differently, put their transformations at serious risk. It is one thing to generate new information; it is another to learn from it and strive to use it to realign your intended results or change process.

This task focuses on the heart of what it takes to lead transformational change—consciously engaging in the process of learning and course correcting. It goes hand in hand with information generation. Because so much is unknown about what to do during transformation and how and when to do it, leaders must strive to stay alert, take action based on their best thinking or intuition, and realign their strategy from what they learn.

The notion of course correction is one of the most valuable, powerful, and underutilized ideas in organizations today. However, because so many organizations have already initiated learning practices in their cultures as a result of the "learning organization" movement, tying learning and course correction together is a great opportunity to build off the existing momentum. Figure 3.1 shows the Course Correction Model.

Figure 3.1. Course Correction Model

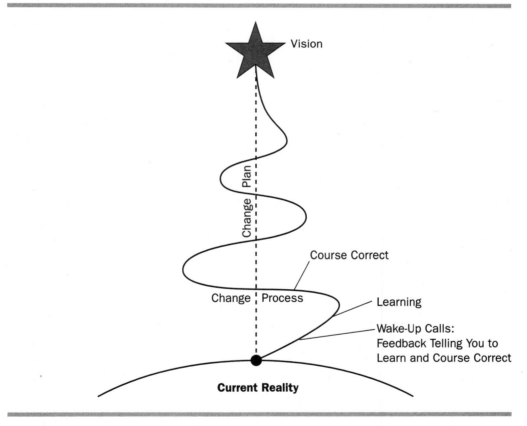

Different from evaluation, measurement, and audit, which are based on the assumption that a preconceived *right* answer or standard exists, the process of course correction consists of:

- Setting a direction based on your best intelligence;

- Commencing action to reach your vision;

- Pursuing feedback, wake-up calls, and new information in the environment and organization for whether you are on or off course;

- Reflecting on the feedback and new information for what they mean about your mindset, knowledge, skills, behavior, and change plan;

- Testing new insights for further learning about what to do differently; and

- Altering both the process and/or the outcome of the transformation based on your latest intelligence.

The notion of course correction requires education, not only of leaders, but of employees as well. Employees, like leaders, typically want security and predictability. Traditionally, they want their leaders to have the answers and tell them the way. If leaders begin to course correct and alter change plans frequently, employees will likely feel that their leaders are lost, adrift in a rudderless boat. That can be very disconcerting and become a good excuse for employees to resist the change.

Change leaders must communicate clearly that information generation and course correction are critical aspects of their change strategy. They must be prepared to model course correction themselves, in their organizational decisions, interactions, and behavior. Then, as they course correct, they can overtly communicate that the alteration is the result of their course correction strategy working, rather than a failure of their initial strategy.

Information generation and course correction are also critical participation strategies. The more people who are generating information for course correction the better. High participation generates more complete information and simultaneously builds commitment and ownership for the change strategy it informs.

Designing and using a widespread course correction system can also have a potent effect on shifting fear-based cultural norms in the organization (for example, "Kill the messenger who brings bad news!") to ones that are based on learning and innovation. If an organization is eager to embrace learning, it has to be willing to shatter the myths that "The leader has all of the answers" and "Having a plan is a guarantee for success." Valuing rapid course correction keeps people vital and attentive, engaged in pushing the envelope of innovation and breakthrough. Exhibit 3.1 offers a checklist for building your course correction system.

Exhibit 3.1. Checklist for Building Your Course Correction System

☐ A philosophy statement linking the system with your leadership style for the change and your new culture

☐ Target areas of assessment or inquiry

☐ People identified and tasked to seek feedback and input on how things are going, representing all levels of the organization, stakeholders, and customers

☐ Ways to ensure that these people fully understand the intended existing direction or outcome of the change, the process for achieving it, and then any subsequent adjustments to the process or outcome (for example, communication vehicles, training)

☐ Means for gathering out-of-the-box data and feedback (Use your information generation strategies.)

☐ A place, person, or group to bring aberrant data or wake-up calls

☐ A process for dealing with and deciding how to use feedback and data

☐ A process for communicating the impact of feedback and data, whether or not it was used, and how

☐ Reinforcement or reward for generating useful data

☐ Ways of stepping back from the course correction system and reviewing its usefulness; course correcting the system itself

☐ Resources to support all of the above

☐ Training to support all of the above, if necessary

Task I.E.8: Design How to Minimize the Human Trauma of the Change, and Initiate Strategies for Helping People Through Their Emotional Reactions

In these initial planning stages of your transformation, inevitably the rumor mill in your organization is in full gear. People in different parts of the organization may be flip-flopping between excitement and anger, fear and hope. Performance may be affected, and the e-mail system is probably loaded with time-consuming commentary about what is going to happen and who is going to get the boot. Several of the top leaders are likely at their wits' end about how to respond to the building crescendo, and a few are likely ready to erupt emotionally themselves. How do you deal with all of this when you haven't actually changed anything yet?

People will have a full array of natural reactions to both the desired outcome and to the change process leaders use to put it in place. Because an organization cannot transform without affecting people, a critical condition for success is designing a change strategy so that it minimizes the negative impacts on people and positions the leaders to respond effectively to people's reactions throughout the process. This task develops strategy, mechanisms, and resources to handle people's reactions.

It is important to note that this task is designed for the change leaders to clarify how they can support the workforce through their emotional reactions. Keep in mind that the leaders *themselves* also need this support. Although traditionally it may not be considered acceptable for leaders to express their own emotional reactions or needs, in a conscious approach, the leaders' humanness is as important as anyone's. If the leaders are upset, hurt, or out of balance, they will undoubtedly miss important signals about what the transformation requires. This is an opportunity for the leaders to model this shift in cultural expectations. Be sure to address emotional support for the leaders in executive and change leadership team development processes and through executive coaching.

How People React to Change

In recent years, many leaders have come to recognize that they must deal differently with people during change. There are a number of valuable models used to educate leaders about how people react to change and how to respond to people's reactions. William Bridges' Transition Model (1991) is particularly useful, as is John Adams' Seven Stages of Transition (1989). The Adams model is shown in Figure 3.2.

The core message of Adams' model is straightforward: People have a series of natural reactions to change. They will lose focus during the process and will enter the "pit" (anger, withdrawal, confusion, victimization, blame) before emerging to deal effectively with their new reality. Leaders throughout the organization must support and facilitate people through the *entire* cycle, even people's descent into the pit. Trying to avoid or rush the pit phase actually lengthens its duration.

Most everything leaders do in change triggers diverse reactions in people. One abusive example is telling people that they no longer have a job by putting the

Figure 3.2. Seven Stages of Transition Model

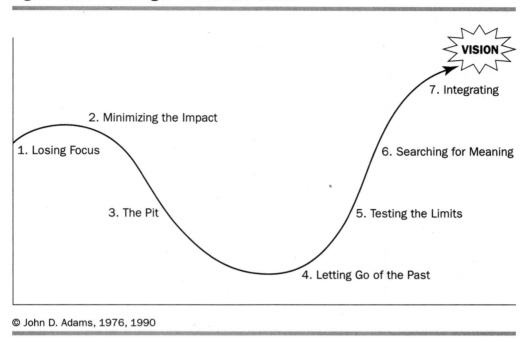

VISION

7. Integrating

2. Minimizing the Impact

1. Losing Focus

6. Searching for Meaning

3. The Pit

5. Testing the Limits

4. Letting Go of the Past

© John D. Adams, 1976, 1990

infamous "pink slip" in with their final paycheck. This is a short-sighted, inhumane strategy. Perhaps the leaders who have used this approach deny the personal trauma they cause because they do not understand how people respond to change, or perhaps it is because they do not want to face the pain or anger their decisions have created in their workers. In either case, it is far more powerful to understand how people naturally react to change, to address people's concerns overtly as much as possible, and to plan the change process to minimize known negative impacts on the people of the organization. A conscious approach also calls for leaders to acknowledge the truth of their own feelings about the pain their actions may cause others.

Conscious approaches to reducing people's trauma include Appreciative Inquiry approaches (see Watkins & Mohr, 2001), dialogue, personalized communications, employee assistance programs, "letting go" rituals, celebrations, stress management programs, large group participation strategies, training, outplacement, learning and support groups, and leadership modeling.

Review your recent and current change strategies to assess their potential for causing emotional upheaval. Redesign them with people's emotional needs in mind. Completing this task does not mean that people won't have bad reactions; they likely will, even in the best of change strategies. The intent, however, is to minimize unnecessary negative reactions and maximize strategies that will engage people in enlivening, constructive ways.

Task I.E.9: Select and Initiate Temporary Change Support Structures, Systems, Policies, and Roles

A classic change implementation scenario is one in which the leaders, without thinking, attempt to force the demands of change on top of people's already overflowing plates, mandating unrealistic timetables and providing no additional resources. Ouch! Transformational change, if it is to succeed, cannot be imposed on an organization that is already at capacity for time, energy, and resources. So how is required change handled in such situations?

Change leaders need to reprioritize the work of the organization to keep what is essential in motion and to delay or stop what is not crucial to the operation while it is transforming. Stop work? Make space? Refocus attention? Delay? Yes! This reflects conscious process thinking and design. The transformation will consume all of the time and resources made available by this reshuffling of priorities.

The organization is entering a unique stage in which it must continue to operate while it undergoes its transformation. This stage is temporary, and it requires temporary supports to enable and accelerate the transformational process. Consequently, temporary structures, systems, policies, and roles must be designed to handle the interim needs of the change and to balance its demands with ongoing operations.

Many of these temporary supports are designed to promote efficiency, streamline decision making, and remove bureaucratic constraints that would otherwise stifle the transformation. Having referred to these supports as temporary, it is important to note that many organizations recognize so much benefit from them that they incorporate them into their "normal" operations, thus overcoming the slowness of the established bureaucracy and enabling faster action as new priorities emerge in the moment. This trend reflects the move toward greater self-organization and the shift of consciousness toward designing organizations to respond to emergent needs, rather than refute these needs because the rigidity of the organization cannot readily adapt to them.

This task introduces various options for designing these temporary structures, systems, policies, and roles and develops those needed to support the transformation. Some of these strategies will be used immediately, some will be implemented later, and some will be adapted throughout the process. All of them will be dismantled or redefined as "permanent" at the conclusion of Phase IX of the change process. We will describe this task in two sections: (1) temporary change structures and (2) temporary management systems and policies.

Temporary Change Structures

You will likely create a temporary overall change structure to coordinate and integrate change activities. There can be many components to this structure. Some will remain through the entire lifecycle of the transformation, while others will have a shorter life span. Aspects of your structure may include:

- Change roles (sponsor, executive team, change process leader, change leadership team, change project team, and change consultant);

- Interim business management structure;

- Special project teams;

- Multiple project integration teams;

- Culture scanning group;

- Change navigation center;

- Information generation network; and

- Barrier buster teams.

Your overall change structure can be organized as either a hierarchical structure or as a network. Samples of both are shown in Figure 3.3. The network structure is more informal and organic, altering shape as the needs of the transformation indicate over time. The figure identifies sample roles for the various rings in the network. You can assign any relevant role to the participants in the rings.

**Figure 3.3. Sample Temporary Change Structure
and Sample Change Team Network Structure**

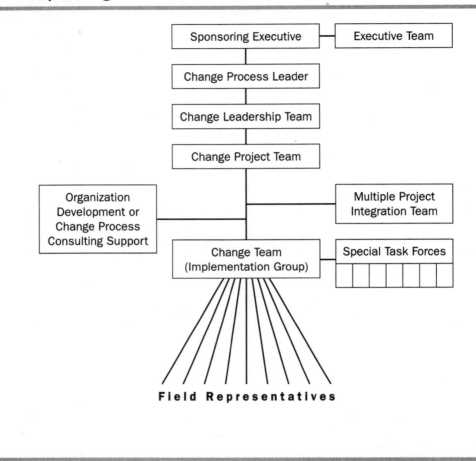

Now let's look at each temporary structure that may be included in your overall change structure.

Interim Business Management Structure and Strategies. Managing the ongoing
business effectively while also making major changes is a critical challenge that can
be addressed with an interim business management structure and strategy. These
are used when leaders recognize that not all of the work currently underway in the
organization can be accomplished "as usual" once the change process begins. The
leaders reprioritize the organization's workload to accomplish *only* what is essen-

**Figure 3.3. Sample Temporary Change Structure
and Sample Change Team Network Structure, Cont'd**

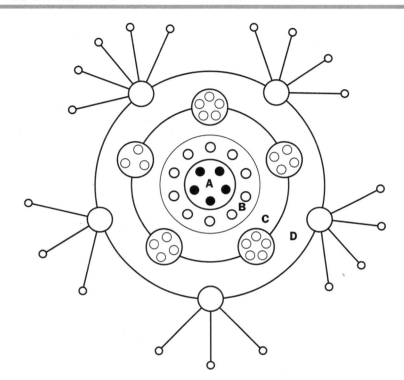

A = Core Change Team (Sponsor, Change Process Leader, Top Change Consultants)
B = Change Leadership Team
C = Nodes of special skills or knowledge needed or special task forces
D = Advocates within the organization or Implementation Teams

tial to maintaining operations and fulfilling current commitments, thereby freeing up resources, time, and attention for the transformation. Because the change leaders are probably already feeling overloaded, given the time they are devoting to the transformation's start-up, they usually have a lively debate when determining what is "essential" to the ongoing operation! Their decision to re-prioritize work is a demonstration that they truly understand the real demands of the transformation.

The interim business management structure is comprised of existing and acting managers in charge of keeping the business operational. Because some leaders might devote their full attention to the transformation, their pre-existing responsibilities must be delegated to acting managers, who then become a part of the interim business management structure. Your succession plan can be very useful for staffing your interim structure, giving your rising stars either line experience or change leadership experience. It is essential that everyone on this team know what the roles and responsibilities are on the change leadership team, and vice versa, so that they can work well together to accomplish both of their missions. Certainly, decision authority and spans of influence must be clear to everyone.

Interim business management strategies include:

- Delegation;
- Acting managers;
- Reprioritization of major tasks, decisions, or projects;
- Altered or expedited decision-making procedures;
- Temporary committees;
- Special meetings;
- Expedited communications;
- Special performance reviews; and
- Coaching and mentoring.

You can design and use any structure or strategy that ensures effective handling of the essential strategic and operational decisions and actions that are required to keep the business going. Keep in mind that these structures and strategies will have to be dismantled once they have served their purpose.

Special Project Teams. The number and types of personnel needed to support transformation will vary with the organization and the complexity of the effort. You may need special teams for any number of change activities, such as to conduct benchmarking, organize your visioning process or large communication events, evaluate new software solutions, engage in design, and so forth. To staff these teams, both internal and external people are selected for their functional expertise, planning skills, and ability to facilitate and model the change. These people may work full-time or part-time throughout the transformation or for short periods until a task is competed. Be certain to start up each team with team building. You may also need to have teams meet with each other to clarify their interdependencies.

Multiple Project Integration Team. In complex transformations, most organizations have many change initiatives, large and small, running simultaneously across or within major segments of the business. A multiple project integration team can be formed to manage the interdependencies and coordination of resources and schedules as the projects are designed and implemented. These teams can save tremendous amounts of time and money as they mitigate the gaps and overlaps among existing projects.

Most leaders have not historically attempted to coordinate and integrate the organization's major change projects. Therefore, you may need to demonstrate this strategy's value before executives will support it. The following case illustrates a powerful strategy for obtaining executive commitment to establish and use a multiple project integration team.

▶ CASE ɪɴ POINT

The leaders of a large research laboratory asked us to assist them in creating a change infrastructure to coordinate the thirty-one change initiatives they had going on in their organization. Things had already gotten out of control, with the sponsors of the key initiatives openly competing for resources, staff, and attention. We asked the executives to identify the most important initiatives underway in the organization. They selected eight and were able to cluster many of the smaller projects under these eight. We called a meeting of the top two people from each of the eight initiatives to obtain progress reports and address coordination issues. Our invitation was met with little enthusiasm. "We're busy enough! Why do we have to attend yet another meeting?" they queried.

We informed the invitees that the meeting was designed to scan all of the initiatives and determine the best allocation of resources and schedules for key change activities. If the change leaders chose not to attend, decisions would be made for them affecting their plans. Of course, they all showed up!

We began the meeting with an overview of goals:

- To inform each change leader about the content and status of all of the projects underway in the organization;

- To surface opportunities to cross-reference, fortify, and communicate a cohesive change message to the organization in word and action; and

- To discover and resolve issues, confusions, and competition among the projects.

To begin the work, we gave each pair of leaders a different colored pad of stick-on papers on which they were to write the key events in their project plans. They were to post the papers on a blank month-by-month calendar that stretched across one whole wall of the meeting room. When each of the teams had completed the task, everyone stood back and assessed the data. Without a word, everyone could see that the current lack of coordination among the eight initiatives would create immeasurable chaos in the organization over the next few months. Four of the eight project teams were independently planning organization-wide surveys in the month of February. Three of them were planning mandated training in the month of April. Three of them were competing for the same personnel to perform design studies. The impact of all this uncoordinated work would be to make the executive team look completely out of control and out of touch with the needs of the workforce. Nothing more was needed to convince these leaders of the importance of integrating their efforts. They agreed to meet weekly during the planning phases and then monthly throughout the transformation. Note how the *information they generated* produced the right action. The CEO did not have to say a word. Neither did we. ◄

Many additional benefits of the multiple project integration strategy were also reaped. The leaders redesigned the reward system that was currently motivating them to compete with each other for their individual projects' success, creating shared rewards. They created a common story among all of the initiatives so the workforce could experience the one integrated transformation they were all serving. They modeled their desired culture of pursuing shared goals and acting as one enterprise and overtly demonstrated new standards for quality and learning, which were the focus of two of the initiatives.

Major political battles were nipped in the bud because the team members agreed to act on behalf of what served the larger organization. Resources were reallocated to places of highest leverage and greatest need. The leaders felt enormous relief when they realigned the timetable of the various changes to better serve the readiness and capability of the organization. Most importantly, by making the progress and course corrections of the team public, the change leaders became powerful models of the collaboration, synergy, and effective process management that were core to the organization's new culture.

Culture Scanning Group. Transformational changes are culture-dependent and require a focused effort to study the organization's current culture and clarify its desired culture. In addition to the classic components of culture (that is, norms, language, stories, and so forth), this includes assessing and shaping the mindset of the organization—its guiding principles, ways of being, assumptions, and values. This work can be accomplished by a culture-scanning group made up of representatives from all levels, areas, business units, and types of employees in your project community. This is a great opportunity for participation, especially for people who are enthusiastic about advocating conscious attention to the human dynamics in the organization.

After the study of the current state, this group can also recommend how the new culture should be reflected in the design of the new organization's operating practices, processes, and structures. Any aspect of culture, mindset, style, and behavior may come under this group's study. Ideally, it has a direct line of communication with the change process leader and change leadership team to raise issues and make recommendations on behalf of the new culture and mindset.

Change Navigation Center. Transformational changes can be supported with a "nerve center," often called the navigation center. This is a meeting place where change leaders make decisions, share information, and shape plans.

Navigation centers can be actual locations, virtual locations, or both. As an actual location, the navigation center is often an office or conference room converted into a headquarters for change activity. As a virtual location, it can be designed in numerous ways. It can serve as a "chat room" for change leaders or be open to the entire organization. It can be a communication board, posting announcements or reporting status, or be part of the information generation system. Often, the change process leader and change teams meet both in the actual navigation center and virtually on the website—for planning and design meetings. The navigation center structure, in whatever public form it takes, provides the organization with a valued sense of strong change leadership.

Information Generation Network. As described in Task I.E.6, information is the "fuel" that drives transformational change (and helps guide other types of change as well). New information can come from anywhere. However, its discovery can be assisted through an information generation network. This network is made up of internal and external people who actively seek "outside-the-box" information. The types of information they seek, the sources of that information, and the methods for obtaining it will depend on each change. A system is required for inputting, considering, and acting on the information generated to support this function. The project community at large can play a vital role in this network.

Barrier Buster Teams. Organizations committed to dismantling bureaucratic cultures and structures during their transformations can form "barrier buster" teams. These teams seek out, assess, and recommend the removal of unnecessary red tape, bottlenecks, convoluted processes, and paperwork—all barriers to efficient and resilient organizations. Barrier buster teams help identify anything that might prevent desired outcomes. They have a direct line into the change leadership team. We have seen several organizations have a lot of fun unleashing and celebrating the success of this team!

Temporary Management Systems and Policies

At times, temporary management systems and policies are necessary to enhance critical steps or functions during the planning, design, and implementation of transformation. Without them, the organization's normal systems and practices might become overloaded bottlenecks when trying to handle the magnitude of activity and urgent pace. Temporary systems and policies can be used to override or accelerate normal procedures.

For example, during a major structural change, temporary selection procedures have to be created to expedite the matching of large pools of candidates with all of the open positions. Standard job posting systems, often taking months to fill a position, will overload and "blow the fuse" of the change process.

Sample Temporary Management Systems

- Staffing system;
- Job design and evaluation system;
- Outplacement: selection and support packages;

- Relocation process;
- Information management and communication systems;
- Team-building processes or new department start-up procedures;
- Accelerated decision-making processes;
- Rewards for contributing to the transformation;
- Approval levels and system;
- Performance reviews;
- Intensive technical or people skills and knowledge training; retraining; cross-training;
- Interim supply, distribution, and materials management systems or policies;
- Interim operations tracking or scheduling procedures;
- Counseling and employee assistance services; and
- Logistics and space allocation/facilities management systems.

Temporary policies may also be needed. For example, if you are able to announce *at the beginning* of a change that everyone will actually maintain employment or retain his or her current salary, employees will breathe a sigh of relief and receive the news of the transformation in a more positive light. These policies can greatly assist you with some of the predictable human dynamics.

Sample Temporary Policies

- Hiring freeze;
- Job reclassification;
- Job security/guarantee;
- Salary protection;
- Mandated training or voluntary cross-training;
- Labor/management agreements;
- Performance-review delays;
- Across the board salary adjustments; and
- Relocation or termination packages.

Be sure to dismantle these temporary management systems and policies publicly when they no longer serve their intended need.

Task I.E.10: Secure Commitment for Resources to Support the Change

Some of the key questions leaders ask before committing to proceed with transformational change are: "How much will this cost us?" and "Will it be worth it?" Fair questions. We have made the assumption that the leaders are already committed to the transformation, given their investment in building their case for change and progressing through the appropriate tasks in Phase I to this point. Until now, resource questions are premature because not enough about the transformation's actual requirements are known. Phase I supports the change leaders to progress far enough in their planning to make sound judgments about resource allocation.

Frequently, leaders want to do the most they can with the least resources, without assessing whether this approach will generate the results they seek. If this is the case, create a dialogue with the change leaders concerning their mindset about resources. They will need to commit to securing an *adequate* resource base for the transformation if they truly want it to succeed. They may have to confront their tendency to have greater expectations for the end result than their resource allocation will support.

Even now, the change leaders will not have accurate numbers about how many resources the effort will require, and they will never have guarantees (remember, transformation is an unpredictable, emergent process). However, they will have to make realistic guesses about the resources necessary, and they will have to commit to provide *sufficient* resources. Allocating ample resources is a telltale sign to the organization that the effort is a true priority, rather than lip service. As more accurate resource needs are determined later in the process, the change leaders can then attempt to secure them.

Each stage of change requires resources. A frequent condition we observe is executives committing high budget dollars to external consulting firms to design the best future scenario and then finding themselves with no money to support implementation. This situation is reflective of leaders who do not see change as a fullstream process. The leaders must accept the fact that transformation is a multi-year endeavor that will require significant resources annually. We suggest that leaders estimate resource needs at least three years ahead.

Another surprise to many leaders is the variety of resources that must be provided. The typical assumption is that they need only money and people. Consider these resources in addition:

- Time required to plan and carry out all of the phases and activities of the change process;

- Types of information needed;

- Information technology: electronic conferencing, communication, and planning systems;

- Access to leaders;

- Training support, especially breakthrough training for mindset, style, and behavioral change;

- Consulting support, both technical and change process consulting;

- Team-building facilitators;

- Conflict-resolution support;

- Equipment and technology;

- Space requirements for overseeing the transformation;

- Meeting time and planning support;

- Graphic support/video production; and

- Communications writing and delivery.

Consultants may need to coach the change leaders to keep their commitment for sufficient resources and to be creative in generating additional resources as necessary. To keep the process conscious, make sure the leaders understand the real implications of their resource decisions on people's ability to deliver what the organization needs.

Task I.E.11: Determine and Initiate Appropriate Measurements of the Change

When executives think about transforming their organizations, one of the most predictable concerns is how to measure progress and results. Logically, leaders want to know how well the transformation is proceeding and whether the outcome will give them the return they expect. The desire for accurate and regular measurement is one reason for the attractiveness of classic project management methods for leading change. These approaches provide good quantifiable measurement and with it some semblance of comfort and control over the change.

This is appropriate when changes are predictable and controllable. However, as we have stated, transformational change is neither. Because transformation requires significant personal and cultural change, it is not predictable, controllable, nor easily evaluated. This makes the objective measurement of it difficult, if not impossible. In addition, because leaders have historically used measurement to control the organization and induce specific types of behavior, people's historical intimidation by measurement may need to be addressed so as not to impede the kind of breakthrough and innovation required for the success of transformation.

We have already made the case that successful transformation requires the organization to respond to emerging, spontaneously occurring dynamics that could not be predicted earlier. Rigid adherence to measures can stifle these critical course corrections by forcing people to continue to conduct activities for predetermined measures when those activities actually need to be altered. Having explicit, preconceived outcomes is not bad; this just needs to be balanced with allowing the measures to change as course correction is required. This is a subtle, but very powerful mindset shift for leaders. Measurement can assist, but it should not drive transformation.

This task designs your measurement strategy. Consider both objective and subjective measures. The change leaders must discuss and determine the following:

- Their need and purpose for having measurements;
- The impacts, both positive and negative, that measurement might have on the change process and outcomes;
- What will be measured both objectively and subjectively (for example, timeliness, goal achievement, responsiveness, units of production, effectiveness of working relationships and communication, demonstrated skill and knowledge, actual and projected costs, customer satisfaction);
- Standards of measurement (frequency, speed, number of occurrences, improvements, learnings); and
- Methods (interviews, surveys, group input).

The change leaders must do this for both the outcomes of the change and the change process itself so that measurement can support ongoing course correction for both.

Task I.E.12: Develop, Communicate, and Initiate Temporary Rewards to Support the Change Process and Outcomes

It is common knowledge that people will do what they are rewarded for. When making major change, especially transformational change, the old reward system frequently motivates behavior that is contrary to the desired state. This task develops, communicates, and initiates new (often temporary) rewards that purposely influence people's behavior to support the change process. These rewards motivate people to make the transformation a reality—personally, behaviorally, and operationally. Then, as part of the new state to be designed in Phase IV, the full-scale reward system can be revised to support behavior required for the new state.

It is essential to realize that fully revamping the organization's reward system at this point usually causes mass upheaval and *should not be done!* This is a major mistake that consistently sabotages transformation. Employees are still assimilating the case for change and what impacts the change *might* have on them. Changing the operating rewards too early can create tremendous resistance and confusion. Focus here on choosing rewards that motivate people to support the process of the transformation.

▶ CASE ɪɴ POINT

In one Fortune 500 company, we brought the executives together to kick off their change process and define their role as change leaders. After appropriate education about change strategy and the Change Process Model, the senior vice president, to whom they all reported, told the leaders they would be held accountable for their influence on the change process and that 20 percent of their annual executive incentive would be attached to their change performance. To make their accountability as change leaders tangible and observable, we gave the executives the task of collectively identifying their own performance standards for excellent change leadership, in specific actionable terms.

After a few minutes of predictable resistance, they saw and accepted the inherent challenge and proceeded to take the information they had just learned about the Change Process Model and create a set of realistic change leadership standards for themselves. Their list included:

- Achievement of specific goals;

- Effectiveness of their communications for creating behavior supportive of the change in the workforce;

- Visibility as a model of the desired behavior;

- Knowledge about the status of the transformation;

- Creation of an effective change infrastructure and conditions for success;

- Timely execution of change decisions; and

- Ability to find adequate resources to support their part of the overall change.

The senior vice president used the list as his guide for evaluating their performance and, in fact, kept his word on tying it to their annual bonus. In hindsight, the executives clearly recognized the power of determining their own requirements for change leadership, which deepened their understanding of the value of wrestling with their own performance standards. ◀

Summary

You have now determined and identified the most appropriate infrastructures for your change effort, including the creation of conditions for success. This work, led by the change process leader, paves the way for a well-supported change effort. Use it as input to your change strategy, which is the last activity of Phase I.

Consulting Questions for Activity I.E: Identify and Build the Infrastructure and Conditions to Support the Change Effort

Task I.E.1: Develop and Initiate Strategies for Dealing with the Politics of Change

- What are the current political dynamics among the leaders and in the organization that may have a direct or negative impact on the success of this transformation?

- Are the leaders able and willing to address these issues together?

- What is the best way to resolve or improve these dynamics among the leaders?

- What ground rules are needed among the change leaders for dealing constructively with the political dynamics that arise as the transformation unfolds? How will you create and monitor these ground rules?

Task I.E.2: Clarify the Process and Style for Making All Major Change Decisions

- How are decisions currently made among the leaders?

- Is this style or process in alignment with the organization's desired culture?

- What are the key change-related decisions to be made? Who "owns" them?

- What is the best style of decision making for these decisions? Which style will best model the desired culture in the organization?

- How will you get the change leaders' agreement to make their decisions in this way?

- Who else has to be informed about how the change-related decisions will be made?

Task I.E.3: Create Conditions for Success

- Do the change leaders understand conditions for success and how they can fortify their transformation?

- How will you facilitate the leaders' ability to determine their conditions for success?

- How will you secure their agreement to commit to the actual creation of these conditions in the organization?

- How will you use these conditions to help manage, measure, and course correct the transformation as it rolls out?

Task I.E.4: Design and Initiate the Overall Communication Plan for the Change and Decide How to First Inform the Organization

- Who is best to create the overall communication plan for this transformation?

- What components will your communication plan include?

- What role will the change leaders play in communications during the transformation?

- Do the leaders understand the "five levels of communication" and how to use them?

- What outcomes do the executives want from their communications?

- How will the leaders communicate about the transformation for the first time, if they haven't already done so?

- If the organization already knows that this transformation is going to happen, what kind of communication is needed to inform it about current plans?

- Is any course correction needed? Do any rumors have to be dispelled?

Task I.E.5: Identify the Process for Creating Shared Vision Throughout the Organization

- What work have the change leaders already done to create a vision for this transformation?

- How willing are the change leaders to engage the organization in the creation of a shared vision?

- How will they do this? What methods will they use to engage managers and employees in shaping this vision? Will they use large group interventions?

- Who is responsible for designing and facilitating the visioning work?

- Once a vision statement is created, how will it be communicated and rolled out in the organization?

- How will visioning be sustained over time?

Task I.E.6: Design Information Generation Strategies

- Do the change leaders and the organization understand what "new information" is and the role it plays in transformational change?

- How will you establish the expectation in the organization for generating new information related to this transformation?

- What systems or processes are needed to support people to seek out new information?

- What will be done with new information when it is surfaced? How will it be screened for relevancy? By whom?

- How will new information be used to course correct the transformation?

Task I.E.7: Design and Initiate the Course Correction Strategy and System

- Do the change leaders understand the notion of course correction?

- Do current cultural norms support giving feedback upward, downward, and across? Do they support learning from mistakes?

- How will you design your system for surfacing feedback and course correcting the change process and desired outcomes?

- How will you establish the course correction system in the organization?

- How will the change leaders communicate course corrections they have made in the change process or outcomes?

Task I.E.8: Design How to Minimize the Human Trauma of the Change, and Initiate Strategies for Helping People Through Their Emotional Reactions

- What past change management practices have caused significant trauma for people in the organization?

- What are the potential negative impacts on people in your current change strategy and plan?

- To what degree do the change leaders understand people's cycle of emotional reactions during change?

- What strategies can the change leaders initiate to help people manage their emotional reactions during the change process?

- What resources already exist in the organization for employee assistance?

- Does the culture of the organization support people to take advantage of these resources?

- What strategies will you use to help the change leaders deal with their own emotional reactions to the transformation?

Task I.E.9: Select and Initiate Temporary Change Support Structures, Systems, Policies, and Roles

- To what degree do the executives and the change leaders understand the function of temporary change structures, systems, policies, and roles?

- How will you introduce these options?

- Which of these mechanisms would benefit the transformation?

- How will each be designed, approved, and established?

Task I.E.10: Secure Commitment for Resources to Support the Change

- What types of resources are needed for the success of the transformation?
- Are these resources currently available in the organization?
- If not, how will you secure the change leaders' commitment to find them?
- If sufficient resources are not available, what will you do to address this issue with the change leaders?
- How will you align the change leaders' expectations for the transformation with the actual resources they provide to support it?

Task I.E.11: Determine and Initiate Appropriate Measurements of the Change

- How has measurement been used in the past?
- Is this approach aligned with the outcomes, mindset, and desired culture for this transformation?
- What do the change leaders want to measure in this change process?
- What is their intention and purpose for measuring these things?
- What types of measurement standards should be used to accomplish this?
- Are all of the target areas for measurement quantifiable? If not, how will you devise appropriate subjective measures?

Task I.E.12: Develop, Communicate, and Initiate Temporary Rewards to Support the Change Process and Outcomes

- Does the existing reward system reinforce leaders' and employees' support for the transformation? If not, what in it is contrary?
- How will you undo existing rewards that may hinder leaders' or employees' support of the change process or outcome?
- What rewards are needed to encourage the behavioral and mindset changes required for the transformation?
- How will you define and establish these in the organization?
- Who will oversee their use?

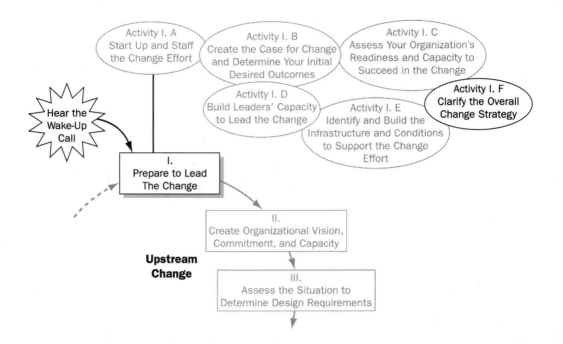

I.F Task Deliverables

I.F.1: The process for creating the change strategy is clear, and the effort has been staffed.

I.F.2: The change leaders are clear about how to lead the transformation as one unified effort.

I.F.3: The change effort is positioned appropriately within the ongoing activities of the organization.

I.F.4: The initial bold actions and strategic levers for making the change have been identified.

I.F.5: Participation strategies for gaining a critical mass of commitment among the stake-holders and targets of the change are clear.

I.F.6: Critical milestones of the transformation have been determined, and the general timeline is established. The integrated change strategy has been developed.

Phase I: Prepare to Lead the Change
Build the Change Strategy

❺VERYTHING YOU HAVE DONE SO FAR in Phase I is input to this activity. Now you will put all of your prior work together into an integrated change strategy for facilitating the complete life cycle of the transformation.

Your change strategy is the ultimate deliverable of Phase I and will influence all remaining phases of the change process. It demonstrates your clarity about what needs to change, sound leadership thinking about how to accomplish your outcomes, and concern for the people who must make the change a reality. The change strategy must reflect your facilitative leadership style.

Recall the discussion in the Introduction to this book of the three elements of change strategy—content, people, and process. Your change strategy summarizes all three elements: What will change and how you will transform your organization in ways that account for people's needs. It makes explicit:

- How you will position the transformation in the organization;
- Core activities for igniting and accomplishing the transformation;

- How management and the workforce will be involved in the effort to create a critical mass of commitment; and

- Your critical milestones and general timeline.

Many of the deliverables of the previous five activities of Phase I shape the change strategy. In Activity I.A, you clarified the current reality of the effort as the starting point for building the strategy, determined the key change leaders and their roles, and identified the stakeholder groups whose needs the strategy will address. The case for change (Activity I.B) determined the content and people drivers of the transformation, mapped the organization's systems dynamics to identify leverage points for change, and also identified your initial desired outcomes. The change capacity assessment (Activity I.C) and change infrastructures (Activity I.E) provide significant information for the people strategy and how the leaders will support the change process. Activity I.D prepares the leaders to build this change strategy and carry it out successfully. Keep all of this information in mind as you review and fulfill the tasks of Activity I.F.

Activity I.F: Clarify the Overall Change Strategy

Task I.F.1: Identify the Process for Building the Change Strategy

Given the amount of input to the change strategy, it is important to be very clear about how to pull it all together. Read the remaining tasks for the key decisions required to create the change strategy. More often than not, the top change leaders perform this work. The leaders cannot delegate building the change strategy and still sustain the knowledge and commitment they need to kick off and carry the transformation forward. This work is not an intellectual exercise; it must carry the same priority as developing business strategy, for without an adequate change strategy, the business strategy very likely will not be implemented effectively.

Create the process for building the change strategy by determining the following:

- How the operating principles for conscious transformation will be used as design requirements for the change strategy;

- Roles for leading and working on the change strategy;

- General timeline for completion of the change strategy;

- Medium and format for recording the change strategy;

- How you will update and course correct the change strategy throughout the change process; and

- How you will communicate the change strategy to the organization.

The operating principles of conscious transformation explored in our companion volume offer a variety of design requirements fit for transformational processes, such as ensuring that the change strategy models the desired culture, supports conditions for success, and encourages continuous learning and course correction. Determining these factors will help make your change strategy conscious and deliberately suitable to the requirements of transformation.

Task I.F.2: Determine How to Lead the Change As One Unified Change Effort and How to Integrate Separate and Distinct Initiatives Within It

The case for change articulates the nature and complexity of the transformation you are about to make. In creating it, you identified your initial desired outcomes and the various drivers of the change, of which there are likely to be several. Many leaders have the tendency to make each outcome and driver—business, organizational, and cultural—into a standalone initiative, such as creating e-business avenues, reorganizing, redesigning a business process, increasing teamwork, and so on. They bless each one, set up teams to handle it independently, and request quarterly updates. However, too many separate changes unleashed simultaneously can overwhelm the organization. Although distinct projects may seem at first to be more manageable, the downstream implications of running them independently complicates the transformation.

Fundamentally, your organization's transformation should be viewed and treated by the people in the organization as one effort—the process of getting from where the organization currently is to where it chooses to be. Your change strategy must spell out how all of the initiatives within the transformation link with and support one another and the overall objectives. In this task, you determine how to unify these initiatives under one transformational umbrella. The infrastructure you design to support them will depend on how you do this. A unified effort streamlines the process dynamics of transformation and provides the workforce greater motivation and understanding than would separate initiatives.

To create a unified effort, clarify the highest level outcome—the big picture within which all of the various content, culture, and people initiatives fit. For example, you may have a number of individual initiatives occurring in the organization, such as restructuring, reengineering your supply chain, revamping your information technology, and redesigning your human resource systems. Why are each of these change initiatives occurring? Perhaps you are attempting to transform your organization to operate over the worldwide web, or perhaps you are transforming from a national to a global company. Employees must understand the highest level intent. Otherwise, each initiative loses its relevance and meaning. We suggest that you use your case for change, initial desired outcomes, and the Drivers of Change Model to tell the story of how everything fits together.

Task I.F.3: Scan All Other Change Efforts Occurring or Being Planned in the Organization to Determine the Fit and Priority of this Effort

In most organizations, change is happening everywhere, and there is no way to sort everything out or know what to do first. This causes confusion and overwhelm, both of which make the start-up of a particular change effort much more difficult. It can be enormously helpful to scan the organization for existing change efforts to assess where this one fits and how important it is in light of everything else that is going on. The leaders may discover that this transformation is more important than much of what is underway and thereby afford it priority status, or they may find the opposite. They may also discover a higher level outcome within which other changes can fit along with this one, and unify the efforts. Certainly, if this is an enterprise-wide effort, then it will receive top priority and all other changes must fit within it.

In any case, the leaders have the opportunity to reduce the organization's confusion by clarifying the position and priority this transformation has among all other efforts. Knowing this helps people put everything in perspective and focus their energy for change.

In their assessment, the leaders may find out that not everything that is going on has to happen in the same timeframe required for the success of the effort they are championing. One guaranteed benefit is that they will gain eye-opening insight into how much change is underway, how appropriate the scope and priorities of the changes are, and the burden they are placing on current operations and employees. This information must be taken into account in the creation of the change strategy.

Task I.F.4: Identify Bold Actions and Strategic Levers for Both the Content and People Changes

Change leaders have two start-up challenges: (1) How to get the organization's attention to take the transformation on and (2) how to mobilize the most powerful strategy to accomplish it. Getting a change effort off and running requires the leaders to overcome inertia. People must recognize that a transformation is underway and that certain action is required of them.

In this task, the change leaders first determine the best way to get people's attention about the importance of the transformation. This action goes beyond sharing information about the case for change; it must alert or stun people into realizing that their world is changing in drastic ways. In situations in which the organization has performed well for years and has become complacent about its success or when leaders have too long ignored the wake-up calls for change, getting the attention of the organization to mobilize for change is a crucial part of your change strategy.

Bold Actions

To do this, change leaders determine what we call "bold actions." Bold actions are highly visible, "outside the norm" moves that dramatically demonstrate that "things are very different around here" or, as we like to say, "Toto, we're not in Kansas anymore!"

Bold actions are emphatic signals that send unequivocal messages about the new direction, like replacing resistant leaders or closing an obsolete plant. Be sensitive that your bold actions do not negate the past, but rather honor it without prolonging it. They must attend to both content and people changes. Consider these other options:

- Establish significant stretch goals and hold people publicly accountable to them;
- Divest a major line of business or operations center;
- Retire an existing product line;
- Hold a funeral for the old way of operating;
- Have all executives take a cut in pay to fund the retention of needed staff;
- Alter rewards to support the transformation process;
- Remove a complete layer of the organization's hierarchy; or
- Significantly alter the allocation of resources, for instance, to fund a new venture that symbolizes the future direction.

Strategic Levers

The second decision in this task is about strategic levers, the key strategies or vehicles the leaders will use to drive the change through the organization, such as reorganization, product integration, or massive training. They describe the essential story line of the transformation. Strategic levers may be identified intuitively or be obvious after assessing the drivers of change. Or they may be dictated directly by your business strategy or from the leverage points for change revealed by the map of your organization's system dynamics. Consider these examples:

- Re-create your brand;

- Develop an entirely new business strategy;

- Significantly alter your business model;

- Re-create the business for e-commerce;

- Globalize the business;

- Reengineer or consolidate functions or business processes;

- Change the whole organization's mindset and culture through massive training and by rewarding new behavior;

- Merge, sell, or acquire businesses or capabilities;

- Replace whole new systems and technology; or

- Downsize.

Task I.F.5: Clarify Your Participation Strategies for How to Gain a Critical Mass of Commitment

One of the most important design requirements for conscious transformation is wide-scale participation by the organization in creating the desired future. Change that is forced on an organization typically generates greater resistance than change that engages people in creating it. Change that is heavily leader-led triggers feelings in the workforce of being "done to" or taken advantage of. People need some way to influence their new reality, both in the process of how it is created and in the actual new state they are to implement. Participation enables this, giving people a focus for their energy and a way to make a positive contribution.

Beyond these beneficial outcomes, participation is required to create a critical mass of commitment to the transformation, which is a key element of the change strategy. A premise of transformation is that until a critical mass of people break through to the new mindset and behave in the new ways, the transformation will never succeed. Participation helps facilitate the breakthrough in mindset and behavior, as well as gives people an avenue to contribute their good thinking to the design and implementation of the content of the change. In this task, the leaders clarify how to create critical mass and what kinds of participation to use to accomplish it.

This task may require some education or discussion about leaders' beliefs about participation. The subject of participation has been in the management literature for a long time. Yet, many leaders are still uncomfortable or unfamiliar with how to determine and customize participation. Many still fear it, believing that, if they ask for input, everything their people request must be acted on or further resistance will result.

Leaders must better understand the direct relationship between influence and commitment. Generally speaking, the higher the influence people have, the higher their commitment to what is being created. Change education (Activity I.D) can address these perceptions and insights.

Different types of participation have different degrees of influence. If people are invited only to stick their toe into the transformational water, they will have a toe-level experience of influence and commitment. If they are invited to dive in head first, they will be immersed in the transformational experience.

There is a range of participation strategies, each with a different amount of influence. Any of them can be used effectively as long as the leaders make the boundaries clear before requesting input. Figure 4.1 depicts a range of six types of participation and the degree of influence each has.

Figure 4.1. Types of Participation

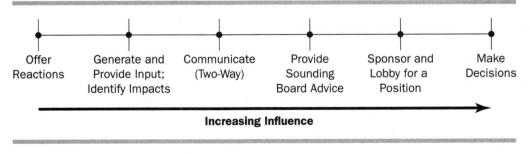

Different tasks in the Change Process Model require different levels of participation. When determining your participation strategies, consider the ideal level of participation for each task. Also, think about obtaining input from sources outside of the organization, such as customers, suppliers, or government officials. Consider using a high-participation strategy as a bold action or strategic lever, such as large group visioning or design conferences, or using an Appreciative Inquiry approach to identify organization-wide recommendations for the design of the future.

The following boxed copy offers a range of audiences to consider for inviting participation as well as types of participation vehicles. Use this list to trigger your discussion.

Audience	Vehicles for Participation
Individuals	Face-to-face, written, or electronic
Intact Functional or Business Process Groups	Focus groups, task forces with mandated or voluntary membership
Organization-Wide, Cross-Functional, or Cross-Process Large Groups	Future Search Model, Conference Model, Real Time Strategic Change Model, Open Space, focus groups with selected or voluntary membership
System-Wide Networks or Communication Vehicles	Ambassadors, representatives, advocates, change agents, advisory councils, newsletter with a response form, e-conference

Task I.F.6: Identify the Critical Milestones and General Timeline for the Change and Complete the Change Strategy

This task, the last of Phase I, develops the integrated change strategy for the transformation, the starting place from which the change leaders will navigate the process. The change strategy is the culmination of the leaders' assumptions and decisions from Phase I for how they would *like* the organization's transformation to unfold. The change strategy also includes the proposed milestone events of Phases II through IX, which can be shown in flow-chart fashion. This macro view of events then allows the change leaders to make an *informed guess* about the general timeline for the transformation, which is a key element of their change strategy. This estimated timeline cannot be used as a rigid measure of the transformation, as it will undoubtedly have to be altered.

Exhibit 4.1 shows a template of the key elements of a change strategy. It includes a list of the critical inputs from Phase I. Use it as a worksheet for your own change strategy. Exhibit 4.2 shows some brief highlights of a change strategy from an organization preparing itself for e-commerce through the realignment of its product groupings, the upgrade of its information management systems, and expansion of its ability to cross-sell products between its dispersed companies.

Exhibit 4.1. Template for Building Your Change Strategy

Inputs from Phase I
- Case for change, including:
  - Drivers of change
  - Initial desired outcomes for the transformation
  - Leverage points for transformation
  - Type of change
  - Scope of the change
  - Targets of the change
  - Degree of urgency
- Project community
- Organizational readiness assessment results
- Leadership capacity assessment
- Conditions for success

Elements of Change Strategy
- How to unify all initiatives under one transformational umbrella
- Position of this transformation in the organization
- Bold actions
- Strategic levers
- Participation strategies for creating a critical mass of commitment
- Change infrastructure
- Milestone events from Phases I through IX
- General timeline

Exhibit 4.2. Highlights of a Sample Change Strategy

Umbrella Outcome: To become a preeminent e-business that sells customized
   families of products

Positioning: Top Priority

Bold Actions

- Conduct large group employee meetings (100–1,000 people) in every market
  worldwide to generate input to the case for change and vision
- Realign executive incentive program to motivate e-commerce support and lavishly
  reward cross-company selling
- Create a high-powered video that dramatizes the vision of worldwide inter-
  company selling over the Internet
- Retire Product X

Strategic Levers

- Incorporate e-commerce strategies in every business
- Reorganize to consolidate interdependent products and services
- Realign worldwide information technology systems to enable cross-selling
- Reposition our image in the marketplace as a one-stop shop
- Reorganize customer point of contact for ease and expansion of sales
- Replace all of Europe's information management systems
- Executive level breakthrough training process for top 2,000 leaders to address
  obsolete mindset, leadership styles, and behaviors

Participation Strategies

- Worldwide information management design input conference
- Cross-company task forces
- International best practices study tour
- Change advocates identified from every product and service line
- Customer Advisory Council

Change Infrastructure

- Top executive change sponsor
- All company presidents on the change leadership team

Exhibit 4.2. Highlights of a Sample Change Strategy, Cont'd

- Information technology change process leader
- All companies appoint top-level change process leaders, linked to worldwide change process leader
- Senior-level change consultants, with consulting support staff in every company
- Open-door network of change advocates for design and impact analysis
- Published conditions for success
- Worldwide, interactive communication plan
- Electronic input of new information to e-commerce change process website

Milestone Events

- January, Year 1: Kick off with interactive video; rollout of leadership breakthrough process
- January–March, Year 1: Team-based communications about case for change, vision, and change strategy worldwide
- March, Year 1: Information technology compatibility assessment; change readiness assessment in every company; sales education process
- September, Year 1: Retire Product X; initiate design process
- January, Year 2: Turn key date for Europe's new information management systems; worldwide impact analysis
- February, Year 2: Develop implementation master plan for pilot test in Asia
- March, Year 2: Pilot inter-company electronic selling in Asia with Products A, B, and C
- September, Year 2: Evaluate pilot and integrate learnings into organization-wide implementation plans
- December, Year 2: Worldwide promotion of e-commerce availability and benefits
- January, Year 3: Worldwide rollout

Timeline

- Year One: Assessment
- Year Two: Design and pilot
- Years Three/Four: Marketing of the e-commerce brand and rollout of the new business

Once the change leaders have created their change strategy, they must plan how to announce it to the organization. Ideally, the change strategy is communicated at the same time as the case for change. However, the change leaders may decide that they want to communicate the case for change long before the change strategy is developed, which also works. The leaders began planning this kick-off communication in Task I.E.4. Now, with more information known, they can fine-tune their communication plan and roll it out to begin Phase II of their change process.

Summary

The first four chapters explored the work of Phase I of the Change Process Model. This phase represents a sizable and significant investment of time and attention. Often work begins in all six activities of Phase I concurrently. How much can be accomplished how quickly depends on the resources and time allotted to setting the change up to be successful. At this point in the process, there are clear leadership roles and working relationships, a compelling case for change, initial desired outcomes, and an integrated change strategy. Your infrastructure and conditions for success have been identified and initiated, the leaders' capacity to lead transformation is increasing, and the organization's level of readiness and capacity for transformation are being strengthened for the most expedient and effective rollout. It is now time to take your initial change plans out to the organization.

Consulting Questions for Activity I.F: Clarify the Overall Change Strategy

Task I.F.1: Identify the Process for Building the Change Strategy

- How will you develop your change strategy? Who will be involved and in what way?

- What elements will you include in your change strategy, and how will you format it?

Task I.F.2: Determine How to Lead the Change As One Unified Change Effort and How to Integrate Separate and Distinct Initiatives Within It

- Is the transformation currently designed as one unified effort or as a collection of separate initiatives?

- How can the "the change" be best described? What is the best strategy for integrating all of these change efforts as one change?

Task I.F.3: Scan All Other Change Efforts Occurring or Being Planned in the Organization to Determine the Fit and Priority of this Effort

- What other change efforts are currently underway in the organization that may have an impact on this one?

- Where does this effort fit among all of the organization's change initiatives? What is its level of priority?

- Do any of the other change efforts fit within this transformation?

- Given the organization's capacity and readiness level for making more change, are all of these initiatives needed at this time?

- If necessary, how will you support the executives' efforts to reprioritize the workload in the organization?

Task I.F.4: Identify Bold Actions and Strategic Levers for Both the Content and People Changes

- How will you determine the bold actions and strategic levers for making this transformation happen in the organization, for both the content changes and the people changes?

- What bold actions will be used to wake up the organization to the necessity for this transformation?

- What bold actions are needed to communicate that the old way of operating is now an honored part of the past?

- What strategic levers will drive this transformation?

Task I.F.5: Clarify Your Participation Strategies for How to Gain a Critical Mass of Commitment

- What are the current norms about using participation in the organization?

- How can you use participation to gain a critical mass of commitment for the transformation?

- Where will you use high levels of participation, and which forms of participation are best for each of these opportunities?

- Who will oversee each of these participation strategies?

Task I.F.6: Identify the Critical Milestones and General
Timeline for the Change and Complete the Change Strategy

- How will you identify the critical milestones for the entire change process?

- Who must be a part of thinking this through?

- How will you graphically portray the critical milestones so that the organization understands the process it is now engaged in?

- How will you establish the general timeline for this transformation?

- How does this timeline match up with the degree of urgency, the resources available, and the organization's readiness and capacity for making this transformation?

- How will you summarize the change strategy so that it can be effectively communicated and understood by the organization?

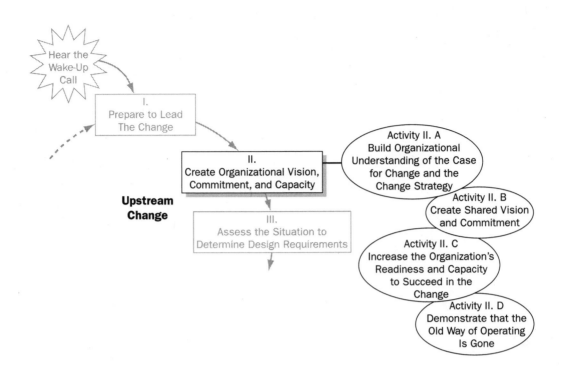

Phase II Task Deliverables

II.A.1: The case for change and the change strategy are communicated to, understood by, and supported by the entire organization.

II.B.1: The entire organization understands the vision for the transformation and is committed to creating it together.

II.C.1: The people of the organization are ready and able to proceed with the transformation.

II.C.2: The organization has begun to build the required change knowledge and skills to achieve the outcomes of this transformation.

II.C.3: The preferred mindset and behaviors are clear and being adopted by all of the stakeholders in the transformation.

II.D.1: The majority of the workforce understands that the old way of operating is gone and accepts the future direction.

Phase II:
Create Organizational
Vision, Commitment,
and Capacity

PHASE II SHIFTS THE ORIENTATION from the leaders preparing themselves and the transformation to succeed to the organization commencing action. The purpose of Phase II is to build organization-wide commitment, momentum, and capacity for supporting and participating in the transformation. It brings people up to speed about the real challenges the organization faces and why this transformation is important to the organization's future. This phase draws people into the change experience, building their understanding of what the transformation is intended to accomplish and what it means to them personally.

Your Phase II goal is to create *collective intention* for the success of the transformation. The broader the shared intention for succeeding in the transformation, the easier the process will be. What do we mean by "collective intention"? This term refers to a critical mass of the people of the organization joining in a concerted effort, with clear purpose and resolve, to create the new outcomes for the organization as quickly as possible. How do you establish collective intention? There is no set formula, yet there are many options. They include:

- Mass participation in building the case for change and the vision for the future;

- Interactive communications that deepen understanding and build excitement;

- Planned experiences that impact people's mindsets, such as leadership breakthrough training or rites of passage from the old to the new;

- Employee input on key change issues that demonstrably influences leaders' thinking; and

- Responsibility for high-leverage action for key players throughout *all levels* of the organization.

You will know you have been successful when a critical mass of people in the project community is moving forward toward the organization's desired future, ready, emotionally aligned, and capable of doing what the transformation requires. This phase is an opportunity for bold action. You will want to design this phase's work to wake up the organization and mobilize action, while minimizing resistance and emotional attachment to the past. There are four activities in this phase to guide you.

Activity II.A: Build Organizational Understanding of the Case for Change and the Change Strategy

Task II.A.1: Communicate the Case for Change and the Change Strategy

In this task, the change leaders and change team members inform the organization about the transformation through their kickoff communication strategy created in Phase I. This communication process is the change leaders' formal declaration to the organization that a transformation is underway. Its content, tone, and delivery have a significant impact on how people respond to the impending challenge. It sets the stage for how the executives will be perceived as leaders of this transformation, how much ownership exists within the organization for the change, and whether employees will buy into the overall change strategy. Make no mistake about it; this initial communication about the case for change and the change strategy is a critical process for aligning the organization, the leaders, and the conditions required to make this transformation successful. It is one of the most important opportunities to mobilize the organization. *It is an opportunity not to be missed.*

Typically, the organization has already heard about the change, and stories and reactions are probably running rampant. Any managers or employees who worked on the case for change and the change strategy will undoubtedly be talking with others about their efforts. It is rare that some information has not already leaked into the organization and is triggering rumors. Therefore, you may want to design your communication to *reorient* people to what the effort is actually about and how it is going to be led. If necessary, use this task to course correct people's perceptions of how the change has been handled to date. Your Phase I project briefing and the assessment of people's capacity for change are good sources of input for this course correction.

This task must be designed as a process rather than as an event. Remember the Five Levels of Communication Model described in Task I.E.4. It suggests that this communication process must include multiple opportunities for employees to hear the messages, formulate their questions, and have their concerns addressed. The intervals between the communications will allow employees to discuss their concerns with their co-workers, which, in turn, will generate more questions to be asked. Eventually, the process will generate greater understanding and acceptance. Honoring the "process" nature of effective communications will help ensure a successful kickoff to the transformation and build the required critical mass of commitments.

People's initial reactions to the transformation may be colored by three dynamics: (1) Their concern for what all of this means to them personally; (2) their complacency about or attachment to the status quo; and (3) the emotions they still have about past changes in which they were adversely affected. If they are having strong reactions, you will definitely have to communicate the same information about the transformation on several different occasions in different ways.

Furthermore, "selling" the future in words doesn't suffice; leaders will have to create a way in which people can *experience* the value of the future for themselves during this series of communications. If the leaders are communicating that this transformation will be very different from past changes, they will have to allow people time to observe whether the leaders' behavior matches their words. People will be watching like hawks to see whether the leaders' intentions to lead this transformation differently are authentic.

Here is one recommended scenario for the design of this kickoff communication process. It attends to many of the common forces at play in the organization. Imagine it occurring as you read, tailoring it to fit the challenges you face today.

An Effective Communications Rollout Scenario

The sponsors, key change leaders, and select representatives of involved managers and employees handle the initial communication—in person, through numerous large group meetings, by teleconference or video. Having more than one person speaking enlivens the delivery, especially if they represent various stakeholder groups. After they have shared the case for change and the change strategy, a series of town meetings cascades throughout the organization, and a live, interactive online conference begins, both of which are led by the executives, as well as the managers and employees who worked on the case for change.

In these meetings, the change sponsors openly discuss what was said in their initial communication, reiterating the facts and their perceptions, hopes, and fears. The managers and employees also offer their perspectives, and the audience asks questions and voices concerns. The leaders of the meeting listen carefully to the audience's questions and issues, responding to all of them. They share their intentions and plans, identify issues that do not yet have answers, and commit to bring the issues back to the planning process for consideration. Through this interchange, the leaders also begin to gather impacts about the transformation that they may not have originally seen.

Facilitated breakout conversations about general reactions or key issues (or online chats) then occur, allowing for active involvement by all participants. Major messages from the breakout groups are brought back to the large group (or main online conference) for presentation to and response by the leaders. The leaders conclude each meeting (or the interactive conference) with a request for volunteers to staff an informal network of change advocates who will be asked for input on the vision of the future and represent their functions' interests as the transformation is planned and implemented.

Over the next two weeks, team leaders facilitate discussions in their work teams about the transformation and its implications for the team and the individual members. The teams are tasked with identifying likely barriers to the effort and conditions for success necessary for the transformation.

The next mass communication vehicle provides a current status report of the transformation effort, highlighting actions taken and outcomes produced as a direct result of employees' previous input. Stories are shared about how various stakeholders have had insights or breakthroughs or have mobilized action central to the transformation's success.

What to Communicate and How to Position the Transformation

The content of the initial round of communications is as critical as the process for delivering it. Often, the content is only delivered by the most senior leaders. We suggest that select managers and employees—also change leaders—take an active role in this delivery as well. Their participation makes the content more credible and demonstrates that change is already occurring. Here is one scenario for what change leaders might deliver.

Imagine the change leaders being genuine, energized, and inviting in their tone. They begin by explaining what has led to this transformation and what has been happening so far. They point out the historical achievements and events they are very proud of and describe how each has contributed to the success of the organization. The leaders are candid about where their own focus has been, sharing how their thinking has recently been impacted by new information and how they themselves have finally heard the wake-up call for this transformation. The sponsors, managers, and employees each speak for their part of the organization. They describe the case for change in powerful terms, including all six drivers, speaking directly to the challenges the organization faces.

The change leaders report how the effort will be led and staffed, especially if their approach will be radically different from the past. The sponsors introduce the change process leader and his or her role and authority. They communicate that everyone in position to add value to this effort is considered a change leader, irrespective of his or her position or level in the organization. Every leadership contribution will be needed. The change leaders describe the key elements of the change strategy, featuring the strategic levers. They announce their bold actions (only if doing so will not steal any thunder when it actually takes place) and other relevant decisions about infrastructure and conditions for success.

The change leaders model the new norm of course correction, admitting that some of the organization's historical change practices must be altered immediately based on new insights. They tell how this transformation fits into the big picture of other organizational events and lay out the required pace of activity and their rationale for it. They convey their genuine understanding of the additional burden this pace may place on the workforce and describe how they will provide adequate resources and support to enable people to create this transformation while maintaining their well-being and current performance.

The change leaders personalize the transformation by sharing what is needed from them as its strategic leaders and as representatives of each level of the organization. They describe how their mindsets and perceptions are changing to enable this effort and how mindset change is also needed throughout the organization. They share how people will be invited to participate, making a compelling case for everyone to pull together and make his or her best contribution. The change leaders tell how this effort will benefit various employee and management groups and speak truthfully about certain groups that will be adversely affected, but treated fairly and humanely.

If appropriate, the change leaders also model new language and behavior, perhaps by emphasizing that they do not have all of the answers about the future and, therefore, want everyone to stay alert for new information and learning, which is different from their normal way of doing things. They describe the transformation as a journey that everyone must undertake together. To demonstrate this, the leaders lay out the upcoming opportunities when people will be asked to provide their input, including the organization-wide visioning process. They reiterate that the transformation is a courageous undertaking and that everyone's full commitment is required for the organization's collective success. They again honor where the organization has been and how this next chapter in its life is the most important and challenging yet. The change leaders conclude with their personal commitment to do whatever is necessary to create this new reality in a way that benefits the organization, its stockholders, and its people, especially the group or level they represent.

Activity II.B: Create Shared Vision and Commitment

Task II.B.1: Roll Out the Visioning Process to Create Shared Vision and Commitment

In Task I.E.5, Identify the Process for Creating Shared Vision Throughout the Organization, the leaders designed a strategy for engaging the organization in the visioning process. For some organizations, the leaders will create the vision of the transformation themselves. For others, the organization will be involved in building the vision. Whatever the strategy is, it is implemented here.

There are three parts to visioning. The first is obtaining agreement about the content of the vision—the actual direction and outcomes of the transformation. The second part is crafting the vision statement in words that capture the compelling possibilities for what the transformation will produce. The third part is ensuring that the entire organization understands the vision and commits to making it real. The outcome of this third piece is creating *collective intention* for the success of the transformation. People must figure out where they personally fit in, what their role in the transformation is, and what action is required of them. If they do this to their satisfaction, people will be on-board with the transformation.

Leaders can choose to do the first two parts of visioning—developing the content and the wording of the vision—themselves or they can use employee participation. It takes about the same amount of time to accomplish all three parts of visioning, whether the leaders develop the content and wording of the vision themselves or use high participation. When leaders develop the content and wording themselves, creating collective intention takes much longer. It can be a slow process to determine the content and wording en masse, yet collective intention is created at the same time.

Determining the Content of the Vision

What is the ideal outcome for the transformation? Exhibit 5.1, Vision for Your Transformation, provides several questions to assist you in building the most powerful vision for your effort. Each question creates a different conversation about the same thing: The outcomes you want the transformation to create. You may not have to use all of the information these questions generate, but their answers will embellish and enliven the pursuit of the vision.

Exhibit 5.1. Vision for Your Transformation

- What is the ideal outcome for your transformation?
- Beyond creating greater profitability, what is your purpose in making this change?
- What difference will it make in the lives of your customers?
- What difference will it make in the lives of the people in the organization?
- How will it add value to each of the stakeholders of the organization?
- How will this transformation help the organization better meet the demands of its marketplace?
- What excites you the most about making this change?
- What would happen if the organization did not complete this transformation successfully? What would be lost?
- How would the organization ideally operate to achieve this reality?

Exhibit 5.1. Vision for Your Transformation, Cont'd

- What are the ideal structural, technological, and financial conditions for supporting this outcome?
- What is the ideal culture for the organization to produce this outcome?
- What are the ideal mindsets, style, behaviors, and values of the leaders and employees to support this transformation?

Writing a Vision Statement

Vision statements are written in words that are compelling and meaningful to people. They should act like a fuel injector for people's excitement. Nice words, safe words, do not jazz people. Vision statements must be bold and challenging. "We want to be the best" doesn't differentiate you from anyone else who is thinking about his or her vision. However, "A computer in every briefcase" or "A cell phone in every pocket" are examples that have some energy to them! Use words that viscerally energize people.

Rather than writing your vision statement in future tense, which describes something yet to be created, it is more powerful if it is written in *present* tense, describing your vision *as if it were your current reality.* This causes people to act as if the vision is already true. It alters people's mindsets about their possibilities and generates positive momentum for bringing these possibilities to fruition.

Building Collective Ownership for the Vision

Prior to or in parallel to creating the vision statement, design a process to build ownership for creating the vision in the rest of the organization. This dissemination does not just mean publishing the words. Many leaders believe that announcing the vision will suffice for its execution. In fact, they are confusing announcement with the emotional integration and commitment required for implementation. Again, remember the Five Levels of Communication. At least the first four levels must be addressed in your vision rollout strategy. People must not only understand and commit to the vision, but they have to know how it changes their work and lives so they can decide whether or not to fully commit to it. If the vision statement is not shared in meaningful ways, a great opportunity for building momentum will be lost. Go back and review the previous task on the process for communicating the case for change and check for applications to your vision rollout.

► CASE IN POINT

In one large telephone company, a very creative strategy was employed to disseminate its new values-based vision. The values group, after completing their statement and the story behind it, designed a pin to symbolize the core values of their vision. They initiated their vision dissemination process by having each group member "pin" two other people out in the organization who were demonstrating the new values by their behavior. Each person being pinned was told the story of the values and given the pin and a card with an oath to be true to the values. The group member then asked that each of those people go through the same ritual while pinning two more people in the organization and telling the values story. Each person was given two pins and cards and the charge to continue the ritual until a critical mass of people had been pinned and had communicated the new vision to others.

The organic nature of the ceremony embedded the values and the vision faster and more sincerely than any formal announcement could have. A large granite version of the pin was placed in the lobby of the headquarters building to represent the importance of its message to the whole organization. Every company building erected a "Values Wall" in its lobby to exhibit photographs of people living the values. These displays were changed monthly to keep the values momentum alive. ◄

Remember that once the vision is shared, each segment of the organization will have to explore the implications it has on its operations and culture. The dissemination process you design should include this tailoring.

Activity II.C: Increase the Organization's Readiness and Capacity to Succeed in the Change

In Phase I, Activity I.C, the change leaders assessed the organization's readiness and capacity for making this change. In this phase, you have the opportunity to provide people supportive and relevant vehicles through which to increase their readiness, knowledge, and skills.

The Phase I assessment should have surfaced information about the true level of readiness and willingness in the organization to move forward with this effort. It should have included an exploration of the current mindset about changing again and the knowledge, skills, and attitudes required for this change's success. Although many organizations have initiated programs to build *leaders'* capacity to lead change in these areas, not many have attended adequately to the workforce's capacity. This activity plans and initiates the process to increase managers' and employees' readiness and capacity for the transformation.

The issue of increasing people's readiness to change can be a sticky one, and it is worth further exploration. A low receptivity to change may be the result of a number of factors, some of which can be changed and some of which cannot. People may be complacent, bored, or resistant. You can impact these states pretty quickly. However, if people are tired, overwhelmed, or burned out from moving at mach speed for too long or from dealing with too many changes at once, you cannot alter this condition overnight. Do you proceed with haste anyway, ignoring their state? Do you pressure people to get on with the work or find another job? Do you put them on a shelf, fire them and replace them with new blood? These can be particularly difficult moral decisions for leaders if they recognize that their people are tired because of years of giving all of their energy to the organization. If the leaders don't recognize this or if they don't care, the usual tactic is to get rid of anyone who cannot keep up with the ever-accelerating pace, despite their years of service. This is no way to retain talent. There is no easy answer in this age of high-pressured change. However, the question cannot go unaddressed and must be reflected in your change strategy and pace.

The decision to provide the organization with change programs that develop knowledge and skills and attend to mindset and behavior is an overt statement by the leaders that people must transform along with the organization's structures and systems. Allocating resources and time to this development communicates how important people are to the future of the organization. We often feel that it is a breakthrough in leadership's thinking to recognize and fund this work. However, we have come to realize that managers and employees are not always receptive to this type of training.

Like the executives, workers may not recognize the need to change themselves personally to support the transformation. They may feel threatened, manipulated, or fearful of engaging in something that they consider to be "personal." Many people will not want to participate unless they first see the executives modeling this work and experience the value it brings. Initially, people may not understand that it is this personal work that is at the heart of the transformation of the organization.

Special consideration must be given to how this type of development is positioned so that it is compelling for people. It is essential to make all of the development relevant to the needs of the organization's transformation and not be about people's behavior outside of the work environment. The focus must be on requirements for succeeding in the transformation, which can be effectively communicated through the story the leaders tell about the drivers of change. People must come to recognize that the change imperatives demand new ways of thinking, behaving, and relating that are of direct value to their performance. In this context, the personal development work has practical relevance and benefit to those who must change.

Task II.C.1: Increase the Organization's Level of Readiness to Change

In Phase I, Assess the Organization's Readiness and Capacity to Succeed in the Change, several factors that influence a person's or an organization's readiness for change, such as stamina, workload, or attachment to the old ways of operating were discussed. The results of the assessment you performed should identify the areas on which to focus your plan for building change readiness in the various groups you studied. In addition to strengthening these areas, your strategy should include helping people identify how they may be holding themselves back from making the change (and perhaps holding others back). The programs and services offered should be designed to stretch people's habitual comfort zones and build their positive energy for the transformation they face.

Strategies for building readiness vary widely. Remember that you cannot force anyone to become more ready and willing to change when they are not. *You can only create the conditions within which they can face, heal, or release whatever it is that is holding them back or identify what would inspire them to move forward.* You may have to address people's mental states, physical states, emotional condition, or sense of meaning and purpose about the transformation. Consider training, breakthrough programs to shift mindset and resolve old emotional issues, communication sessions, dialogue meetings, large group events or rituals, time off, or any of your bold actions. Acknowledging people's true condition without judging or condemning it goes a long way to facilitate their ability to change their state of readiness.

Task II.C.2: Initiate the Plan to Build the Organization's Change Knowledge and Skills

Building people's *ongoing* ability to change is a major investment in the organization's future. Teaching them how to embrace the transformational journey is a strategic lever for bringing that future into being. All organizations have experienced major change. Some have done it well; most have struggled. Not very many have taken the time to learn from their experience and integrate their learnings into how they plan and run their next changes.

In the Introduction to this book, we presented our assumptions that change is now the norm in organizations and that leaders increasingly recognize the strategic advantage of establishing change leadership capability in-house. It is also our assumption that change leadership does not just live at the top of the organization. Change leaders are needed throughout the organization; anyone can directly support the creation of the desired future state. The first step in developing change capacity is assessing the need for additional change knowledge and skills, which you likely completed in Task I.C.1. The Appendix of *Beyond Change Management* offers worksheets to assess the skills, knowledge areas, and behaviors for building conscious change leadership. Use these as well to add to your assessment.

This Phase II task formalizes the awareness, skills, and knowledge various people or groups in the organization require to best support the transformation, then initiates this development. Included is likely education about known best practices for change, the Change Process Model, conscious process thinking and design, and change leadership competencies.

Whom do you target for development? Consider the individuals and groups in your project community. You already have a process in place for the core change leaders (Task I.D.4). Now consider upper and middle management, first-line supervisors, project managers, staff groups involved in the change, in-house change agents and consultants, the union, and other groups. If there are external consulting firms helping you with this change, ensure that each has an understanding of the Change Process Model and how it impacts their work for you and with each other. You might also involve customers and suppliers if they must participate in your change process in an informed way.

We recommend conducting training programs to introduce your change methodology and apply it to the actual change initiatives each group is responsible for. Application materials and tools, in paper or electronic versions, can be very useful for assisting change agents and managers throughout the organization to learn as they work. In Chapter 14, we outline a consulting strategy that develops understanding of the Change Process Model on live cases. It is called "just-in-time consulting" and is a very powerful, albeit experimental, method for assisting busy managers to use and learn the methodology on the fly.

Task II.C.3: Initiate the Plan to Promote the Mindset and Behavioral Changes Required to Support the Transformation

All transformational changes require new ways of thinking and behaving. Many transitional changes do as well. However, organizations rarely focus sufficient attention on the new mindset and behaviors, for all of the reasons we have been discussing.

Our experience with some of the most advanced, creative high-tech giants has shown their reluctance to deal with anything "personal." It has been very interesting for us to observe the difficulties a number of these organizations are facing, which we attribute in part to their over-focus on external results and neglect of human development. In this methodology, executives, managers, and the workforce actively participate in personal transformation that is directly relevant to creating their new business outcomes.

In this task, you design and initiate a "breakthrough process" of self-awareness and transformation that involves at least a critical mass of the entire organization. The context of the process is created through your case for change, and the process is sustained throughout the life of the transformation. It should be integrated with the leaders' breakthrough process begun in Activity I.D.

Some of this work can be done within existing work groups, while some can be accomplished in training settings or large group meetings where a shared experience is more easily created, such as the one described in the leadership breakthrough process in Activity I.D.2. The DTE Energy case described in that activity provides a good example of how this process can work.

Activity II.D: Demonstrate that the Old Way of Operating Is Gone

Task II.D.1: Demonstrate that the Old Way of Operating Is Gone

The process dynamic at play here is inertia. This phenomenon is very real in organizations that have become accustomed to their normal way of operating or attached to their current level of success. People must recognize that the future promised by this transformation is better and more essential than the past or the present. Otherwise, they will not be willing to change. Depending on the magnitude of the transformation, people may have reactions about leaving behind the work they have been devoted to. *Until people let go of the reality they are living in, they will not be able to embrace something new.* No amount of pleading, selling, or coercion will force them to let go.

There are two basic approaches to this task—abrupt and gradual. You can conduct activities that are loud, graphic, wake-up calls that the old is gone, as in the two following cases, or you can gradually deliver this message over time through more subtle actions. Our preference is to use both approaches. Be sure to use your bold actions to demonstrate that the existing way of doing things has served its purpose and the door to the future is open.

▶ CASE IN POINT

A steel company's leaders gathered the members of one of its plant management teams together early one morning. They wanted to read the managers the town's newspaper headlines in person. Unbeknown to the managers, the corporate leaders had printed a special "in-house" edition of the newspaper, just for this meeting. Their goal was to give the managers a very loud wake-up call.

The newspaper headlines read, "Steel Plant to Close for Lack of Performance. Town Goes Belly up!" It took several seconds for the impact of the headlines to register with the managers. The leaders silently let the weight of the trumped-up news sink in. Then they revealed that the newspaper was a prop, and the discussion about the impending change began. ◄

▶ CASE IN POINT

A manufacturing company's leaders wanted to signal to their organization that their old successful product line was going to be replaced by more technologically advanced versions. Not wanting to tarnish the respect and fame that the old line had produced, the leaders unveiled a museum in their corporate headquarters lobby. Under glass, in the most revered display, were prime samples of the long line of products that had been previously retired, including the most current versions. The products were honored, and the message was clear that each was now a "thing of the past." ◄

This task is a tricky one in cases in which the current reality must continue, but in a lesser or different way. In the electric utility industry, for example, there will continue to be regulated businesses. Rather than being the only show in town, though, they will now share the stage with more entrepreneurial businesses. The challenge remains for how to maintain the current operation while still clearly signaling the need to move the organization ahead.

Summary

You have now begun to build momentum for the transformation. The organization understands the case for change and the change strategy and has participated in creating a shared vision of the future it will create. You have initiated strategies throughout the organization to increase readiness, knowledge, and skill for succeeding in the transformation, including mindset and behavioral change for the workforce.

Consulting Questions for Activity II.A: Build Organizational Understanding of the Case for Change and the Change Strategy

Task II.A.1: Communicate the Case for Change and the Change Strategy

- How will you communicate the case for change and the change strategy? How will you ensure that they are understood and supported?

- How will you handle resistance and upset about what the organization is planning to do in this transformation?

- How do the change leaders want to be perceived in this communication? Who will support them to achieve this intention?

Consulting Questions for Activity II.B: Create Shared Vision and Commitment

Task II.B.1: Roll Out the Visioning Process to Create Shared Vision and Commitment

- How will you engage the organization in either building or understanding the vision for the transformation and for the change process itself?

- How will you build commitment for the vision and what it requires?

- How will you ensure that all segments of the organization understand their part in creating the vision?

Consulting Questions for Activity II.C: Increase the Organization's Readiness and Capacity to Succeed in the Change

Task II.C.1: Increase the Organization's Level of Readiness to Change

- How will you use the assessment data you have about the level of readiness in the organization for making this transformation?

- How will you increase the levels of readiness where needed?

- How will you know when you have succeeded?

Task II.C.2: Initiate the Plan to Build the Organization's Change Knowledge and Skills

- What groups will you target for developing change knowledge and skills?

- What specific change knowledge areas and skills will you develop?

- How will you build the required change knowledge and skills?

- How will you make this development relevant to the participants and the work of the transformation?

Task II.C.3: Initiate the Plan to Promote the Mindset and Behavioral Changes Required to Support the Transformation

- How will you position this work in the organization so that it is acceptable and relevant to people?

- Will you use external expertise to facilitate this work? What criteria will you use to select a vendor?

- What part will the change leaders play in this process? How can they assist it while furthering their own mindset and behavioral change?

- How will the breakthrough trainings for the workforce integrate with the leaders' own breakthrough process?

- How will you reinforce these new mindsets and behaviors?

Consulting Questions for Activity II.D: Demonstrate that the Old Way of Operating Is Gone

Task II.D.1: Demonstrate that the Old Way of Operating Is Gone

- How will you demonstrate that the old ways of operating are gone?
- How will you pay respect to the past?

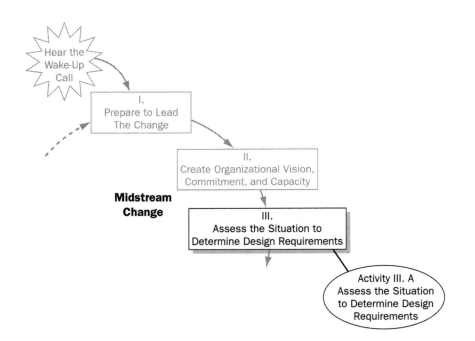

Phase III Task Deliverables

III.A.1: The assessment of the organization's current reality against the vision of the change is complete. Aspects of the organization that must stay in place, be dismantled, or be created have been identified.

III.A.2: Relevant best practices from other organizations have been identified.

III.A.3: Customer requirements are clear.

III.A.4: The statement of design requirements is complete.

6

Phase III: Assess the Situation to Determine Design Requirements

PHASE III IS THE LAST PHASE IN THE UPSTREAM STAGE of change. You have set your foundations for success; you have a clear vision of your desired future and are increasing momentum for the transformation throughout the organization. It is now time to begin to get specific about what the future state will look like and how it has to operate to meet the expectations of your vision. To do this consciously, you must generate accurate and adequate information to guide the design process coming up in the next phase. How will you know which road to take? How will you know what currently exists in the organization that can be brought forward into the future? How will you know which of the possible scenarios to make a reality?

People are generally all too eager to jump headlong into designing various future state scenarios based on their opinions or political positions, rather than on relevant information. Phase III surfaces information that defines what success means and what the organization already has in place that supports this success. This information is formulated into tangible *design requirements* for the future. These requirements are used to shape the future state to satisfy the transformational imperatives for change.

This information is generated through a series of assessments—of the current state of the organization, of other organizations that have engaged in similar changes, and of customers' needs. Your design requirements are the culmination of the four tasks of this phase.

There are several benefits from clarifying your design requirements:

- They articulate clear expectations for what you want and need to achieve to be successful;

- They influence the creation of various design scenarios;

- They can be used to evaluate design options;

- They can trigger needed course corrections during implementation;

- They can be a part of your evaluation of the desired state after implementation is complete; and

- They can further clarify what in your current organization supports the future state, what must change, and what must be left behind.

Activity III.A: Assess the Situation to Determine Design Requirements

Task III.A.1: Assess Current Reality Within the Organization Against Your Vision for the Change

Your vision of the future is by definition different from the current reality in the organization. In order to know just how different the two are, an assessment is designed and performed to compare them. The assessment focuses on the requirement the vision has in both the business/operational aspects and the human/cultural aspects of the organization. It is important to know the following:

- What already exists in the organization that supports your vision in each of these areas;

- What will have to be changed or dismantled; and

- What has to be created from scratch.

This information is essential to shaping your design requirements. Information is sought from any or all of the members of your project community, especially people who are deeply involved in the transformation, impacted by it, or have a stake in it. Customers and others outside your organization can be a valuable source of insight.

Change assessment studies are different from generic survey research assessments performed in traditional organization development practices. Generic organizational studies are typically open-ended and general, searching out anything that is not working well in the organization. Change assessments are purposely designed to provide *specific* information necessary to create a realistic outcome for your future state. For instance, if your transformation is focused on e-commerce, you would ask about products and services that could be sold over the Internet and how selling such products might best be handled. You would not want to hear about other matters occurring in the organization that do not specifically relate to the e-commerce vision.

Change assessments can be used to raise people's expectations and investment in the transformation. For instance, you might ask people their opinions about the three most important features required for the new organization to succeed or what they believe to be the three greatest hurdles to that success. You might ask what the managers or workers see that they think the executives may be overlooking as they plan for the future. Clearly, you would ask about the types of design requirements you are investigating.

Exhibit 6.1, Determining Your Design Requirements, lists several types of design requirements and gives examples of each. You may find that other types of requirements are essential to your design as well. Be sure to clarify the types of design requirements you are researching before conducting your assessment. Use this worksheet to assist with your own determination of design requirements or customize your own worksheet based on the types of design requirements you are investigating.

Exhibit 6.1. Determining Your Design Requirements

Organizational Constraints, "Givens," or "Must Haves"

What factors must absolutely be included in the design? Categories might include finances, customer requirements, equipment, people involved, management processes, etc.

Examples: Maximum staff size; required use of existing technology

Exhibit 6.1. Determining Your Design Requirements, Cont'd

Mission, Vision, and Business Imperatives

Examples: Enables e-business marketing and sales; allows an integrated product sales approach

Assessment Issues

Any concern or benefit raised in the assessment study

Examples: Enables a ten-day or faster production time; enables on-time delivery

Job Requirements/Tasks

Any requirement for workflow or content of jobs or functions

Examples: Centralizes scheduling function; maximizes innovation and group interaction

Organizational Mindset and Behavior

Any requirements for modeling and demonstrating the organization's desired mindset and behavior

Examples: Ensures early customer input to new product designs and upgrades (market-driven mindset); enables teamwork, shared responsibility, cross-boundary communication

Exhibit 6.1. Determining Your Design Requirements, Cont'd

Political Implications

Any relationship or circumstance that involves political influence, turf, reputation, or power

Examples: Retains strategy-level decision making in the office of the chief executive; titles reflect contribution, not hierarchical power

Cultural Imperatives/Values to Model

Examples: Ensures and rewards new information; reduces job title and level differentials

Technological Needs

Examples: Uses existing plant equipment; enables smooth assimilation of software upgrades

People Requirements

Examples: Maintains existing complement levels; enhances on-the-job development opportunities and cross-training

You may also want to generate ideas for design requirements by answering the following:

- "We want an organization (or system, or culture, or process) that is able to. . . ."
- "This organization (or system) will be successful if it. . . ."
- "In order to meet customer requirements, we must have an organization that. . . ."

The assessment methods you choose—be they individual or group interviews, large group interventions, or a general survey—will influence the level of receptivity for the transformation. The act of inviting participation in the study fuels positive momentum. People then expect some result to occur and will expect to hear back from you. Be sure to plan how you will inform your assessment participants about the results of the study and how these results will be used to influence the design of the future state. Feed the assessment results into your communication plan to keep the greater organization abreast of progress in the transformation process.

Task III.A.2: Benchmark Other Organizations for Best Practices

Since the quality movement began, benchmarking has become common practice. Fortunately, it is seen as an honor to be perceived publicly as a "benchmark organization" with best practices in specific areas. Because benchmark organizations are open to sharing their "secrets" with the world, learning from them can be very valuable at this point in your process. Their relevant best practices can be strategically used to help define your design requirements.

The first step in this task is to uncover the organizations that are "top in class" in the specific content areas of your change (for example, customer service, manufacturing processes, e-commerce) or in the culture or organizational structure you seek (for example, shared responsibility, learning-oriented, autonomous work teams). Set a clear scope for your search before beginning. Your process might include site visits, telephone interviews, literature searches, web searches, or any other form of research that will surface recommended design requirements.

Task III.A.3: Clarify Customer Requirements

Some of the most critical factors for shaping your desired state are the needs of your customers. Your customers' requirements are key drivers of the transformation and will define your success. This task provides a way to work with your customers in clarifying how your organization must change to serve them better. How you go about contacting, interviewing, and relating to your customers can pave the way for long-lasting and mutually satisfying relationships. The more you create partnerships with them, the better your chances of learning about their evolving needs and serving them over time. When you assessed the drivers of your change in Task I.B.2, you identified marketplace requirements and customers' needs. Be sure to build on this work.

Which customers are your best sources of guidance? How will you use this inquiry to strengthen your relationship with them? Consider creating a customer council to advise you throughout your transformation. Be aware of the mindset shifts that you are making and whether your customers are thinking outside of their own boxes in giving you guidance. You may have to create a mindset—shifting strategy for your customers so that, together, you can push the envelope of change.

This is one area where an integrated effort is critical. Be sure to ask all the change process leaders of all major change initiatives in the organization which customers they will be speaking to. You do not want to alienate your customers with multiple requests.

Task III.A.4: Write the Statement of Design Requirements

The output of Phase III is your statement of design requirements. The process for creating this list begins with the compilation of your organization's assessment results, the best practices from other organizations, and your customers' requirements. Review these inputs in light of your vision and note any gaps. This review will reveal the high-leverage requirements for the design of your desired state.

Summary

You have now competed the upstream stage of change. Take a moment to glance back at the ground you have covered. The effort has been staffed, its leaders have been developed to lead it collectively, and the workforce has been motivated to make the transformation a reality. Your reason for transforming is clear and compelling. Your change strategy provides the level of guidance necessary for an integrated and efficient rollout. The change infrastructure provides the resources and support for handling the transformation in the midst of everyday pressures. And you have prepared yourself and the organization to design its future. We now proceed to Section Two, the *midstream stage* of the change process.

Consulting Questions for Activity III.A: Assess the Situation to Determine Design Requirements

Task III.A.1: Assess Current Reality Within the Organization Against Your Vision for the Change

- What aspects of your current organization will you assess to determine the gap between what you have and what your vision demands?

- What assessment methods will you use?

- Which people or groups will participate in this assessment?

- How will you position this work to continue to generate energy for your transformation?

Task III.A.2: Benchmark Other Organizations for Best Practices

- What will you benchmark in other organizations?

- How will you identify benchmark organizations?

- How will you carry out this research, and who will do it?

Task III.A.3: Clarify Customer Requirements

- How will you determine your customers' requirements?

- What kind of a process will you use to keep your customers involved in shaping the outcomes of your transformation?

- Who are your best customer contacts for this work?

- Who will decide which customers are to be contacted?

Task III.A.4: Write the Statement of Design Requirements

- How will you compile your design requirements from all of the data you have collected?

- Who must approve these requirements?

- How will you ensure that your design requirements drive the creation of your design scenarios?

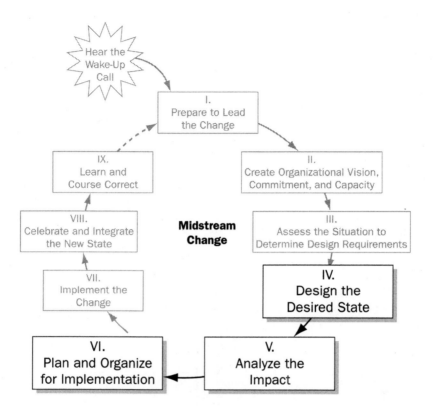

Midstream Change

Section Two
Midstream Change

Phase IV

Chapter 7: Design the Desired State   159

Phase V

Chapter 8: Analyze the Impact   171

Phase VI

Chapter 9: Plan and Organize for Implementation   181

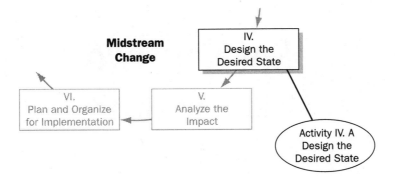

Phase IV: Task Deliverables

IV.A.1: The process for designing the desired state has been defined, staffed, and mobilized.

IV.A.2: A preferred desired state scenario has been created and approved.

IV.A.3: The desired state has been tested in preparation for planning its implementation.

IV.A.4: The desired state has been effectively communicated to the organization.

7

Phase IV: Design the Desired State

THE MIDSTREAM STAGE OF CHANGE FOCUSES ON designing the desired state, assessing the magnitude of work and resources required for it to operate successfully, and preparing the organization for implementation. The upstream preparation you have done will make this stage go more smoothly and expeditiously.

The purpose of Phase IV is to design the specific organizational and cultural solutions that will enable the organization to achieve its vision successfully. Let's clarify the difference between the *vision of the transformation,* which has already been determined, and the *design of the future state.*

The vision of the transformation creates a compelling picture of the organization's reality when the transformation has been successfully implemented. It is, by definition, a quest, a dramatic stretch that energizes and motivates the organization to pursue this very different and exciting outcome. Metaphorically, the vision is the picture of the future from the 30,000-foot level. The vision is directional and inspirational, not necessarily tangible.

The design of the desired state is the view of the future from the 5,000-foot vantage point. It is the organization's best guess at what *specific* changes are required to accomplish or progress toward the vision. The design is much more tangible and will likely include particular changes to structure, systems, processes, technology, work practices, jobs, mindset, relationships, and culture. It is still a picture of the future, but much more concrete.

To balance both the organizational and the human requirements for success, make sure that your desired state design serves the people who must make it work, not just the results it is designed to produce. The culture, relationships, rewards, and technology interfaces have to be created to support the people of the organization as well as its operations and outcomes.

The activities of this phase use the design requirements created in Phase III to develop the best future state scenarios, test them, and determine which one is the most likely to create an organization that will be successful. From this point on in the process, the transformation is driven by the design of the desired state.

Activity IV.A: Design the Desired State
Task IV.A.1: Create the Process and Structure to Design the Desired State

There is a wide range of strategies for designing the desired state. Your process will vary depending on the type and scope of the change, style of the change leaders, and degree of in-house ability to design the desired state. The process you use will impact not only the resulting design scenario, but also the organization's understanding and commitment to it.

The design process should reflect the mindset and cultural norms espoused in Phase I. There are a number of political considerations to keep in mind in how you design the desired state. For instance, who gives input, what design features are given priority, and which design is selected will all have political implications. Keep these factors in mind as you proceed with this phase.

If you are using in-house resources to create the design, consider forming a design team of expert personnel or representatives from a cross-section of the organization impacted by the change or creating a Future Search Conference or other large group intervention.

Exhibit 7.1, How to Develop the Desired State Design, offers several questions to guide your thinking for this task.

Exhibit 7.1. How to Develop the Desired State Design

- Who will perform the work to create optimal desired state scenarios? Will you use external content expertise, do the work in-house, or both?
- If you use external consultants as well as in-house resources, how will the two groups work together?
- Who will lead this effort from within the organization?
- What role will the change leaders and the executives play in design?
- What training or professional support does your in-house design team require?
- How will the actual desired state scenarios be generated? How will you use your design requirements to guide this work?
- How will the various design scenarios be evaluated?
- What is the timetable for this entire phase?
- How will the effort be supported and given resources?
- How will the decision about the best desired state scenario be made?

Use of External Consulting Services

When the magnitude of the transformation and the need for specialized expertise are great, many organizations turn their design effort over to external consulting firms. This can be a very effective approach—if these expert consultants are integrated into the overall process and style of the transformation. Problems arise, however, when the organization's executives make two serious mistakes: The first is when leaders believe change happens through only two stages, design and implementation (midstream and downstream stages). With this mindset, it seems reasonable to think that a consultant could come in, determine the best design, and then leave the organization to its own devices to implement the solution. In this case, the design phase is not seen as part of a fullstream change process and often has little or no connection with the upstream stage of change, if one even occurs.

The second major mistake happens when leaders think only about changing "content"—the formal aspects of their organizations, such as structure or business processes. Remember the three elements of a comprehensive change strategy—content, people, and process. The narrow focus on content inadvertently causes upheaval for the people of the organization and for the change process. We have seen far too many organizations retain consulting firms that, under the promise of providing help and efficiency, come in, take over, alienate key internal stakeholders, neglect the human dimensions, and behave in ways that are counter to the mindset and culture in the existing or desired state. This usually does more harm than good.

These problems arise because so many expert consulting firms have a limited view of the process of change and don't fully understand the transformational dynamics of employee ownership or people's normal reactions, mindset, culture, and behavior. They are not trained or experienced in these areas and often prefer to stick to their technical specialties. Unfortunately, they are not exempt from negatively impacting the change process or the culture and human dynamics that surface strongly during the design phase, especially if the change is transformational. If left on their own, they can seriously complicate the political and emotional dynamics of your change effort. Because the consultants cannot be isolated from the organization's operating style and culture, they must at least take these factors consciously into account as they work, if not attempt to model *your* culture.

Having said this, we also support the use of expert consulting firms when leaders need their content expertise in the design phase of their overall transformation. However, leaders must be purposeful about how these consultants are used. Always ensure that these consultants gather data from a full range of stakeholders about what they think will work best in your organization. Be sure they do *not* attempt to sell you on a design just because it worked somewhere else.

Many organizations are beginning to form partnerships between content consultants (internal and external) and organization development practitioners (internal or external) to take advantage of the important process and people expertise OD brings. This is a relatively new approach and requires emotional maturity from everyone to succeed. Decision-making authority, spans of control, roles, and professional contributions must be clearly differentiated, and the means for monitoring and course correcting the interactions among all parties must be firmly in place from the onset. It is essential that change leaders set very clear ground rules for how they expect the different consulting groups to work together, because the relationships can be very messy if left without accountability or coordination. Done well, this strategy can leverage the unique value each consulting firm brings, plus streamline the number and types of consultants being used.

Most of the major expert consulting firms have recognized the problem of having inadequate people and process expertise and have been building in-house capability to incorporate this expertise into their content design services. Where many firms still separate people and process from content, some are attempting to integrate the three. They are also attempting to provide implementaton services to support their design deliverables. From our observations, however, no one firm has yet mastered either of these integrations throughout the ranks of consultants who do the actual work in their client organizations. Where the requirements for these integrations may be clear with their practice leaders, the online delivery staffs usually still have much to learn.

Integrating Design Efforts Across the Organization

Most organizations have many change initiatives underway that may be in their design phase at the same time. Task I.F.4 recommended that you perform an organization-wide scan of all change initiatives that may impact your current transformation. This scan should be able to tell you which initiatives are currently in design and, of those, which should be integrated into your transformation's design work, which have to be coordinated in parallel with it, and which are totally separate. This information should be reflected in your strategy for creating the design process to support the overall organization's transformation.

It will also be useful to find out what design approaches are being used throughout the organization and whether creating a design process "operating system" to integrate all of them would be of value and acceptable to all the players. Coordinating integrated design activities is relatively simple when the various initiatives are each using this Change Process Model as their roadmap.

Task IV.A.2: Design the Desired State

Once the people selected to develop the desired state are on board, educated for their task, and working well together, they proceed with the important work of designing the actual future for the organization. They use the design requirements developed in Phase III to craft various scenarios for consideration.

Using the facilitative leadership style will influence the role of the executives and change leaders in design. Most executives want to stay very close to the design events, usually to ensure that things are going the way they want. This can be advantageous as long as roles and decision making remain consistent with your previous start-up agreements or are *overtly* altered and agreed to by everyone. Having people in power inappropriately step in and exert control at this juncture can do tremendous damage to the culture change momentum that has been building. Be sure to review the executives' roles in the entire design process and decision before you begin.

The scope of the transformation will indicate what the design work has to cover. Design may be needed for any relevant aspect of the organization—product or service development, business process development, organization and/or work redesign, culture, technology, information systems, or software design. These areas require their own unique design processes. Be sure to seek out expertise for the best designs for each of the featured content areas of your transformation.

Design scenarios usually reflect levels of design. We describe four levels of design: vision, strategic, managerial, and operational. The first two are more abstract or conceptual (vision and strategy) and the second two are more concrete (managerial and operational). Note that each of the words, "vision," "strategic," "managerial," and "operational" refers to a level of design; none of them refer, in this case, to the organization's vision, its strategy, its management, or its operations.

To complete your design scenario, you will have to work through all four levels, starting with vision and ending with operational. If you skip one of the higher levels, your managerial and operational designs may not function the way you intend, or they may actually compete with your desired outcomes. Figure 7.1 illustrates the levels and gives some general examples of what is typically included in each level. The following boxed copy applies the levels of design to the specific example of a reorganization.

Levels of Design Example Applied to a Reorganization

Vision Level	Streamlined organization, efficient and resilient, close to the customer
Strategy Level	Consolidate functions A, B, and C; move to strategic business units; create single point of customer contact within each business; create shared services
Managerial Level	Executive committee composed of all strategic business unit presidents; create cross-business councils; define shared services for all affected functions; put business planning expertise into each strategic business unit; use interdependent customer service systems
Operational Level	Twenty customer service centers staffed by fifty customer service representatives; customer satisfaction measurements; standardized information processing procedures; job descriptions

---

Figure 7.1. Levels of Design Model

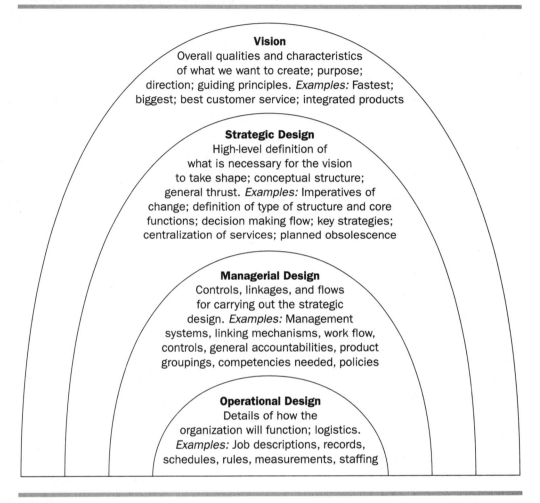

It is essential for the people doing the design to be clear about what level they are designing and what information exists about the levels above their current level of focus. Nothing is more frustrating than working diligently on an operational design and discovering that the strategic design is either not clear or emphasizes a different direction. Too often, leaders delegate the task of operational design without having thought about or reached consensus on the strategic or managerial levels, causing costly political and emotional battles. A very helpful design practice is to complete one level of design and have it approved before fine-tuning the next more tangible level. Remember to use the decision-making style and process you decided on earlier.

It is a common strategy to complete the vision, strategy, and most of the managerial levels of design during this phase. Frequently, operational design must wait for more information to be available or for the people who will actually be living with the day-to-day workings of the desired state to do this work to suit their needs. Keep in mind that some design work will also be accomplished during Phase VI, Plan and Organize for Implementation, when the impacts of the desired state are resolved and translated into specific actions for implementation.

The design process will uncover a lot of information, opinions, and positions about the organization's future. It may even identify the next likely wave of change that is too big, too risky, or too premature to do now. This information must be channeled to the appropriate people on the change leadership team for decision or action. You may wish to use your information generation system (Task I.E.6) for tracking this new information.

Task IV.A.3: Pilot Test

Sometimes the design of the desired state is so radically different from the old way the organization operates or so complicated, costly, or risky that the change leaders decide to test the design before they proceed with full-scale implementation. This task guides planning and executing a pilot test, learning from it, and refining the design of the desired state (if necessary) before gaining full approval to proceed.

When designing a pilot, determine the scope of your test, the outcomes you are after, the political implications of the site or areas you select for the test, and what criteria you will use to evaluate the results. Some organizations attempt to run pilots as if in a "pure" laboratory environment, just setting it up in standard form and letting it unfold as it will. Others set the pilot up using their conditions for success and vision of the future, giving the test the greatest likelihood of demonstrating what they hope to achieve with their transformation. While either approach is valid, the latter moves the process along with greater intention. Both approaches can generate valuable data for the refinement of the desired state scenario being tested.

▶ CASE IN POINT

In one organization we worked with, the change process leader, a very conscious and creative man, decided that the organization needed to run a pilot program. Concerned about resistance, he announced to the organization that a pilot test would be run on the desired state scenario and that two sites would have the opportunity to contribute to the organization's future by testing the desired state, as well as be a year ahead of the game if they were successful in their efforts. He invited any site that was interested in pioneering the future to tell him why and how they would proceed. Much to our surprise, more than half of the thirty potential sites submitted proposals. At the time, the desired state scenario was defined through the managerial level of design, requiring the chosen test sites to complete their own operational-level design as they figured out how to implement. Two sites were chosen; the test period was to be one year.

The two sites represented two very different leadership styles and cultures within the organization. One was more controlling, conservative, and pressured; the other was more facilitative, open, and risk taking. The conservative site rolled out its implementation with no consulting help, little margin for error, and minimal foundation setting. The innovative site used the internal organization development consultants, selected its own change team to design the change strategy, spent considerable effort to identify and create conditions for success, and involved the front-line teams that were the most impacted by the desired state design.

Upon completion of the pilot program, both sites reported important findings about the desired state, the change strategy used for their rollout, and the receptivity of the various target audiences in the organization. The results of the pilots revealed predictable outcomes—the more innovative site that took a proactive and participative approach proved to be the more positive. The conservative site was also considered successful, although the culture, morale, and performance of the innovative site had observably more vitality, commitment, and buy-in. It was clearly the preferred wave of the future. ◄

Task IV.A.4: Communicate the Desired State

Once the desired state is decided, you communicate it to the targets of the change, the organization, and all stakeholders. Because the change is transformational, it carries no guarantees, and the leaders must communicate the preferred future state with a caveat: "This desired state is the organization's current best guess about what will bring it success. As the transformation toward this new state proceeds, everybody has to be on the lookout for emergent information or feedback that something better may still be required. Full commitment to this future state is critical, along with the understanding that the organization is in a learning process and that the future will continue to evolve."

This caveat is extremely important for transformational change to be successful. It reinforces the very nature of transformation and helps to further dismantle the mindset that the leaders always have the right answers or that once a plan is put in motion, it must be completed with blind faith. This communication is a central part of waking up the organization's members to being full players in its *conscious* transformational process. Everybody has to be willing to provide feedback for course correction without being afraid of attack or becoming disheartened when further adjustments are needed. You want to prevent the common reaction that "the organization didn't get it right the first time." Instead, you want to instill the idea that course correction is the essence of transformation.

Summary

You now have a desired state scenario that meets your design requirements. It is your best estimation of what will create your transformational outcomes. The organization now understands what its future looks like and can proceed with the next step in making it a reality. The desired state is, by definition, different from the current reality in the organization. This fact brings us to the next critical phase in the change process, Analyze the Impact.

Consulting Questions for Activity IV.A: Design the Desired State

Task IV.A.1: Create the Process and Structure to Design the Desired State

- See Exhibit 7.1 for Consulting Questions on this task.

Task IV.A.2: Design the Desired State

- How will all four of the levels of design be handled?

- Who has to approve each level of design for each aspect of the desired state scenario?

Task IV.A.3: Pilot Test

- If a pilot test is required, how will you determine the best site(s) for the test?

- Will you set up your pilot test intentionally with conditions for success or allow it to unfold in the organization naturally?

- How will you measure the effectiveness of your pilot test(s)?

- How will you deal with data that surfaces in your pilot(s) indicating the need to course correct the desired state design?

- What is your timeline for the pilot(s)? Does this timeline allow for an adequate test?

- If your pilot(s) reveal the need to further refine the desired state scenario, how will you handle this work? Will you involve everyone from the original design process or select a few for fine-tuning?

Task IV.4: Communicate the Desired State

- How will you communicate the desired state to the entire organization? How will you position it with the "transformational caveat" to allow for its continuous evolution?

- How will you communicate where you are in the overall change process and what the organization can expect next?

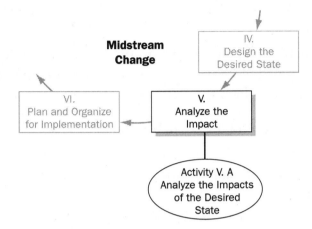

Phase V Task Deliverables

V.A.1: The impact analysis process has been designed, communicated, and initiated.

V.A.2: The impacts of the change effort have been identified, categorized, and assigned for resolution.

V.A.3: The magnitude of individual and collective impacts has been assessed for system-wide implications in the desired state design.

V.A.4: The desired state has been refined, as necessary.

V.A.5: The targets of the change, the organization, and all stakeholders understand the summary results of the impact analysis and the newly refined desired state.

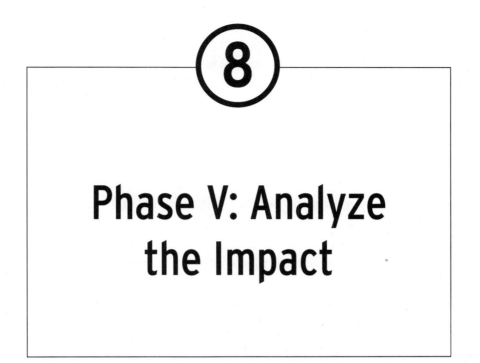

Phase V: Analyze the Impact

TOO OFTEN, EXECUTIVES ANNOUNCE THEIR DESIRED STATE
and then proceed headlong into its implementation before having a realistic sense
of how disruptive the change will be on their operations and people and how best
to handle its complexity. They assume that people will deal with whatever is
required by the change effort on their own. By diving into implementation without forethought, they force their organizations into the reactive mode, not knowing what they are really dealing with and not caring about how burdensome the
transformation will be for those who must make it happen. This phase is designed
to prevent this costly and stressful mistake.

Phase V accomplishes two important functions: (1) It clarifies the magnitude of
work required by the desired state and (2) it ensures that the desired state will
function effectively as an integrated system. To handle the first function, Phase V
assesses the impacts of the desired state on the current organization and its culture
and people. In essence, this function is a detailed gap analysis, determining the differences between the old state and the desired state. This impact analysis surfaces

specific issues that must be addressed in order to plan how best to implement the desired state and identifies the issues that remain before a clear plan can be devised. The actual planning for implementation occurs in Phase VI, based on the lists of issues identified during this phase.

The second function looks at all of the variables built into the desired state design and projects how they will interact over time. In essence, it assesses the system dynamics of the future state. If the interactions are unclear or costly to the system's effectiveness, they are noted or redesigned to support desired outcomes.

This impact analysis differs from the initial impact analysis you performed when building your case for change. Your initial impact analysis was used to assess the general magnitude of your transformation for determining its scope. Now that you have created a more precise picture of what your new state will entail, you can perform a more comprehensive analysis with which to plan your implementation.

There are three areas of focus for generating impact issues: (1) The formal organization, including structures, management systems, business processes, skills, numbers of people, technology, and work practices; (2) the human and cultural aspects of the organization, including mindset, behavior, relationships, and all elements of culture; and (3) interactions between any of the factors on either list.

The tool you used to perform your initial impact analysis (see Chapter 1, Task I.B.4, Exhibit 1.4) can be used for the first two parts of this assessment as well. It covers both the formal elements and the human elements of the organization. Scan it again with the desired state scenario of your transformation in mind, adding any additional items requiring attention in this detailed assessment.

Interactive impacts can be identified through open dialogue among key change leaders or by creating a hypothetical systems diagram of the desired state. Although there will be numerous assumptions embedded in this diagram, it will prove very useful to further stimulate conversation.

Each of the impacts identified has to be fleshed out to focus the study, information, or work required to plan implementation. Although the actual resolution of these issues is accomplished in Phase VI, during this phase, you simply identify the issues that require further work. For example, impacts may include:

- Study the organizational structure for how to reduce it by one or two layers of management;

- Research how to consolidate products X and Y for ease of sale and delivery to customers;

- Redesign the resource allocation process;
- Assess cultural norms in sales to identify how to build stronger and more sustainable customer relationships;
- Study how to broaden the "abc" family of products (for example, acquisition or in-house start-up?);
- Figure out how to overcome the attitude of entitlement in the R&D department; or
- Redesign the reward system to motivate greater team performance and reduce rugged individualism.

One of the prime benefits of the impact analysis process is ensuring a valid new state design. If you surface impacts that are too radical or costly for the organization to handle, you can alter your design to lessen them. It is better to uncover such impacts now, on paper, rather than during implementation when redesign is much more difficult. The unwise scenario, of course, is ignoring major impacts and plodding ahead as if they don't exist.

The impact analysis deepens understanding of the transformation and the desired state for both the change leaders and the workforce. It secures greater buy-in from those who have had a chance to give input and helps you develop a realistic change plan. Handled well, it is the turning point in the process from imagining the transformation to acting on it.

Activity V.A: Analyze the Impact of the Desired State

Task V.A.1: Create the Process for Conducting the Impact Analysis

There are many ways to go about analyzing the impacts of the desired state and many areas to study. The impact analysis process looks different for every change effort. In some cases, it may be a formal study; in others, an intuitive scan. The study can be designed to involve all levels of the affected organization in order to build greater investment in the transformation. Who knows the impact of a future scenario better than those who will be directly affected by it?

This activity is a particularly valuable one in which to use participation, especially from resistors. Your goal is to discover all that stands in the way of the transformation happening successfully. The identification of obstacles, issues, and conflicts is welcome information at this point, and the act of listening to and validating the perceptions of the "nay-sayers" gets their good ideas on the table, reduces their resistance, and engages them more in the transformation. Their input may even change the face of the effort! Remember to include representatives of all groups who have a stake in the transformation, especially those who will be most impacted by it. They are primary sources of impact issues and information.

This first task creates the process for conducting the impact analysis. Read over the remaining tasks before designing the study process. Exhibit 8.1, Designing the Impact Analysis Process, includes several questions to consider for this task. The change process leader typically guides the design of this work.

Exhibit 8.1. Designing the Impact Analysis Process

- What structure will you use to generate impact issues? Consider study teams, large group interventions, or surveys cascaded through your formal organization or informal networks. Will you use external consultants?

- Is education needed about how to perform an Impact Analysis?

- What will be the scope of the study? What areas will it address?

- What degree of detail is desired in identifying issues? Consider using the Levels of Design Model for consistency (that is, vision, strategic guidance, managerial input, operational detail).

- In what medium do you want the impact issues to be recorded, and how they will be managed?

- Who are the best people to perform this work? What criteria will you use to select them?

- What is the appropriate pace and resource base for this work?

- How will you divide the issues into categories or groups of similar issues?

- How will you identify the best people to assign as impact group leaders? How will you ensure that they work well as a team?

- How will you assess the magnitude of the impacts? What criteria will you use? Who will do the magnitude assessment?

- How will you monitor for political, emotional, and cultural dynamics triggered by issue identification?

- How will you communicate the impact analysis process and results to the organization?

Task V.A.2: Conduct the Impact Analysis of the Desired State

The impact analysis process identifies all of the important impacts of the desired state and determines the work required before implementation can accurately be planned. In most transformational changes, a thorough impact analysis can generate hundreds of issues. This can cause the dynamic called "analysis paralysis." The transformation may be so complex that the number of issues identified overwhelms people. Be aware of this tendency, especially in organizations with cultures that support detail and thoroughness. Your challenge is to design this activity in a way that gives you the most accurate and realistic information and continues to engage the organization without bogging it down.

To address this dynamic and assist with managing the issues, the impacts are grouped into categories of similar interdependent topics, such as human resource issues, cultural issues, structural issues, sociotechnical issues, or issues relating to a specific product or business process. The categories will depend on the transformation and the desired state design. Exhibit 8.2, Ways to Categorize Impact Issues, offers a list of typical categories.

Exhibit 8.2. Ways to Categorize Impact Issues

- By customer requirement
- Within a function
- Across specific functions
- Between specific levels of the organization
- Between stakeholder groups
- If a design issue (managerial or operational design)
- By business line
- By geography
- By specialty
- If people or human resources related
- Technical training needs
- Mindset and behavioral training needs
- Management development training needs

After lists of issues have been generated and grouped, assign someone to be responsible for resolving each of the categories, which is work that occurs in the next phase. We call these people "impact group leaders." They must have direct access to the executives who own the ultimate design decisions, as some of the issues may require some redesign of the desired state. The impact group leaders will "own" their issues, resolving, integrating, and presenting their solutions during the development of the Implementation Master Plan, which also occurs during the next phase. It is important to remind impact group leaders that their allegiance is to the overall success of the transformation, not to their impact group. Group leaders must work well together for the good of the whole effort.

Task V.A.3: Assess the Magnitude of Impacts, Individually and Collectively, to Discover System-Wide Implications of the Desired State Design

Once the impacts are grouped, they must be evaluated for the magnitude of changes they require, the cost of making those changes, and the future system dynamics they will likely produce. The impacts must be evaluated collectively as an integrated system, not just individually. Costs can be assessed in terms of dollars, time, energy, resources, expertise, culture shock, or morale. This information is used to determine the viability of the desired state design and to obtain a more accurate sense of the level of effort and emotional stamina the transformation will require. The most informed people review the impact issues for this information, as well as for potential red flags that can be obstacles to the effectiveness of your desired state or even prevent its implementation. These people determine whether any of the issues demand refinement or alteration of the desired state. If key issues must be resolved before they can be accurately assessed, then that work, which occurs in Phase VI, happens concurrently with this task.

Task V.A.4: Refine the Desired State as Necessary

If you discover impacts that are of a magnitude that require you to refine or alter the desired state, those changes are made here. Revisit your design requirements. Sometimes this refinement calls for only a minor adjustment to the design—other times a major overhaul, especially if system dynamics are uncovered that will seriously impair the functioning of the desired state. The time needed for this course correction is a worthy investment in creating the outcome you want.

After the desired state has been redone, perform another impact analysis on the latest iteration to ensure that it is now viable and capable of being implemented. From here on in the transformation, you will continue to gather impact analysis data as it shows up, incorporating it appropriately into the change process.

Task V.A.5: Communicate the Summary Results of the Impact Analysis and the Newly Defined Desired State to the Targets of the Change, the Organization, and All Stakeholders

The results of the impact analysis and the possibly refined desired state must be communicated to keep everyone apprised of the status of the transformation. Every communication from the change leaders generates more valuable information back to them about the viability of the desired state, the readiness of the organization for the next phase in the transformation, and implementation requirements. This communication can increase people's readiness and further develop employee commitment. It is yet another opportunity for the change leaders to walk their talk, as they will again be modeling the new norm of continuous course correction. As always, be sure to use the Five Levels of Communication to design your communication.

Summary

You now have a detailed assessment of the magnitude of work required to plan implementation. You, and all of the people who contributed to the impact analysis, have a more thorough understanding of the workings and requirements of the desired state. Phase VI moves this understanding toward action, in preparation for implementation.

Consulting Questions for Activity V.A: Analyze the Impacts of the Desired State

Task V.A.1: Create the Process for Conducting the Impact Analysis

- See Exhibit 8.1 for questions.

Task V.A.2: Conduct the Impact Analysis of the Desired State

- How will you organize and categorize the impact issues?
- Who are the best people to lead your impact groups through to resolution?

Task V.A.3: Assess the Magnitude of Impact, Individually and Collectively, to Discover System-Wide Implications of the Desired State Design

- What criteria will you use to assess the magnitude of your impact issues? How will you determine whether they have system-wide implications for the design of the desired state?

- Who are the best people to assess the magnitude and implications of the impact issues and whether a refinement is required in the desired state?

- How will you clarify their roles and decision-making authority?

Task V.A.4: Refine the Desired State as Necessary

- What are the political implications of refining the desired state at this point? How will you deal with them?

- What process will you use to refine the desired state?

- Who will do this work and who must approve the new design?

Task V.A.5: Communicate the Summary Results of the Impact Analysis and the Newly Defined Desired State to the Targets of the Change, the Organization, and All Stakeholders

- How will you communicate the newly refined desired state to the organization?

- How can you position this communication to build further readiness and reinforce the norms of continuous learning and course correction?

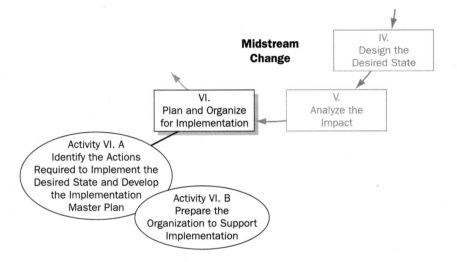

Phase VI Task Deliverables

VI.A.1: The process for developing the Implementation Master Plan has been created and approved.

VI.A.2: Solutions for individual and interdependent impact issues have been identified.

VI.A.3: Solutions have been translated into actions and compiled into the detailed Implementation Master Plan.

VI.A.4: Strategies to sustain the energy for the entire transformation have been designed and integrated into the Implementation Master Plan.

VI.A.5: Based on the magnitude of implementation work, the pacing strategy and a realistic timeline have been determined and applied to the Implementation Master Plan. The Implementation Master Plan is approved.

VI.B.1: The infrastructure and conditions to support implementation are in place.

VI.B.2: Strategies for supporting people to embrace the desired state and manage their reactions to the transformation have been identified and initiated.

VI.B.3: The targets of the change, the organization, and all stakeholders understand the Implementation Master Plan.

Phase VI: Plan and Organize for Implementation

THE IMPACT ANALYSIS ALWAYS GENERATES A LOT OF ENERGY for the change. It widens your lens for understanding the breadth of what is required to implement the desired state. Now the challenge is to focus all of that energy and channel it into a viable plan of action. At this point in the process, the impact issues must be resolved before implementation can be planned. This phase resolves these issues, translates their solutions into implementation actions, and develops the Implementation Master Plan.

The Implementation Master Plan is the guide for how the transformation will proceed. This plan is the detailed version of the critical milestones from your change strategy, adjusted, of course, to fit the circumstances of the current transformational reality. The plan enumerates the what, who, where, and when of the implementation phase of your transformation. Its purpose is to facilitate and coordinate the multitude of activities necessary to create the desired state in a way that reflects its new culture, mindset, and style.

"The rubber meets the road" in this phase. The number of actions required and their prioritization and sequencing are key steps in determining the real magnitude of the transformation. Because there are likely to be many issues that are interdependent, their actions have to be integrated as much as possible before being compiled in the Implementation Master Plan.

A complete Implementation Master Plan would overwhelm and perhaps alienate any organization that was not prepared to receive and respond to it. Therefore, the second activity of this phase prepares the organization to support the plan through the refinement and creation of the conditions, structures, systems, policies, and resources required for successful implementation. The speed and ease of implementation will be a direct result of this work.

Activity VI.A: Identify the Actions Required to Implement the Desired State and Develop the Implementation Master Plan

Task VI.A.1: Create the Process for Identifying Actions Required to Implement the Desired State and for Developing the Implementation Master Plan

The work of this task is critical to the success of the transformation. It translates the impact issues into design solutions for the transformation and then translates these solutions into specific implementation actions, both of which are required steps for developing a realistic Implementation Master Plan. The process you use in this task can make this complex activity either smooth or very cumbersome.

Because this work is facilitated by the "impact group leaders," it is best for them collectively to design how to accomplish it. They must determine how to resolve and integrate their impacts, to identify the actions required to implement the desired state, and to input all of this into the development of the Implementation Master Plan. Ideally, their process will enable integrated solutions within and between impact groupings. Completing this work now will save many conflicts and delays later and will ensure optimal use of time and resources.

When the impact group leaders design this process, have them consider the questions listed in Exhibit 9.1. It covers Tasks VI.A.1, 2, and 3. Because this is one of the most intensive and complicated phases in the change process, it is essential for them to have clear procedures and aligned leadership.

Impact group leaders should choose the most knowledgeable, action-oriented people to participate in the resolution and integration process. They might create special study teams, hire external consultants, or give issue responsibility to the

Exhibit 9.1. Questions for Resolving Impact Issues and Developing the Implementation Master Plan

- Who will lead the overall process design effort? Will all of the impact group leaders participate? How will they be helped to accomplish this work?

- Who will be involved in the work of resolving each impact group's issues? How will you ensure optimal participation in the process? How will you organize these people?

- Is education needed about the impact resolution and action planning process?

- How will the impact group leaders track impact issues and their solutions?

- What scope of detail do you want when determining actions?

- How will the impact group leaders accomplish the integration of impact solutions and actions across impact groups? Who will facilitate this process?

- How will you address the political dynamics that arise during the integration and planning tasks?

- How will you determine who is responsible for carrying out the various actions in your plan during implementation?

- How will you format your Implementation Master Plan?

- How will you discern the appropriate priority and sequence of actions within the plan? How will these be aligned with the events and priorities underway in the ongoing business?

- How will you inform the change leaders and/or executives about the entire roster of implementation actions? How will you ensure their agreement about the magnitude of the work required for this transformation to be successful?

- How will you determine the appropriate pacing strategy for the plan?

- How will you handle updating the plan over time?

most competent individuals in the organization. Where appropriate, we strongly advise creating diverse teams, including synthesizers, systems thinkers, detail lovers, and complexity masters. These people can be brought together for team development to ensure that people with different thinking styles have a say. All of this should be reflected in the process designed for this task and be facilitated by competent OD practitioners.

Task VI.A.2: Create Plans to Resolve the Individual Impacts of the Desired State

In this task, the impact group leaders facilitate the resolution process for each impact and between impacts within their group. They are responsible for ensuring that the issue solutions reflect the required transformational breakthroughs. Education about the desired mindset and vision of the transformation, creative problem solving, open systems theory, and the operating principles for conscious transformation can be used to align the solutions with the goals of the transformation rather than the old way of doing things.

The people assigned to the issues identify the desired outcomes, actions, resources, and cultural norms required to implement the solutions, using what is best for the overall desired state as their guide. For instance, let's say a team is asked to design a fully integrated knowledge management system that enables the global sharing of information. The team will explore the implications of this activity on related important issues, perform the study, determine what this new system will be, and clarify how the system supports worldwide collaboration. They will work with any other team addressing issues that impact their outcome. The team then identifies the resources and actions for how to purchase and/or create this system and how to put it into place in the organization so that the desired outcome occurs. The actions they identify will be integrated into the Implementation Master Plan.

Issues in one area inevitably ripple out into other issues within an impact group. The leaders must proactively work with their teams to integrate or combine related impacts to minimize redundancies, prevent negative system dynamics, and optimize the needs of the whole system.

Task VI.A.3: Integrate Individual Impact Plans to Identify Actions for the Detailed Implementation Master Plan

To ensure the most streamlined, cost-effective resolutions for their collective impacts and to support the creation of positive system dynamics, the impact group leaders work together to integrate resolution plans across impact groups. Their goal is to combine their solutions where appropriate and determine the most effective and efficient actions for achieving the outcomes needed for the desired state to function optimally. In organizations in which managers have historically focused only on their own functions, there will be resistance to the need for cross-functional integration and even the sharing of information. Often, serious political struggles surface. If this occurs, completing this task successfully could require a significant mindset and behavior shift. Good OD support is essential.

► CASE ᴵᴺ POINT

In one very large telephone company, this lesson created a turning point in how the leaders thought about running their new integrated company. The leaders were redesigning their organization to improve functional efficiencies across several states. At this point in their change process, each state's change leader was asked to come to an organization-wide meeting to present his or her plans for resolving impacts. They resisted attending the meeting, complaining that their functional plans were clear and that they were ready to implement. The change sponsor insisted, and all of the leaders attended.

During the reports about the critical events and actions required within each function, one leader announced the need to downsize a key function in one state by 150 people. The next leader then offered his report and announced a critical need to hire fifty new people to staff his function. It happened that these new people were needed in the same state in which the prior leader planned to downsize.

The two men looked at each other, "mental gears" turning, and agreed to meet to integrate their plans to support one another's outcomes without costing the organization or the affected people beyond what was necessary. Whereas the old culture had never required these leaders to communicate across the boundaries of their functions, the leaders immediately recognized that their own successes, as well as the effectiveness of the integrated organization, were suddenly dependent on this kind of cross-boundary communication and teamwork. ◄

The second requirement of this task is for the various impact resolution plans, whether for individual impacts or for related impacts, to be compiled and sequenced into a detailed Implementation Master Plan.

There is a range of style options for how to compose and format your plan. Detail-oriented organizations may dive into capturing the fine points with relish and create detailed electronic project plans. Fast-moving organizations, such as high-tech and e-commerce firms, may be far more macro in their plans and depend more on the implementers' real-time decisions about how the details should be handled. Adapt your style and format to your desired culture. Figure 9.1 shows a partial Implementation Master Plan in a flow-chart format.

Figure 9.1. Sample Flow Chart of an Implementation Master Plan

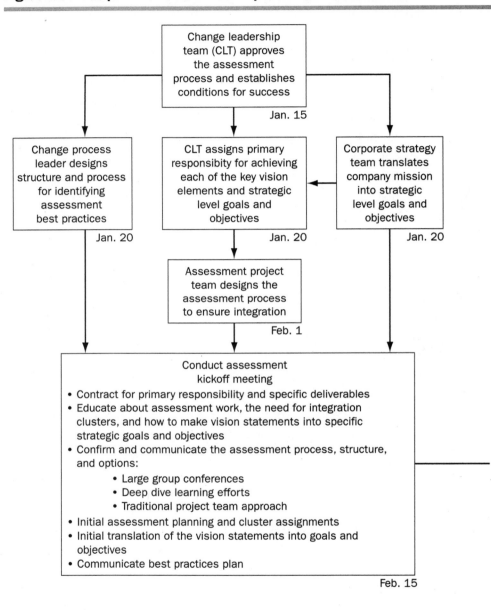

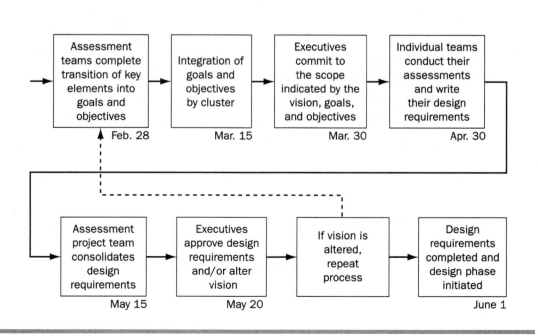

There are five major elements in the Implementation Master Plan:

- The sequenced actions required for implementation;
- Who will accomplish these actions;
- When the actions will be initiated and completed;
- Where in the organization the actions will occur; and
- The resources required for all of this to be completed effectively.

Think through how to format and publish the plan, who will have access to it, and who will oversee updates to it.

Task VI.A.4: Design Strategies to Sustain the Energy for Change Throughout Implementation and Integrate Them into the Plan

Because transformational change typically takes so long to implement, it is essential to determine strategies and actions that will help sustain the momentum and intention for the change over time. Too often, large-scale implementation plans consist of a barrage of planned activity at the beginning and then a dramatic drop-off. This pattern often leads to the failure or "drifting" of the change effort, as there is no clear way to sustain it or to follow up consistently. Change leaders can prevent this effect by consciously planning to sustain the energy for the change and identifying the actions required to see it through over the long term. Build these momentum-sustaining plans into the Implementation Master Plan and continuously tailor them as new needs arise during the dynamic course of implementation.

In addition to planning these strategies formally prior to implementation, it is also critical to use them during course corrections to the change process. People often need an energy boost when they have to alter course repeatedly. Because this is common in transformational change, energy-sustaining strategies are key throughout the rollout. The following boxed copy offers several examples to integrate into the Implementation Master Plan. Some are one-time events; others are ongoing.

Energy-Sustaining Strategies

- Publicize and celebrate progress in the change process;
- Grant periodic surprise rewards, outside of the norm;
- Periodically review conditions for success, and re-establish those that are faltering;

- Neutralize or remove blockages quickly;

- Remove major bureaucratic red tape and any barriers to information flow and participation;

- Hold large group meetings with senior leader involvement;

- Introduce new symbols, mottoes, or language;

- Create group rituals or rites of passage;

- Debunk rumors;

- Create champions of the transformation;

- Encourage naturally emerging forays into new state scenarios and out-of-the-box possibilities;

- Hold a burial for the past;

- Hold a contest for solving some quandary in the transformation;

- Design a media blitz, internally or externally;

- Tell the story of the organization's history, where this transformation fits in it, and the next series of chapters yet to be "written";

- Conduct special luncheons for change team members;

- Expose and dismantle negative system dynamics;

- Model and celebrate learning opportunities; and

- Secure newspaper and television coverage.

Task VI.A.5: Determine the Pacing Strategy and Timeline and Apply Them to the Implementation Master Plan

Once you have compiled the Implementation Master Plan actions, you then assess how much time the plan will take to accomplish. In Phase I, the change leaders developed their change strategy with a proposed timeline. Their timeline was based on strategic-level information and, in truth, either good guesswork or political pressure for speed. This "guesstimate" may or may not prove to have any basis in reality. It is only now, after you have completed the actual planning for implementation, that a more accurate timeline can be determined. This is essential to the Implementation Master Plan being approved for rollout.

The data generated by the impact analysis, plus the results of the Phase I assessment of the organization's capacity to take on the transformation, provide the basis for making a more realistic decision about the timeline. Keep the human factors in mind for this decision. Too often, we find competent people having emotional breakdowns over unrealistic time pressures they cannot renegotiate because the change sponsors lack awareness or openness about this issue.

There are a number of decisions to make about timing, wrapped up into what we call a "pacing strategy." A pacing strategy consists of the speed of change, the scope of the organization that is changing at any one time, and the rollout sequence of actions. Speed is determined by the time actually required to complete the work of implementation. "Scope of the organization" refers to the parts of the organization to be involved in making the change, such as functions, levels, locations, business units, and so on. The rollout sequence involves the selection of one or more of the following strategies:

- All at once;
- By phases (usually overlapping and ongoing);
- By independent sequential steps (that is, implement one aspect fully, then another fully, then another); or
- Gradual, incremental, evolutionary change over a long period of time.

Keep in mind the requirements for the ongoing operation as you determine the pacing strategy.

▶ CASE ɪɴ POINT

A major oil company was undergoing a massive restructuring of its refining organization. The restructuring required eight months for implementation, based on the impact analysis. The change leaders designed a pacing strategy to be completed in three phases. The strategy prioritized the most critical organizations and functions that had to and could move first. It initiated these moves while preparing for its second-phase moves and then its third-phase moves. At one point, all these phases were in motion. By the time the third-phase moves were integrated into the new structure, the new state organization was largely functional and disruption was minimized. ◀

When you have determined a realistic pacing strategy, compare it with the original timeline created by the executives in Phase I and renegotiate it, given the reality of the work required. As mentioned above, unrealistic timetables are a leading factor in the failure of transformation. If you think about it, a realistic judgment about how long implementation will likely take can only occur after you have determined the impacts of the change and clarified plans and actions for how to resolve them.

Once you have an agreeable pacing strategy, apply it to the Implementation Master Plan and proceed with securing approval for the plan.

Activity VI.B: Prepare the Organization to Support Implementation

Task VI.B.1: Refine and Establish the Conditions, Structures, Systems, Policies, and Resources Required to Support Implementation

In Activity I.E, the change leaders predicted what infrastructure and conditions would ensure a successful change effort. They created ways to support both the process and people's needs. Now, with the Implementation Master Plan in hand, they can more accurately refine what is required to further support implementation and the people who must make it happen. Once identified, they establish these structures, systems, and policies in the organization in the appropriate sequence and pace. The plan for doing this is incorporated into the Implementation Master Plan. The relevant decisions the change leaders made in Activity I.E include the following:

- Strategies for dealing with the politics of the transformation;
- Conditions for success;
- Communication plan;
- Strategies for generating new information;
- The course correction system;
- Ways to help people through their emotional reactions to the change;
- Temporary change support structures, systems, policies, and roles;
- Measurement standards and methods for the new state and the change process; and
- Rewards to support the change process and outcomes.

Use this list to prompt your thinking about how to support implementation.

Task VI.B.2: Initiate Strategies for Supporting People to Embrace the Desired State and Manage Their Reactions to the Change

In Task I.E.8, Design How to Minimize the Human Trauma of the Change and Initiate Strategies for Helping People Through Their Emotional Reactions, you began the process of planning how to deal effectively with the human impacts of the transformation. Back then, your planning was mostly conceptual, based on how you thought people would react, and dealt mostly with peoples' reactions to the *thought* of change. Now, with implementation just around the corner, you can take a more realistic look at how to support people through the *actual* changes impacting them. With the information you now have from people's reactions to the effort so far, you are better able to create specific, tangible strategies to meet their current needs and maximize support for them. This task provides another powerful opportunity to demonstrate the fundamental value that people are important and deserve to be treated with respect and concern.

Most organizations have a variety of pre-existing services and policies for providing people support. Begin with these existing services and policies. The following boxed copy lists several to consider. Tailor them to the particulars of the transformation. They can help reduce some of the stress induced by the change, as well as help shift the organization's culture by modeling increased concern for people. Communicating these policies and services in advance of implementation adds to management's credibility, company loyalty, and positive morale at a time when they are needed most.

Suggested Ways to Support Your Workforce

- Employee assistance counseling;
- Management counseling;
- Career development counseling;
- Outplacement services, job placement;
- Coaching;
- Training on managing stress and handling emotions;
- Job-request system;
- "Grandfathering" or "red lining" salary policy;
- "No demotion" policy;
- "Guaranteed job with training provided" policy;

- Skills training (technical or professional);

- Mindset and behavior training, management development;

- On-the-job training;

- Financial assistance counseling and training; and

- Support groups.

Be cautious about how you communicate and monitor these support mechanisms. Too often, employees and managers avoid using them because they fear being labeled as weak or inadequate and therefore less valuable to the organization. These approaches must be encouraged and made easy to pursue and receive. In one "model" client organization of ours, the senior vice president funded *anonymous* and *confidential* counseling for anyone who wanted it if the person had scored high on a stress test administered during a series of "breakthrough trainings" we provided. Employees were thankful for this service, and we were able to provide support when it was very much needed. Such gestures go a long way toward rebuilding trust in leaders and represent the type of organizational values that attract and retain talent.

Review the Implementation Master Plan to identify actions or events that may be the most difficult or challenging for people to accept or embrace. Ask your OD specialists or human resources people for input. Or, as a developmental exercise, the change leaders can scan the plan for their predictions about people's reactions. This work is well worth the time and effort. It is now that people's true reactions to making the transformation will emerge and now that your earnest efforts at involving people, minimizing trauma, and supporting people emotionally will pay off. If necessary, course correct your Implementation Master Plan to incorporate any required changes.

Letting Go of the Past

In Task I.E.9, we presented Adams' Individual Transition Model of the emotional cycle people experience when undergoing change. One critical phase is the "pit," which requires people to let go of the past in order to move into more productive phases. Creating strategies to assist employees to let go of their old ways of operating and providing assignments to take on and succeed at the new ways are essential to supporting people through the inevitable "pit." The following boxed copy lists several strategies for letting go. As you consider them, plan to do more than you think people need.

Strategies for Letting Go

- A "roast" of the old way;
- A final meeting of a group or team to acknowledge their ending and celebrate their past;
- Celebration events of the new ways of working;
- A ritual "wake" or burial of the old ways;
- A museum to honor the old; putting the old products under glass or in display cases to be respected, but not touched;
- Videos or slide shows commemorating the past;
- Counseling;
- A bonfire, with speeches and mementos;
- A "final edition" newsletter;
- A televised ritual to tear down or dismantle old equipment, factories, or products;
- Stories of individual successes and breakthroughs to the new ways;
- Extra time for people specifically to practice, learn, and gain confidence in new state practices;
- Behavioral and skill training for new state requirements; and
- Team debriefings and "post-op" learning sessions.

Be sure that most of the required letting go work occurs in intact work teams. The heart of this process must occur among people who work together on a daily basis. Letting-go rituals can be a collective rite of passage when done as a shared experience. Be cautious not to rely solely on the organization's formal or en-masse letting go rituals. Those driven by the executives can be beneficial, but should not be thought of as replacing more intimate events during which workmates directly relate to one another.

▶ CASE IN POINT

We helped to create a letting-go strategy for two organizations that were being merged. We planned a dramatic event for both groups with the intention of demonstrating that their old organizations were "a thing of the past" and that they were becoming a part of something completely new.

The leaders asked everyone to come to a very large open field and to bring with them all of their old organization's forms that had their old company name and logo. People came with letterhead, business cards, and manual forms. In the middle of the field, in a fire pit, was a huge rectangular box adorned to look like a coffin. Each organization's attendees were asked to file past the box and throw their papers in. When all of the people had offered up their materials, the box was closed and the newly announced president ignited it.

A huge bonfire ensued, symbolically cremating the old organizations. While it burned, the new executives of the merged company talked about the value of each old organization and the vision for the new one that all of the attendees would create together. Plans were communicated about the change strategy and timeline. People were asked to talk about their memories of working together in the past. They honored their history, and the future was born.

To end the session, the people from both organizations were asked to mingle together and were given IOU's for new business cards with the name of the new company on them. People felt valued and supported for their past efforts. Moreover, the message was very clear about moving into the future. ◄

Such rituals should be emotionally uplifting. This one certainly was.

Task VI.B.3: Communicate the Implementation Master Plan to the Targets of the Change, the Organization, and All Stakeholders

After the communication of the case for change, vision of the future, and the change strategy, and the communication of the design of the desired state, this communication is the fourth most critical of the entire change process. The change leaders outline the Implementation Master Plan and the infrastructure and conditions designed to support the transformation to occur smoothly. They link this information to the original change strategy or announce how the strategy has been course corrected. It is important for the leaders to demonstrate and reinforce that the organization is in the "process" of planning and carrying out its transformation and that this communication marks a major milestone in the journey.

This communication is a primary opportunity for the change leaders to demonstrate their commitment to the transformation, the workforce's well-being, and the future. The leaders' ability to walk the talk of the transformation will become evident in what they communicate and how they come across at this important juncture. Review your communication strategy for input to this task.

Ensure, again, that you treat this communication as a "process" of multiple, reinforcing opportunities for people to explore what the core messages mean for them personally. Well-designed communication processes will support people to move through and out of the "pit" and on to making a positive contribution to the future.

Summary

You have now planned the implementation, created the most realistic pace for action, and put in place key support mechanisms to enable the transformation to roll out smoothly. This completes the midstream stage of the process. Having communicated how everything is designed to work, you are ready to enter the downstream stage and implement the transformation.

Consulting Questions for Activity VI.A: Identify the Actions Required to Implement the Desired State and Develop the Implementation Master Plan

Task VI.A.1: Create the Process for Identifying Actions Required to Implement the Desired State and for Developing the Implementation Master Plan

- See Exhibit 9.1 for Tasks VI.A. 1, 2, and 3 consulting questions.

Task VI.A.2: Create Plans to Resolve the Individual Impacts of the Desired State

- See Exhibit 9.1 for Tasks VI.A. 1, 2, and 3 consulting questions.

Task VI.A.3: Integrate Individual Impact Plans to Identify Actions for the Detailed Implementation Master Plan

- See Exhibit 9.1 for Tasks VI.A. 1, 2, and 3 consulting questions.

Task VI.A.4: Design Strategies to Sustain the Energy for Change Throughout Implementation and Integrate Them into the Plan

- What strategies will you use to sustain the energy for the change?
- How will you determine when to use them?

**Task VI.A.5: Determine the Pacing Strategy and Timeline
and Apply Them to the Implementation Master Plan**

- How will you determine the best pacing strategy?

- How will you analyze the Implementation Master Plan for the realistic amount of time required to carry it out effectively?

- How will you handle any differences in speed from the original pace outlined in the change strategy? If you have to renegotiate this initial timeline, how will you do this?

- How will you apply the pacing strategy and timeline to the Implementation Master Plan?

- Who has to approve the Implementation Master Plan? How will that be handled?

Consulting Questions for Activity VI.B: Prepare the Organization to Support Implementation

Task VI.B.1: Refine and Establish the Conditions, Structures, Systems, Policies, and Resources Required to Support Implementation

- Which conditions, temporary support structures, systems, policies, and resources must be refined to help the organization succeed in implementation? How will you put each into place?

Task VI.B.2: Initiate Strategies for Supporting People to Embrace the Desired State and Manage Their Reactions to the Change

- How will you support people to manage their reactions to the implementation in real time?

- Is further education or coaching required for the change leaders and management to be able and willing to support people as implementation rolls out?

- Do you need to create "letting-go" strategies? If so, what will they be?

Task VI.B.3: Communicate the Implementation Master Plan to the Targets of the Change, the Organization, and All Stakeholders

- How will you communicate the Implementation Master Plan to the organization?

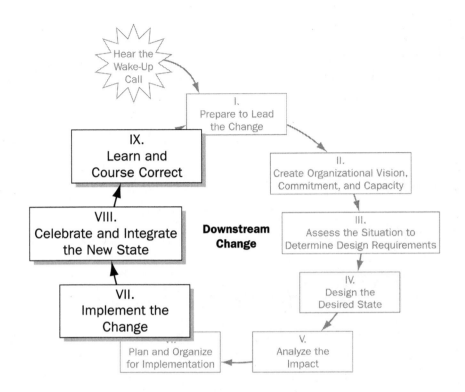

Downstream Change

Section Three
Downstream Change

Phase VII

Chapter 10: Implement the Change   201

Phase VIII

Chapter 11: Celebrate and Integrate the New State   211

Phase IX

Chapter 12: Learn and Course Correct   223

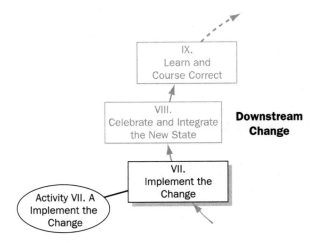

Phase VII Task Deliverables

VII.A.1: The Implementation Master Plan is being rolled out. Leaders and key stakeholders are modeling the new mindset, behaviors, and relationships of the desired state as they carry out change activities.

VII.A.2: The implementation process is being course corrected as required.

VII.A.3: The desired state is being course corrected as required.

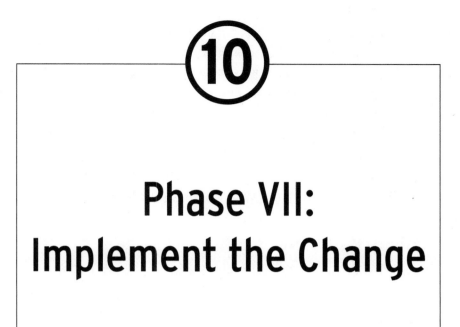

Phase VII:
Implement the Change

WITH THE INITIAL PLANNING AND PREPARATION BEHIND YOU, you now enter the downstream stage of change implementation. Actually, certain types of implementation have been happening all along, particularly the personal changes required to clarify and plan for the transformation. This stage, however, is where most of the content or "external" changes occur. The organization now takes on the tangible form of the desired state. You will need to continue to support the "internal" personal changes throughout implementation and beyond.

The purpose of this phase is to carry out the Implementation Master Plan to achieve the desired state and to course correct *both* the change plan and the desired state as the needs of the organization and its environment require. During implementation, the bulk of activity takes place to dismantle the old ways of working and thinking, to learn the new ones, and to monitor whether the organization is on the right track. Many of the people dynamics, for which the leaders so diligently prepared, will now play out.

There is no set formula for how implementation occurs. Every transformation is different. One hopes that all of the planning, analyzing, and designing the change leaders have done will create a smooth implementation.

The change leaders must actively attend to what is actually happening in the organization as it is changing, as implementation will inevitably go differently than planned. This is the leaders' opportunity to accept that they can't "force the river." Their toughest internal work begins now—allowing the implementation to take on its own life, learning from what occurs, influencing appropriately, and course correcting intelligently.

Activity VII.A: Implement the Change

Task VII.A.1: Roll Out the Implementation Master Plan

The organization now makes the content aspects of the transformation a reality. It is always eye-opening to look back at all of the preparation you have done; it has been a long runway until takeoff! So many organizations move into implementation immediately after announcing that a change is going to happen. Imagine all of the confusion and turmoil that would ensue if you had not planned for this implementation and prepared the leaders, the organization, and all of the stakeholders for its rollout!

Because your Implementation Master Plan is your guide, we cannot speak to how it will or should go. However, we will discuss some of the people and process dynamics to be aware of as the action unfolds.

Dealing with Resistance

Many change models emphasize the need to overcome people's resistance during implementation. This focus becomes necessary because these models put so little attention on the up-front work that the Change Process Model covers in Phases I and II, which prepare the leaders and the organization for the transformation. If you are using the nine-phase Change Process Model for the first time, you likely will see much less resistance in people than you might have expected. Even with good upstream planning, however, some resistance is inevitable. It is a natural phenomenon and should be embraced as a normal part of change, along with people's other emotional reactions. Resistance is a person's behavioral expression of either not feeling aligned with the new or not thinking it is what should be happening or what is best for him or her personally or for the organization. Rather than be reactive to people's resistance when it shows up, conscious change leaders must actively seek to understand what is causing it and what value it serves. Our advice is simply to set up a safe environment in which to explore people's resistance and then to listen, listen, listen. People need to have their concerns heard. True listening is the most powerful and direct way to defuse resistance. People's issues might even surface a different perspective for more effectively guiding the implementation.

Attend to People's Reactions

During implementation, people will be realizing the full impact of letting go of their old way of operating. If they are committed to the overall transformation, this reaction will be small. If they are not, the reality of the change will come crashing in on them now. We hope that you have put sufficient strategies in place in Phases I through VI to deal with the emotional roller coaster that may be unleashed. Because this part of the process is so unpredictable, be prepared to give additional attention to the human dynamics during implementation. This applies equally to the leaders and managers, who are not exempt from their own personal reactions during this volatile time. Consultants should be prepared to spend significant time coaching leaders and counseling key players.

Walk Your Talk and Support People's Internal Changes

During implementation, the leaders must actively walk their talk, modeling the new mindset, behaviors, and ways of working that they espoused during the earlier phases of the transformation. Employees will be highly critical of leaders who are not acting in the new ways. Yet when transformational change requires significant mindset and behavioral change in people, how fast can this personal transformation reasonably occur? Is the implementation phase long enough to *complete* this process? How do you make personal change coincide with the organizational changes during implementation?

There are no easy answers to these important questions. Let's look at some of the dynamics at play to understand better how to address these issues.

It is to be expected that not everyone will have fully integrated the new ways of thinking and acting during implementation, even when this work begins in Phase I. In their own ways, everyone who has committed to the transformation will be attempting new behaviors and trying hard to function successfully according to desired state expectations. Inevitably, however, people will unintentionally slip back to their old behavior, again and again, long after implementation. *This is normal.*

To address this dynamic, the change leaders must create public understanding of the process of personal transformation and how to support it so that the organization can develop a cultural norm of tolerance and continuous learning. Otherwise, when people revert to old behavior, blame and distrust will follow, rather than constructive feedback and support.

Deep personal change cannot be "scheduled" to coincide with the formal organizational shifts that occur during implementation. People must understand this reality and allow both to occur in their rightful time.

When people, especially the leaders, fall back into their old habits, their quick and overt course correction is essential to maintain credibility and sustain the "walk the talk" requirement. Leaders have a valuable opportunity to model learning, human vulnerability, and the new "process-oriented" reality being created in the organization as they undergo their personal changes.

This dynamic provides important learning about conscious process thinking. Given the process nature of change, we know that the personal aspects of transformation, so critical to success, occur over time. In more control-oriented and reactive organizations, it is logical for leaders and employees to assume that when leaders announce their intention for a certain type of new behavior, people should then act that way immediately and exclusively. This doesn't happen. Mindset changes, reflected in behavior, words, and interpersonal skills, take time to integrate. Although these changes begin the moment people choose to change, they take much practice to master. Deep personal change can actually take years for leaders and employees.

It is one thing to know this intellectually. It is another to set up this understanding to be conscious and overt in the organization, as everyone is collectively undergoing his or her own transformation, and the organization is being changed as a result. It is important that the change leaders take the time to recognize and publicize this critical aspect about how transformational change—on the individual level—takes place. Any assumption otherwise causes unnecessary turmoil. People must be encouraged and supported for making this effort on behalf of the organization's, and their own, transformation.

Whether you clarify this notion in Phases I and II as part of the leaders' and employees' breakthrough training or as you prepare for implementation, it is critical to instill conscious process thinking and understanding about personal transformation into the organization.

Task VII.A.2: Monitor and Course Correct the Implementation Process

No matter how well you planned for implementation, it will unfold differently than you expect. In Phase I, you developed a course correction process and system for overseeing your change process. Ideally, everyone in the organization participates in course correction, monitoring how the transformation is going and offering recommendations for improvement.

However, change is commonly seen as the "leaders' thing" and is rarely presented as everyone's responsibility. Traditionally, the leaders do their planning and announce the change. The people of the organization then help or hinder its progress, depending on how they feel about what is going on. In this scenario, employees view change as something that is done *to* them. This circumstance creates a reactive orientation, fraught with unnecessary difficulties.

By doing the early Phase I and II work, you have established the change effort as a conscious and collective endeavor. We have a motto for how this collective effort works. It is: "Everyone is responsible. No one is to blame." If you have created a critical mass of support for the transformation, everyone shares responsibility for making the change process a success.

There are many topics that require monitoring during implementation. Exhibit 10.1, Change Process Topics to Monitor During Implementation, offers a checklist of things to observe. Use the checklist to guide your expectations for this task.

Exhibit 10.1. Change Process Topics to Monitor During Implementation

- ☐ Communication delivery and impact; rumor management;
- ☐ People's reactions and how they are being dealt with;
- ☐ Mindset and behavior successes or failures;
- ☐ Need for more training and coaching;
- ☐ Cultural norms that need to be changed;
- ☐ Commitment to the transformation from the leaders or key stakeholders;
- ☐ People's capacity to engage in the transformation as well as perform their ongoing responsibilities;
- ☐ Opportunities to celebrate and recognize milestones, best practices, and new behaviors;

Exhibit 10.1. Change Process Topics to Monitor During Implementation, Cont'd

☐ Political dynamics that hinder progress;

☐ Unforeseen relationship issues;

☐ Operating problems in sustaining the ongoing business;

☐ Conditions for success;

☐ Resources needed;

☐ Pacing;

☐ Team effectiveness;

☐ Information generation and how new information and feedback are being handled;

☐ Effectiveness of decision making;

☐ Needs of the project community; and

☐ Appropriateness of the temporary support structures, systems, policies, and roles.

Task VII.A.3: Monitor and Course Correct the Desired State

Like your implementation process, the desired state will inevitably take shape somewhat differently than intended. During this task you must monitor new information signaling that the design of the desired state needs to be altered. The alterations will mostly be at the operational and managerial levels of design. For the most part, these modifications are better made now, while implementation is underway, rather than later when people are trying to adjust to the new state once it is in place. Exhibit 10.2, Desired State Topics to Monitor During Implementation, provides another checklist to assist your planning of this work.

Exhibit 10.2. Desired State Topics to Monitor During Implementation

☐ Fulfillment of your design requirements;

☐ Fulfillment of customer and marketplace requirements;

☐ Measurement of the desired state;

☐ Completion of the operational design;

☐ Effectiveness of each aspect of the new organization (structure, business processes, work practices, management systems, policies, technology, facilities, culture, skills, and so on);

Exhibit 10.2. Desired State Topics to Monitor During Implementation, Cont'd

☐ How well the new organization works as an integrated system;

☐ Forays into out-of-the-box new state solutions;

☐ How well the new organization manifests its vision;

☐ Competencies of management and the workforce to succeed in the new organization;

☐ Effectiveness of decision making, knowledge management, and information systems;

☐ Fit of the new culture with the requirements of the operation; and

☐ Ability to integrate and model the new mindset and culture.

In our experience, the most common change to desired states is the recognition that some people dynamic has been missed and must be incorporated formally into the new state if it is going to succeed. As much as the Change Process Model stresses attention to the human dimension, inevitably during implementation, unforeseen people requirements show up.

▶ CASE ɪɴ POINT

In the oil company case, the new organizational structure at the refinery management level was to be a matrix. The refinery managers would have three "bosses," the vice presidents of the organization's three new business units. The change strategy included special training to introduce the managers to their new multi-headed chain of command.

During implementation, after the training had occurred, it became apparent that a more formal system was going to be required to assist the refinery managers to manage the communications and work priorities coming from their three bosses. A new priority management system was established for the business line vice presidents and the refinery managers. A group meeting was conducted to clarify relationships, the mechanisms for determining priorities that benefited the overall organization, and how to handle competing demands and conflicts of interest. The desired state design was effectively course corrected to accommodate these needs. ◀

Summary

You have now implemented and course corrected the Implementation Master Plan, putting into place the desired state. Most likely, operational implementation will continue as the desired state is established, bringing you to the next phase, Celebrate and Integrate the New State.

Consulting Questions for Activity VII.A: Implement the Change

Task VII.A.1: Roll Out the Implementation Master Plan

- How will you ensure that the change leaders remain committed to modeling the new mindset, behaviors, and relationships during implementation?

- How will you build understanding that people changes take time and support to occur?

- How will you establish the expectation that all stakeholders are responsible for the successful implementation of the desired state? Does everyone know what to look for to support success?

Task VII.A.2: Monitor and Course Correct the Implementation Process

- How will you oversee the implementation process and course correct it? What aspects of the process will you observe?

- Who must be involved in hearing and integrating feedback about how the change process is proceeding?

- How can you leverage learning opportunities about process design and change process leadership during this phase?

Task VII.A.3: Monitor and Course Correct the Desired State

- How will you assess the appropriateness of the desired state as the organization puts it into place?

- What aspects of the desired state will you monitor?

- How will you communicate to the organization necessary course corrections to your change process and desired state during the implementation phase?

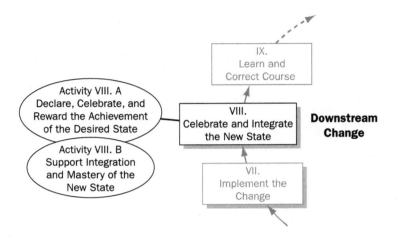

Phase VIII Task Deliverables

VIII.A.1: The achievement of the desired state has been declared and celebrated. People throughout the project community have been recognized and rewarded for supporting the successful creation of the desired state.

VIII.B.1: Individuals and intact work teams understand how best to work together and how they fit into the big picture of the desired state.

VIII.B.2: A critical mass of the organization understands how the overall new state operates and how to support its optimal performance.

Phase VIII: Celebrate and Integrate the New State

©ONGRATULATIONS! THE DESIRED STATE of the transformation—now the organization's "new state"—is largely up and running. It may look like what you originally intended, or it may have been adapted several times during prior phases. In either case, to address the dynamics of this phase, assume that the organization has begun to operate in ways that produce your intended outcomes.

Having reached this point, the organization needs and deserves to know that it is now officially living in its "new state." The purpose of this phase is to celebrate the great milestone of achieving the desired state and to support people's integration and mastery of the new mindset, behaviors, skills, and work practices that make the new state successful. This phase allows the people of the organization to settle in, learn about, and ultimately master their new way of working and relating.

This phase creates an essential psychological and physical "pause" that nurtures the well-being of the organization, as well as giving it an energy boost through celebration.

This phase is not a vacation, however; you accomplish very important work here. This work assists people to reorient more rapidly to their new reality and appreciate what they have achieved while making it better. This outcome enables them to produce quality results and become ready for the next evolution, which is a condition that change leaders must consciously support. Otherwise, they promote burnout in their employees, cause their organizations to become averse to change, and jeopardize the smooth functioning of the new state they have worked so hard to create.

Activity VIII.A: Declare, Celebrate, and Reward the Achievement of the Desired State

Task VIII.A.1: Declare, Celebrate, and Reward the Achievement of the Desired State

In the first activity of this phase, the change leaders officially acknowledge that the organization is now operating in its new state. They sponsor celebrations of all change process work up to this point, rewarding the people and teams who most directly supported the transformation and, in particular, modeled its new mindset, culture, and desired behaviors. Celebrating the new state allows people to enjoy the fruits of their hard work and is an opportunity for the change leaders to reinforce the new culture further. You may have been holding mini-celebrations during each of the prior phases of the change process, which is a wonderful way to sustain the energy for the transformation. This celebration, however, is your milestone celebration, and it should be given extra attention.

Celebrations can take many forms. Consider the following:

- Electronic or video celebration addresses;
- Written announcement or special edition newsletter;
- A party, festive dinner, or luncheon;
- Large group awards meeting;
- Rewards such as bonuses, personalized appreciation letters, momentoes, or tickets to sporting or cultural events;
- Family gatherings at work to show off the tangible changes;
- Media coverage; or
- Time off for key people or groups with publicity as to why.

Because so many organizations are traditionally too busy to celebrate, this point in the change process is an opportune time for changing this norm. When planning the celebration strategy, consultants and change leaders must design it so that it clearly reinforces the vision and desired outcomes that have been driving the transformation. You can also use this strategy to recognize best practices for conscious change leadership.

▶ CASE ɪɴ POINT

In a manufacturing facility located in Louisiana, the plant manager wanted to reward his entire organization for its efforts in transforming its structure from a functional, compartmentalized one to a completely integrated production process. The culture of the plant was undergoing a radical shift to support this new structure, requiring people to play many roles and serve many masters.

To celebrate the achievement of the new structure, the plant manager decided to invite the entire organization to a Monday breakfast "fish fry," which was considered a very fun and rowdy kind of event. The plant manager spent his weekend catching and preparing fish for the event and was the lead cook at the breakfast. His intention was to demonstrate his willingness to serve his people and to reinforce that working together could be a lot of fun. The event was the first of many such uplifting gatherings used to energize the new culture. ◀

There is a specific risk inherent in celebrating the achievement of the new state that you must be aware of and minimize. The risk is communicating that "change is over" and that the organization has arrived where it ultimately wants to be. Given the process nature of transformational change, this is *never true.* In good conscious process thinking fashion, people have to understand that change is ongoing and that everyone is expected to continue to improve the organization as it strives to reach its vision. People must understand this, especially if the organization is already engaging in its next transformation.

Activity VIII.B: Support Integration and Mastery of the New State

We are at times astounded by leaders who assume that when the organization's new state is in place, their people should be immediately able to function at full capacity within it. When you became old enough to drive, even after you took your driver's education class, you were not a fully competent driver. Driving takes practice; competent driving takes experience. People have the same needs when they are required to operate in new and different ways at work.

The second activity of this phase supports individuals, intact work teams, and the organization as a whole to further integrate and master the new state and how it operates. What do we mean by "integration" and "mastery"? By *integration,* we mean assimilating change so that it becomes the norm. Integration occurs when a person moves from their "discomfort zone" of *trying* to function in new ways to their "comfort zone" of being *competent* to perform effectively. Learning, trial and error, and course correction are essential to people integrating the new state.

The following list describes an ideal state of integration. Consider how productive and satisfying the work experience will be when any or all of these items are *clear and mutually understood* by all who are involved in the new state! Consultants, change leaders, and organizational managers can target any of these outcomes to improve their group's or organization's effectiveness.

Integration Has Occurred When You Have:

- Completed an operational impact analysis and worked out the operational kinks;
- Initiated adjustments and course corrections to the new state;
- Identified and shared best practices;
- Initiated learning about the optimal way of interfacing with others in the organization;
- Clarified and strengthened new working relationships;
- Created and accepted new concepts and terminology;
- Begun new norms and rituals;
- Established new power, influence, and support norms;
- Clarified how to communicate with one another;
- Agreed on how decisions are made;
- Clarified how conflicts are handled;
- Created mechanisms for monitoring and course correcting the mindset, behaviors, and practices of the new state; and
- Identified further support needed and figured out how to obtain it.

By *mastery*, we mean the continuous process of developing your skills to new levels of excellence, both individually and collectively. Mastery results from advanced learning; it is an ongoing way of being and working, not an absolute end result. We list several indications of mastery below. Again, consider how responsive and resilient the new organization will be when these are living characteristics of how it operates in real time!

Mastery Is Occurring When You Are:

- Fully competent in your current state, yet committed to improve continuously;
- Able to perform routinely at "best of class" levels;
- Continuously learning and pushing the next edge of innovation or breakthrough;
- Inquiring about different ways to do things; thinking out-of-the-box;
- Taking on new challenges;
- Mentoring and supporting the excellence of others;
- Embracing different people's ideas and approaches; and
- Achieving new performance levels.

First, we will address integration and mastery of the new state at the individual and intact work team level, then address it for the organization as a whole.

Task VIII.B.1: Support Individuals and Intact Work Units to Optimize Their Performance by Increasing Their Integration and Mastery of the New State

Metaphorically, this task is the bridge between a couple's honeymoon and actually being able to live together happily in the marriage. This task focuses on clarifying roles and straightening out the kinks of working together in a new way. Carrying the metaphor further, you will be figuring out who cooks and who cleans, whether you push the toothpaste from the bottom or the middle, how to handle disagreements, and how to make financial decisions.

In this task, individuals and intact work units learn how to operate most effectively to fulfill their requirements for the larger organization. They work out their own kinks and learn what they must know and do and how they have to behave to succeed in the new state. Dispersed or virtual teams also undertake this work, but in a way that enables them to operate optimally from their own locations.

When the change leaders provide overt attention and encouragement for this kind of learning at the "local" level of the organization, they directly accelerate integration and mastery of the new state. Support for integration also enables people to further their personal change process and embrace their new reality more fully. Everybody needs to know where he or she fits in and adds value to the organization. This work meets those needs. Again, competent OD practitioners can offer invaluable assistance.

There are two main requirements for individuals and work units to integrate and master their roles in the new state. First, they must fully understand what it takes to make their part of the organization function effectively at the day-to-day, pragmatic level. The steps for accomplishing this are:

1. Identify new ways of thinking and behaving, new work practices and relationships, and supportive norms that are essential to making this part of the new state work.

2. Practice, test, and fine-tune these.

3. Share best practices about these new ways among those involved or impacted by the person's or group's work.

4. Achieve and celebrate competence in these new ways.

There are many ways to accomplish these steps. Exhibit 11.1, Integration and Mastery Strategies, offers a checklist of options for this work. Review it to shape your thinking.

Exhibit 11.1. Integration and Mastery Strategies

☐ Classroom training and follow-up application meetings;

☐ Coaching and mentoring;

☐ Identifying and rewarding best practices and desired behaviors;

☐ Further impact analysis and working sessions to resolve issues;

☐ Job, project, and skill clinics;

☐ Further benchmarking of other organizations;

☐ Process improvement;

☐ Dialogue and learning groups;

Exhibit 11.1. Integration and Mastery Strategies, Cont'd

☐ Computer conferencing to support learning, questions, and resolution of issues;

☐ Assessment meetings to look at both operational and emotional needs;

☐ Relationship/partnership contracting;

☐ Counseling to reinforce mindset and behavior changes;

☐ On-the-job training; and

☐ Ensuring the right people are in the right jobs.

The second requirement of this activity is for individuals and work units to understand how their part of the organization fits into and contributes to the larger organization. This brings us to the second task of this activity.

Task VIII.B.2: Support the Whole System to Optimize Its Performance by Increasing Its Integration and Mastery of the New State

Learning to drive a car requires more than knowing how to steer and how to press the gas pedal or the brake. Every part of the car—inside the engine and in its body—is required for the smooth functioning of the vehicle. As the driver, you must know how to operate the car as well as learn the laws and etiquette for competent driving. All of this comes together as systemic requirements for excellent and safe driving. The same is true in learning how the entire new state operates in order for it to achieve its vision and business goals. System-wide integration of the new state is essential to establish the big picture of success in the organization. It also sets the expectation for strengthening any aspect of the new state so that it better supports the effectiveness of the whole.

This task designs and carries out a process to ensure that all key players understand how the overall organization has to operate to meet the needs of its marketplace and changing environment. You are actually making people smarter about how to support the new state by expanding their view of the organization. Through this task, each part of the organization—functional groups, divisions, product or service lines, or geographical regions—gains a greater appreciation for how the whole system now functions and how each part contributes to the greater good. In addition, the change leaders discover what aspects of the new state need fine-tuning, where the gaps and redundancies in its operation are, and where there are opportunities for further breakthrough in system dynamics or performance.

▶ CASE IN POINT

A manufacturing company revamped its business strategy, structure, management processes, culture, and decision making to create strategic business units. After the majority of the organization's changes were in place, we designed a system-wide integration strategy to unify the whole and fortify the leaders' collective understanding of how the new organization worked.

Every functional leader was asked to prepare a creative presentation of his or her purpose, contribution, responsibilities, and assets. In addition, they presented their views of what services or resources they offered to other key functions and what they needed from others to carry out their roles effectively. They also identified the relationships they had with the other leaders that were in good working order and those that were in need of clarification or support. Everyone was encouraged to ask for the participation of their staff to widen the organization's involvement.

In the logical sequence of business workflow, the leaders presented their input. As the organization's total functioning was pieced together like a complex puzzle, the beauty of the whole picture began to take shape. Rather than understanding just the theory behind the new design, the leaders saw how each of them was essential to the success of the whole. They saw that the total organization needed their individual functions to work optimally. And they pinpointed where new relationships were required, how to improve their effectiveness, and how the culture of shared responsibility and teamwork was essential to the company's new business direction.

The senior leaders used the meeting to reinforce their new expectations of management, to put some old negative political and behavioral patterns to rest, and to reward examples of breakthrough thinking and acting. The participants went away with a much broader perspective and much sharper directives to share with their staffs. ◀

One critical human dynamic to be wary of in this process is the return of old state political battles. Even though leaders may be in entirely new roles and have very different relationships and positions of influence in the new organization, their old behavior patterns may not have been resolved. If you have set the ground rules for how to deal with these dynamics in advance, you can avert much of this. If you haven't, give some thought to how to address these issues if they show up as the new organization refines its optimal way of performing. This work is yet another culture change leverage point.

The above example included mostly middle and upper management, but you must accomplish the intent of this task throughout the organization. The more people who understand how the organization operates as an integrated whole, the more people you have who can intelligently course correct and improve it over time. By definition, this task is complete when a critical mass of the organization has attained this understanding and their behavior and working relationships reflect it.

Summary

At this point, you have truly succeeded in implementing the new state. You have celebrated the achievement of your intended outcomes and supported individuals, teams, and the entire organization to function effectively and to understand how each contributes to the greater good of the organization. From this place, you can now "close" this chapter of change.

Consulting Questions for Activity VIII.A: Declare, Celebrate, and Reward the Achievement of the Desired State

Task VIII.A.1: Declare, Celebrate, and Reward the Achievement of the Desired State

- How will you announce to the organization that the desired state is now in place?

- What methods will you use to celebrate and reward the efforts of creating the new state?

- How can you use this announcement and celebration to further reinforce the mindset, values, norms, and behaviors required for the success of the new state?

- How will you ensure that the organization understands the need for further changes, even though the new state has been achieved?

Consulting Questions for Activity VIII.B: Support Integration and Mastery of the New State

Task VIII.B.1: Support Individuals and Intact Work Units to Optimize Their Performance by Increasing Their Integration and Mastery of the New State

- What strategies will you use to support individuals and intact work units to optimize their integration and mastery of the new state?

- How will you handle this work within dispersed or virtual teams?

Task VIII.B.2: Support the Whole System to Optimize Its Performance by Increasing Its Integration and Mastery of the New State

- Is education required for the change leaders to agree to support an organization-wide integration and mastery process?

- What strategies will you use to support the whole organization to optimize its integration and mastery of the new state?

- Who are the appropriate attendees for organization-wide integration meetings?

- Should you invite customers or vendors to such meetings? What outcome would you want?

- How will you present the purpose, content, and norms of these meetings to the attendees? To employees?

- What topics will you ask the participants in this process to present as their contribution to the overall integration effort (for example, their role, responsibilities, deliverables, relationships, assets, resources, services, products, needs, and so on)?

- How can you ensure that the senior leaders model the new behaviors they want to reinforce in the organization during the integration and mastery process?

- How will you keep old political dynamics from creeping back into the new state at these gatherings?

- What strategies will you use to deepen front-line employees' understanding of how the new state functions as an integrated whole system?

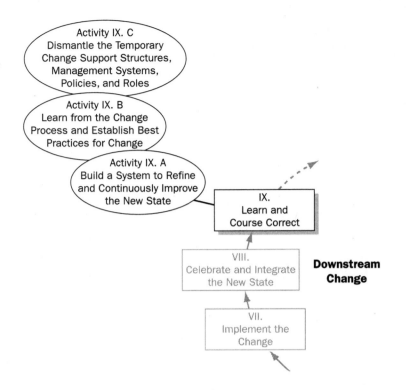

Phase IX Task Deliverables

IX.A.1: A system to refine and continuously improve the new state has been designed and implemented.

IX.B.1: Learnings about the change process have been identified, communicated, and integrated into the organization's way of leading change, including best practices for change.

IX.C.1: The temporary change support structures, management systems, policies, and roles that are no longer relevant have been dismantled and communicated as complete.

The support structures, management systems, policies, and roles employed in the change process and useful in the new organization have been tailored, formalized, and communicated as continuing.

The targets of the change, the organization, and all stakeholders understand that this current iteration of change is now complete.

Phase IX: Learn and Course Correct

THROUGH THE LENS OF CONSCIOUS PROCESS THINKING, the new state is never considered the "be all and end all" guarantee of success for the organization. The environment and marketplace continue to change, as do the dynamics inside the organization. Although reality remains in flux and the next wave of change may already be underway, the majority of people have a need for completion. Attention to the "ending" of this round of transformation is a requirement of the process.

The three activities of this final phase, then, are designed to accomplish the following:

- Create mechanisms for continuous improvement of the new state;

- Put in motion ways to evaluate and to learn from how the change strategy and process were designed and implemented;

- Initiate actions to improve the organization's readiness and ability to facilitate future changes successfully; and

- Close down the existing change process by dismantling the temporary infrastructure and conditions that no longer serve the needs of the new organization.

This task is essential to the process of supporting the organization as it evolves in a balanced and healthy way. Endings leave a lasting impression that will impact the beginning of the next iteration of change in the organization. What you do here to prepare for the future and put closure on the past will influence the degree of readiness, willingness, and capacity in the organization for continued transformation. This is a primary responsibility of the change leaders, who must continue to pave the way to the future.

Activity IX.A: Build a System to Refine and Continuously Improve the New State

Task IX.A.1: Build a System to Refine and Continuously Improve the New State

This task formalizes how the organization will continue to improve its new state and, therefore, ensure its ongoing success. This practice of continuous improvement must be overt and be seen as the normal way of doing business. Your goal here, from a process perspective, is to create an organization that remains viable over time and responsive to new demands as a matter of course. This attitude cannot be left to hope. It is both a part of transforming the culture and the way the organization operates.

In this task, you design a system to monitor and refine the new or now "current" state. The system focuses on the organizational and technical aspects of the business, as well as on the human and cultural aspects. The organizational and technical changes will likely be implemented long before the desired culture is fully integrated. Therefore, the culture change strategy has to ensure that the cultural work continues.

The system you design should shape how the organization monitors and responds to changes in the requirements of its stakeholders—its customer base, industry, workforce, and community. It should include how the organization will scan the external and internal environments for new wake-up calls, as well as how it will keep its vision alive and evolving.

What types of people are good at this function? Consider people who are highly perceptive, love change, and are always looking out into the future. In one organization, the leaders selected their most "maverick" thinker, a person who was known to rock the boat and had difficulty fitting into the status quo of anything! When given overt permission to identify areas in need of tinkering or wholesale revamping, he thrived and the organization benefited.

Exhibit 12.1 is a checklist of options for promoting continuous improvement in the new state. Review these with the new leaders of the organization, and tailor them to fit your situation.

Exhibit 12.1. Mechanisms to Continuously Improve the New State

- ☐ Stretch goals to seek opportunities for course correction;
- ☐ Public recognition and communication about people who have suggested valuable ideas;
- ☐ Wake-up call recognition system;
- ☐ On-line information generation network;
- ☐ Leave the change process leader in place to oversee ongoing learning and course correcting or to bridge this transformation with the next;
- ☐ "Office of the future" to research new trends;
- ☐ Customer input board;
- ☐ Stakeholder input board;
- ☐ Future Search conferences;
- ☐ "Skip level" dialogues about how to course correct;
- ☐ Periodic visioning processes;
- ☐ "Barrier busters" group;
- ☐ Quality improvement tools and teams;
- ☐ Performance reviews that assess tangible support for learning and course correcting; and
- ☐ Rewards for learning and course correcting suggestions.

Activity IX.B: Learn from the Change Process and Establish Best Practices for Change

Task IX.B.1: Learn from the Change Process and Establish Best Practices for Change

Inasmuch as you have monitored and course corrected the change process in every phase and acquired best practices along the way, this task *formally* looks back at the entire transformation process with "20/20 hindsight" and identifies learnings from the experience. It is based on two assumptions: (1) Change is continuous, and (2) you are committed to strengthening the organization's capacity for future transformation.

This task focuses on identifying an array of best practices for change, including strategies, skills, knowledge, mindsets, behaviors, tools, and techniques. It is a high-gain effort to determine how you would design and facilitate your next transformation—what you would do similarly and what you would do differently.

Some organizations have used the results from this task to help shape their programs for developing change leadership capacity. Many have taken the data and incorporated it into their existing or new curricula for management, supervisory, and leadership development. Others use the information to influence the competencies they look for in new hires. Others have used it to customize a change process model that uniquely fits their new organization or melds with their strategic or business planning models. The tailored change process model can be implemented across the organization and can become the standard operating system for all subsequent changes. Each of these strategies delivers a substantial return on investment.

Depending on the time, resources, and commitment available to this task, you can select any number of approaches for learning and evaluation. Organizations that are committed to creating a learning-oriented culture typically emphasize this task and plan a comprehensive and formal evaluation strategy. Others take a less formal tactic and design a self-reflective, qualitative approach to evaluate how well they did.

Whose input will you seek? Be sure to include the key members of the project community—the change process leader, sponsor, change leadership team, executive team, union leaders, employee groups or change advocates, and other key stakeholders. Also consider including all consultants and trainers and representatives from the organization's external constituents, such as customers, clients, and vendors.

In selecting what to study about the change process, consider using the relevant measurements that you identified for the change process in Task I.E.12, Determine and Initiate Appropriate Measurements of the Change, and your conditions for success. In addition, Exhibit 12.2 offers a checklist of many more options. Select and add items that fit your learning needs and the goals for your change leadership development strategy. Use the results of this study to determine the best practices for change for the organization.

Exhibit 12.2. Assessing the Change Process to Identify Best Practices

☐ How well you met the expectations for the change process as set by:

- Your vision for the transformational experience;
- The overall change strategy (for example, bold actions and strategic levers);
- Conditions for success;
- Participation strategies;
- Measurements of the process; and
- Desired culture.

☐ How well the change strategy balanced speed with thoroughness;

☐ How well the deliverables of each phase and each task were created, used, and received (Be sure to assess each phase and/or activity independently.);

☐ Performance of the change leaders, change process leader, change team members, and change consultants, including how well they modeled and walked the talk of the transformation;

☐ How much trauma was created for people adversely affected by the process, and how well people were supported through their reactions;

☐ How effective the strategies were for building readiness and capacity to change in the leaders;

☐ How effective the strategies were for building readiness and capacity to change in the organization;

☐ How well the leaders assisted people through their resistance;

☐ How well relationships and partnerships were created, developed, managed, and maintained to support the change process;

☐ How clear and effective the decision-making processes were;

☐ How well you were able to determine and secure adequate resources;

Exhibit 12.2. Assessing the Change Process to Identify Best Practices, Cont'd

☐ How effectively the leaders dealt with political dynamics;

☐ How well new information was handled, generated, and used for refinements and course corrections;

☐ Responsiveness to the needs of the organization as it changed; balancing ongoing business requirements and stakeholder needs with the emerging requirements of the transformation;

☐ Effectiveness of communications (evaluate for attention to all five levels);

☐ Ability to course correct the process quickly and effectively;

☐ How well you handled changing the mindset, culture, and behavioral aspects of the organization to support its success in the present and the future;

☐ How much more capable the organization is in keeping itself on the cutting edge and continuously adapting than it was before this change;

☐ Effectiveness of the temporary change structures, management systems, policies, and roles;

☐ How much more capable the executives are as change leaders after building their capacity to lead the transformation individually and as a team;

☐ How flexible, responsive, and sensitive the change leaders were to unpredicted disruptions, conflicts, or changes in direction; and

☐ What condition the people of the organization are in as they "conclude" this change effort.

Activity IX.C: Dismantle the Temporary Change Support Structures, Management Systems, Policies, and Roles

Task IX.C.1: Dismantle the Temporary Change Support Structures, Management Systems, Policies, and Roles

Now that this particular change effort has been "completed," it is time to dismantle the temporary support structures, systems, policies, and roles put in place to support the change process. This task identifies which of these have served their purpose and have to end. All too often, project teams and committees continue to exist long after their mission is accomplished and their value has been realized. This "bureaucratization" of change structures justifiably creates a negative perception among employees and must be avoided.

In this review, many organizations discover that some of their temporary mechanisms have actually made life in the organization much easier and more effective and, with some tinkering, can be valuable additions to the organization's normal operations. The structures or systems that still serve a useful purpose can be realigned as formal parts of the new state.

A part of this task is ending the special roles people have played to support the transformation. Many of the people who have served on special teams or in temporary roles will now go through their own transitions as they settle back into their old roles. For those moving into new state positions, this is still somewhat true, but less so, especially if their new roles are attractive to them.

Special attention is required for both categories of people, particularly if they became engrossed in their temporary assignments, as many do. They are not the same people they were before the transformation; their views of both the organization and their individual contribution to it have been altered and expanded, and this must be recognized and considered. Be sure to celebrate their successes overtly and create formal closure to their participation with their teams. Be especially cautious of placing people who have thrived in these dynamic and influential change leadership roles back into more static, routine jobs. We have often seen talent leave the organization because their post-change jobs lack the thrill and challenge of leading transformation.

▶ CASE ɪɴ POINT

In one oil company's transformation, the change process leadership role was filled by two people—a business-savvy individual and a process-savvy person who was the head of Organization Development and Human Resources Planning. The effort was successful, and both individuals were profoundly impacted by what they had been able to do together to plan and facilitate this complex and challenging three-year process.

At the conclusion of the change, both people were given bonuses for their contributions. The business leader, near retirement, was given the job of continuously improving the business operations of the new organization.

This was the perfect placement for him. The OD leader, young and ambitious, was offered the job of managing compensation and benefits. For her, the change process leadership role had been fast-moving and challenging—greatly expanding her horizons and sphere of influence in the organization. She was disappointed by her offer, feeling that it was a lateral move into a function that, although important to the human resources department, was confining and static. Despite the executives' appreciation for her talents on the transformation, they were too busy to consider another, more dynamic position for her, and she left the company to form her own change management business. Her departure was the company's loss, given how much change it faced in its next several years. ◀

There are many things to consider when designing the strategy for this task. As this case demonstrates, this part of the process has many subtle human dynamics to which change leaders must be sensitive. Exhibit 12.3 offers a checklist of several to consider. Think through the outcomes you want in completing this effort and the types of support you have to give to the organization as it readies itself for the next round of changes.

Exhibit 12.3. Designing Your Dismantling Strategy

☐ How will you determine which structures, management systems, policies, and roles have to be dismantled and communicated as complete?

☐ How will you determine which of these need to be continued to serve the new organization?

☐ How will you tailor, formalize, and communicate the change structures, management systems, policies, and roles required in the new state?

☐ How will you provide a formal ending and celebration for teams within the temporary structures?

☐ How will you place key members involved in the transformation into the new state organization and provide them with the required emotional support for their transitions?

Exhibit 12.3. Designing Your Dismantling Strategy, Cont'd

☐ How will you assess whether or not to keep the temporary rewards created for the change process, and, if you do keep them, how will you integrate them into the organization's existing or redesigned reward system?

☐ How will you communicate to the targets of the transformation, the organization, and all stakeholders that this current iteration of change is now complete?

☐ Will you have an ongoing culture committee to continue the development of the desired culture and the dismantling of old norms and practices that inhibit the organization's progress?

Summary

Phase IX completes the downstream stage of change and brings you around to the beginning of the Change Process Model once again. You have implemented the transformation, supported the organization to build its understanding and capacity to succeed in its new state, and completed this particular transformation in preparation for the next. If they haven't already been heard, new wake-up calls await you.

We hope that this descriptive journey through the process of transforming the organization has prepared you to take on your next real transformational challenge. The last section of the book explores how people typically respond to the Change Process Model and how to leverage its value.

Consulting Questions for Activity IX.A: Build a System to Refine and Continuously Improve the New State

Task IX.A.1: Build a System to Refine and Continuously Improve the New State

- How will you ensure that the new organization continues to stay current with the ever-changing needs of its environment and marketplace?

- How will you ensure that the leaders of the new organization understand the need to build ongoing change capacity into the organization?

Consulting Questions for Activity IX.B: Learn from the Change Process and Establish Best Practices for Change

**Task IX.B.1: Learn from the Change Process
and Establish Best Practices for Change**

- What aspects of your change process will you study?

- Who will evaluate the effectiveness of your change process and build your best practices for change?

- How will you measure the effectiveness of your change process? Will you attempt to quantify it? In what way?

- How will you document, communicate, and educate the organization about your best practices for change?

- How will you incorporate the results of your assessment into your existing or new leadership or management development programs?

Consulting Questions for Activity IX.C: Dismantle the Temporary Change Support Structures, Management Systems, Policies, and Roles

Task IX.C.1: Dismantle the Temporary Change Support Structures, Management Systems, Policies, and Roles

- See Exhibit 12.3 for these questions.

Section Four
Leveraging the Change Process Model

Chapter 13: Reactions to the Change Process Methodology   235

Chapter 14: Opportunities for Leveraging the Change Process Methodology   247

Chapter 15: Continuing the Journey to Conscious Transformation   261

Reactions to the Change Process Methodology

NOW THAT YOU HAVE READ ABOUT THE CHANGE PROCESS **MODEL** in its entirety, you have undoubtedly surfaced a number of reactions and questions about it. This chapter addresses the reactions we most commonly hear about the model, as well as several key questions about how it is used. Where people are in their professional development as change agents or change leaders impacts their reactions to the methodology, as does their ability to use it to their advantage. We will be discussing this further. We hope that this chapter helps you understand your own reactions and gives you some answers so that you can take full advantage of the potential the methodology offers.

This chapter explores four areas influencing how people respond to the model. These areas are:

1. The model as a multi-dimensional thinking discipline versus an instruction manual of prescribed sequential actions;

2. Developmental stages of learning to master the Change Process Model;

3. Common reactions to the model and how people's reactions influence their ability to take advantage of it; and

4. Perceptions that the model recommends a "top-down" approach to change versus a more organic, multi-directional approach.

The Model as a Thinking Discipline

The nine-phase Change Process Model has an appealing logic and flow to it. Some leaders and consultants may inadvertently assume that this logic implies that transformation is controllable and predictable and that the model is meant to be adhered to rigidly and followed sequentially. These assumptions would neither be wise nor beneficial. As we noted in the Introduction to this book, the Change Process Model is not a cookbook for how to orchestrate transformational change. The model is designed as a *thinking discipline,* a guidance system for navigating the complexity and chaos of transformation in a conscious and thoughtful way. The organization it provides is meant to support your thinking, not necessarily to order your actions. We encourage you to revisit this discussion in the Introduction now that you have read about the model in its entirety.

No doubt you have been applying the Change Process Model to your current change effort or to a past experience as you read the last three sections of the book. In working with change leaders and consultants, we have discovered that a person's level of professional experience as a change agent influences his or her reactions to the model. We have identified four levels or stages of development that have an impact on how the model is perceived and used. As we overview the stages, we encourage you to find yourself within them.

Developmental Stages for Learning the Change Process Methodology

We have identified four stages of growth for practitioners of change—novice, basic, proficient, and master. These apply both to consultants and to change leaders. The four stages are shown in Figure 13.1, which indicates that they nest *within* each other rather than replace each other sequentially. Our descriptions of the stages will be brief, only giving general characteristics of each.

**Figure 13.1. Developmental Stages for
Learning the Change Process Methodology**

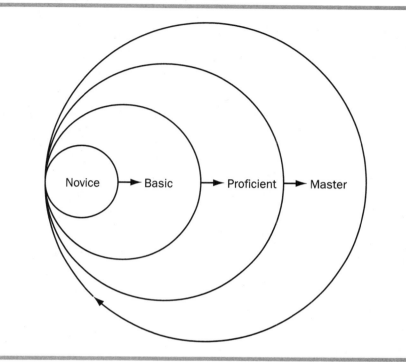

Novice practitioners are new to change leadership and consulting. Their eyes are wide open to discovery, and they take everything they are learning in with equal enthusiasm. This absorption of the totality of every new approach can often overwhelm them or make them anxious about not "getting it right" or doing it "by the book." They often assume they have to do everything suggested in the model in the right order for fear of missing something important. Their ability to discern what is needed, what can be skipped, and what should be tailored to the reality of a particular situation has not fully developed.

Novices often carry documentation of the entire methodology everywhere, as if having it with them will give them greater assurance of success. They look to the methodology continually to help guide their planning and to ensure they are "on track." Inasmuch as they fear making mistakes, they can also enjoy the latitude of trial and error if they make their minimal experience known to the people they work with. This latitude for experimentation can help accelerate their learning process and is far more comfortable for them than pretending that they are more advanced than they are.

Basic practitioners have less anxiety than novices about doing everything in the model and exercise more choice about how to apply it to unique situations. They will carry the Change Process Model in outline form, yet still check themselves often against the more detailed versions of its tools. They understand the methodology more than novices and have greater experience, but have not yet integrated the model fully into their worldview or thinking. Basic practitioners are most comfortable working with proficient or master practitioners at their sides, only venturing out alone in settings where they feel the risk is minimal or where a plan for action has already been developed. They often seek out opportunities to test their wings and appreciate having the safety net that the model offers.

Proficient practitioners understand the entire methodology and are comfortable applying it selectively, tailoring it when the situation calls for customization. They know the model well enough to teach it to others. They can integrate it with other models and competencies in their consulting and management repertoires, yet still reference the Change Process Model outlines and workbooks periodically to check their thinking and course correct. Proficient practitioners are competent in the most complex of change efforts and like the challenge of transformation. They can be good models of the conscious mindset, behavior, and strategies the model represents if they have developed their internal selves as much as their external expertise.

Master practitioners have all of the experience and comfort of their proficient counterparts, with the additional capability of easily changing and evolving the methodology as the situation indicates. They typically are consciously observing emergent patterns in the transformational process and the people involved in the change and testing out new hypotheses and approaches. They may present or write about their theories and experiences for the consulting profession or at leadership conferences.

Achieving mastery requires practitioners to develop themselves mentally, emotionally, and spiritually; acquiring change skills is simply not enough for mastery. Without significant personal transformation, the subtle yet significant nuances of organizational transformation go unseen or unappreciated.

Their personal development gives masters the gift of being authentic models of the conscious approach to transformation. They demonstrate their own learning, course correction, and personal breakthrough when they encounter a live opportunity to do so. Their personal presence in these situations is always a powerful illustration of how people's consciousness is always evolving, at both the individual and organizational levels.

Our intent here is only to overview these developmental stages, not to address how to advance from one stage to another. We describe the knowledge areas, behaviors, and skills of conscious transformational leaders and consultants in the Appendix of *Beyond Change Management,* in the context of planning for their development. Further exploration of the developmental process for consultants and leaders is the topic for another book.

Keep the four developmental stages in mind when considering how to teach and mentor people in the Change Process methodology. It is also very important to hire people—employees or external consultants—who actually have the level of expertise you need. This often requires a proficient or master-level practitioner to participate in the interview process. Change leaders who don't yet understand transformation or change process models will not know what to look for in candidates. Many an effort has crashed and burned due to staffing at too low a level of competence for the complexity of the changes required. Most importantly, hire people who are devoted—first and foremost—to their own personal transformation. These people always make better change leaders.

As we noted earlier, people's different levels of expertise in leading change influence their impressions about the Change Process Model. Let's explore the various reactions we encounter.

Reactions to the Change Process Model

Through teaching hundreds of people this methodology over the years, we have observed a range of reactions to it. These reactions either support or hinder people's use of the model. Some people's reactions cause them to adopt the model in its entirety, almost as the "savior" of their change effort, while others' reactions cause them to reject it outright, even if pieces of it serve their need.

As a consultant or leader facing major change who has chosen to read this book, you are more than likely looking for insight, tools, and techniques to help guide your efforts. If you have not used a change process model before, after reading through the description of all nine phases of the change process, you are likely experiencing one of three reactions—or something similar.

Reaction 1: Structure and Security

"Finally! A structure I can follow! I knew a lot of this had to be done; I just didn't know how to get it all organized. Now it is all in one place, in sequence! I'm relieved to I know I am on the right track."

This first reaction infers that the model provides a sense of security in its organization and comprehensiveness. For individuals who have a basic level of experience in leading change, the reaction expresses relief that their strategies are sound. We often hear this, even from proficient practitioners.

This reaction is common in organizations that value a fairly clear and structured approach to things, such as engineering, utilities, traditional manufacturing, or other organizations that are highly regulated in their operating practices. The people in these settings appreciate the structure of the methodology and its all-inclusiveness. It provides a comprehensive roadmap for planning their change process and guiding their decisions along the way.

There is a downside to this reaction, however. These consultants or leaders put themselves at risk in believing that the model is a "silver bullet," the answer to the discomfort and chaos of transformation. If these people rely too heavily on the model for lockstep instructions, they are in danger of thinking that they really are in control. Worse yet, they may think that following everything the model suggests will guarantee their success. Clearly, this is not true.

As a consultant or change leader, your reality will always dictate how to proceed and should supercede your strict adherence to this or any model. Be cautioned. No change model takes the place of your own experience and expertise, conscious perception, and intuitive evaluation about the situation you face. If you try to use any of them, including this one, as a formula or cookbook, you are making a strategic mistake.

Reaction 2: Aversion to Complexity

"This is far too complicated for me. I had no idea that all of this work was required! I'd rather go back to my simple view of change and struggle through like I always have."

This reaction, which is very human, is an example of an "ignorance is bliss" orientation to life. It is interesting to observe how many people have a genuine aversion to the complexity of transformation and resent discovering that transformation is so "messy," let alone that they have to be conscious of so many dynamics, especially in themselves. In our view, these people's resentment causes them to reject the model and its thoroughness, *as if not using it will diminish the complexity of the reality they actually face.* They throw the baby out with the bath water and succumb to a reactive mindset.

Transformational efforts all have some degree of complexity, some more than others. Your change effort will possess the complexity it has, no matter what approach you take. The choice to use a simpler change model will not alter the actual complexity you face. Instead, it may cause more messiness if you overlook critical activities as you proceed.

This aversion to complexity is most common when the Change Process Model is viewed as a rigid prescription for *required action* rather than a *template* for consciously thinking about your options for how to proceed. The Change Process Model is intended to describe most of what *might* have to happen in your transformation, allowing you to consciously decide exactly what actions are required for your particular situation. The model can assist you to streamline the activities of your change process to be the most influential and help you avoid complexities that result from neglecting mission-critical actions.

Most people who have used less extensive change models discover that the nine-phase model offers essential additional guidance. Rather than forcing a choice between models, consider integrating the parts of each model that seem to fit your style, perception, organizational culture, and change needs. No one model has to be the "be-all-and-end-all."

Reaction 3: Go Faster!

"I don't begin to have the time or patience to do all of this. This will take way too much time. I want something that will accelerate the change, not slow it down with all of this activity."

If leaders assume that all of what is detailed in the nine phases is necessary, the model could appear as a work-generating, time-consuming burden that is impossible to overlay on an already overwhelmed organization. Parts of this worry are sometimes true; the organization is too burdened to undergo transformation. However, this has nothing to do with the Change Process Model.

The complexity of the transformation process itself—not the comprehensiveness of the model—creates enormous discomfort and anxiety for people who feel a deep need to have their transformation happen lightening fast. Often, the organizations these people live in are moving at warp speed. Change is happening everywhere in them, and there is no end in sight. In these settings, the leaders typically make the assumption that they can mandate the pace of transformation despite its complexity or people's readiness or stamina. They believe that the transformation must be made immediately, no matter what approach they use. When these leaders establish and sustain high-pressure conditions inappropriately, employee morale usually goes down, resistance goes up, and implementation flounders, all of which slow down the effort.

Even if the organization has a change model, most leaders in these harried organizations believe that the best way to speed things up is to skip or abbreviate steps in the process; to set urgent, if not impossible, timelines for change; and to mandate action under some real or imagined threat. Such actions carry risk and cost because the organization is not a machine with a gas pedal but a living system with human needs.

Much to the frustration of these pressured leaders, the transformation process always seems to have its own clock. Change can sometimes be accelerated, but not merely by someone's will. Leaders must make sound strategic choices about which change process activities to do and which to skip and then use effective methods to accomplish the actions they select. Helping make these conscious choices is the role and benefit of a comprehensive change process model.

The right actions, carried out consciously, build speed and momentum by delivering what the organization needs and by positively impacting people's commitment, readiness, and ability to act. People have to understand the case for change and the vision. They must have frequent communication and involvement. They need time to develop their change skills and, mostly, to assimilate the impact the transformation has on them personally and emotionally.

Remember the "Go slow to go fast" operating principle of conscious transformation. Establishing the conditions for success that enable you to move expeditiously often means investing time to set them up correctly in the beginning. This investment always brings a significant return.

Having said this, there is merit to the "go fast" orientation of reducing planning time and adopting an act first, "ready—fire—aim!" orientation, but only if leaders overtly build continuous learning and course correction into their change strategy. When leaders rigidly demand that the transformation be done right the first time, they are setting up the organization, and themselves, for failure. The best solution seems to be equal parts of conscious planning, "ready—fire—aim," real-time learning from mistakes, and the ability to course correct as you go.

Let it be stated for the record that we do not have "the answer" about this dichotomy of desired speed versus required action. However, we are experimenting with different ways to solve this dilemma, which we will discuss in the next chapter.

A Top-Down Versus a Multi-Directional Approach to Change

The OD field features many approaches to change, some of which are leader-led and most of which involve people throughout all levels of the organization. In fact, the field of OD purports a value of supporting the people of the organization to be responsible contributors to, if not masters of, their own organizational reality.

Although you might recognize that we also support this value, you might also be experiencing an underlying concern or disconnect in that the Change Process Model is designed as a change *leadership* approach, with heavy leader involvement. Most of our discussion in this book makes reference to the leaders of the change determining the change strategy and the importance of the executives being sponsors and models of the organization's transformation. The Change Process Model clearly focuses on the important role of leaders in how transformational change is handled. Does this mean it recommends a "top-down" approach to change? Well, yes and no.

In order to clarify where we stand on this issue—top down, bottom up, or middle out—we must explain our views further, including why we focus Phase I on leaders, who the "leaders" of the organization are, and what transformation demands of "top" leaders.

First and foremost, we believe that transformation will only succeed if the whole system transforms. It can be initiated anywhere and mobilized in any direction—top down, bottom up, or inside out. The work of each phase of the Change Process Model, theoretically, must be accomplished for the transformation to occur. Who does this work is less important than the fact that it be done consciously to influence how the transformation is designed and facilitated.

Phase I of the model, "Prepare to Lead the Change," specifically addresses the top *leaders* of the change effort, who can establish the initial infrastructure and conditions for success. It begins with these leaders hearing the wake-up call for change and initiating the transformation by clarifying change leadership roles, creating the case for change, and building the change strategy for how the transformation will be led. Then, in Phase II the model recommends that the top leaders take the change effort out to the organization. Even if Phase I work is done in parallel with Phase II work, the emphasis of Phase I is on the leaders, with Phase II being on the organization. This is partly to help organize the multitude of change activities, and partly because achieving leadership alignment and setting up conditions for success as early as possible greatly accelerate the change process.

In Phases II through IX, you *could* construe that the change process design work is the responsibility of the top change *leaders,* along with their change teams. You could construe that the *leaders* ask their managers and employees to be involved in design, impact analysis, and implementation as the top *leaders* see fit. This would be an easy interpretation of the structure and language of the model.

This interpretation would be accurate if the change leaders designing the change strategy and process were all selected from the *top* of the organization being changed. However, we do not recommend that change leaders only come from the top of the organization. We believe that both design and implementation are best accomplished with the whole system being represented in both of these activities. The work of all the key change activities is best accomplished through whole-system participation. That is why we emphasize high-participation strategies. Therefore, when we speak of change leaders in Phases II through IX, we do not necessarily mean only the top leaders in the organization.

Second, our discussion has focused on organization-wide transformation, assuming that the "organization" in question is, in fact, the whole system. However, more often than not, transformation is occurring or at least starting in some part of the whole system—a business line, division, or plant. In these cases, the "leaders" we reference in Phase I are those in charge of the organization undergoing the transformation. The change leaders referenced in Phases II through IX can and should include top leaders, as well as mid-managers and front-line employees who are key stakeholders in the change.

We must also clarify that it is our intent to support everyone who has a possible influence on the transformation—be they executives, employees, or consultants—to view themselves as "change leaders." If they are intentionally making a real contribution to the effort, we consider them change leaders.

The third reason we emphasize top leaders in Phase I is because transformation can be squelched most easily by top leaders, especially if they have not heard the wake-up call or resist the requirements of the transformation. Therefore we focus significant attention on their role. This doesn't negate a bottom-up or middle-out approach; it simply ensures that the top leaders engage in the transformation in ways that are critical to the effort's success, especially at the beginning.

In situations in which the leaders are operating "unconsciously"—in traditional command-and-control fashion—they often do not understand or support the requirements of transformation. In these cases, Phase I work has to focus on leadership breakthrough and change education to help leaders "wake up" to these requirements, including whole-system participation, and mindset and behavior change, especially for the leaders.

It has been our experience 100 percent of the time that, when the entire system must transform, even if the change ignites in the middle or bottom of the organization and then spreads out, if the senior executives do not eventually get on board with the shift in consciousness and behavior required for the transformation to succeed, the transformation eventually dies on the vine or goes underground. It is put aside until the top leaders get a painful enough wake-up call that they finally recognize the need to change.

We have seen and assisted successful efforts that begin at the grass-roots level of the organization or in a discrete segment of the business before spreading to other parts of the system. We have supported several transformational pilot efforts in divisions that were ready and excited to pioneer their future and pave the way for the larger organization. Most of these efforts were successful ventures in and of themselves, and they all applied the Change Process Model at their level of the organization and did the mindset work. A key enabler in each was top leader support.

We have witnessed countless examples where conscious, proactive, upper or middle managers and supervisors courageously engaged their own parts of the organization in a well-designed transformation, only to hit the wall of a resistant mindset in the top echelon when the content or personal changes required extended beyond the managers' sphere of influence. The managers' mindsets had evolved, but the executives' mindsets had not.

Mindset can be either the key that opens the door of transformation or the key that keeps it locked shut. Mindset change is best accomplished through simultaneous efforts throughout the whole organization. From our experience, this whole-system effort has the best chance of succeeding when it is sponsored by a senior executive who can pave the way and keep less "conscious" leaders from stifling the transformation. Acknowledging this, we emphasize that the top leaders of the organization that is transforming must become models of the mindset and behavior change required for the whole organization to transform as early as possible in the effort. They are the ones who set up the safe conditions for the rest of the organization to engage in the personal work required for the transformation to succeed.

Summary

If after having read the description of the Change Process Model, you have concerns about its length, order, or level of detail, we encourage you to remember that the model is designed as a thinking discipline rather than a prescription for action. Suspend your judgments and ask yourself how *your* process can be shaped to be of value to *your* organization's change efforts. Success is in your ability to discover the right balance of structure, order, and speed to match the real people and process dynamics of your transformation as it is happening.

In this chapter, we discussed four stages of development that influence people's effectiveness in using the model. We explored how people's reactions to the methodology impact their ability to use it, and we addressed the issue of tailoring the model to fit the culture and needs of the organization, making it top down, bottom up, or middle out, depending on what is suitable. We will now turn our attention to various strategies for using the Change Process Model to your organization's greatest advantage.

Opportunities for Leveraging the Change Process Methodology

ONCE YOU DECIDE TO USE THE CHANGE PROCESS MODEL, you must figure out how to gain the greatest value from it. We have discovered several special ways to use and leverage the unique attributes of the Change Process methodology that are worth exploring:

1. Using the Change Process Model as an operating system to integrate all of the organization's change initiatives;

2. Strategically deciding who "owns" the change methodology in the organization;

3. A consulting strategy designed for "just-in-time" application of the model; and

4. Accelerating the change process.

To begin, we offer a change leadership strategy for using the methodology that, once in place, can greatly reduce time, confusion, and the cost of change across the organization.

Using the Change Process Model as an Operating System

At any point in time, most organizations have many improvement programs underway. These change efforts may or may not appear to be related or integrated. In fact, most often, they compete with each other for time, attention, and resources. Most all are run using different and inconsistent methods, producing confusion in the organization and slowing down their completion. No wonder the workforce resents the "flavor of the month" syndrome and loses faith in leadership's ability to lead!

The Change Process Model is a tool that can make all ongoing or upcoming change initiatives run easier and faster, especially when integration of initiatives is required. The most value-added context for the change methodology is that it becomes the *operating system* for how all existing and future change efforts are led.

Much like Microsoft's Windows™, or the MAC-OS™ systems that support the consistent running and cross-referencing of myriad software programs, using the Change Process Model as the operating system for all change initiatives ensures that they all run in a manner that promotes integration across business content, people, and process issues. Without a change process operating system, the various initiatives cannot be integrated to serve the overall good of the organization.

If you decide that having a change process operating system would be helpful, you should be aware that there is a serious risk in asking an already overloaded organization to learn a new methodology for leading change. The initiative leaders may view the methodology as yet another change program, something to be added on top of all of the other change initiatives underway. In fact, the Change Process Model is not something else to be done *on top of* existing efforts and must not be positioned that way. Instead, it should support *the way in which the existing efforts are accomplished.* It should inform decision making and shape the change process by guiding how all initiatives are led, planned, and run, not by being seen or positioned as a new initiative. Of course, learning the change methodology does take additional time on the part of the organization's change leaders and consultants who will apply it. If leaders recognize, in advance, that the organization must improve its change leadership capacity before it is fully immersed in change, then this learning can take place in advance as well. Let's explore the operating system analogy further by using a case example.

► CASE IN POINT

We worked with one organization that had over thirty "priority" change efforts underway simultaneously. The people of the organization were exhausted and frustrated with their leaders. The executives engaged us to help organize, prioritize, and coordinate their many initiatives into one unified approach and build the organization's understanding of its transformation. Consistency and integration of the discrete efforts were desperately needed across the organization, as many of the initiatives were competing with each other when their outcomes could only be achieved through synergistically working together. Nearly every one of the initiatives was being run using a different change model, if one could even be deciphered. This made collaboration nearly impossible. Like different computer platforms, the initiatives could not "talk" to each other. They needed a common language and approach.

We helped the change leaders prioritize their top initiatives and educated them and their internal consultants about the Change Process Model. The training was all "case-based," and the change leaders applied the model to each of their top initiatives as they learned it. Having a change process operating system became a strategic advantage that provided them a basis for consistency, integration, and flexibility. With this approach, their multiple changes could coexist, work in tandem, and be communicated as one overarching transformation. The methodology allowed them to lead all of the changes in a coherent, yet customized fashion. With continuous follow-up, application clinics, and coaching, the leaders created a system that met the majority of their needs as well as accomplishing their transformation. ◄

Are you a candidate for this strategy? Exhibit 14.1 lists several questions to assist you in thinking through what is required.

Exhibit 14.1. Determining the Value of Using a Change Process Operating System

- Does your organization have more than three major change initiatives underway? Do these efforts impact each other or depend on each other to be successful? Are they transformational?

- What current problems does the organization experience in not having a common change methodology among its initiatives? Are both change frameworks and change process models being used?

- How would a change process operating system benefit these initiatives? How would it benefit how the organization leads its change efforts in the future?

- How would you determine which change methodology would work for the organization? Would you create one or acquire one?

- How would you tailor a change methodology to fit the culture and readiness of the organization's change leaders?

- How would you position the integration of a change process operating system so that leaders in charge of change initiatives would want it?

- How would you design the process of educating all change leaders and consultants in the organization about the change methodology?

- How would you create consistency while allowing for necessary customization and flexibility?

- How would you support each change leader to apply the model to his or her ongoing changes?

- How would you ensure follow-up and continuous learning about the change methodology?

- Who is the best person to head up the decision about using a change process operating system for your organization?

- Does the organization have the resources to support this effort adequately?

- Does the organization have internal change consultants who can take the lead on applying the process and the methodology? Would you also need external expertise?

- What would have to happen for this strategy to succeed?

The benefits of using a consistent change process operating system include:

- Increased speed in both design and implementation, as well-integrated efforts have fewer competing challenges;

- People become familiar with a consistent change process being used, significantly reducing resistance and confusion about it;

- People expect and embrace temporary change structures, systems, policies, and roles;

- Change leaders automatically set up conditions for success that smooth the way for expedient design and implementation;

- Change leaders can readily share learnings with others, creating a natural process for continuously increasing the organization's change leadership capacity and building best change practices; and

- It increases the organization's change capability.

More than anything, a change process operating system strategy supports clear thinking and action on behalf of the whole organization by integrating all related initiatives into a common transformational direction.

Once you decide to use the change methodology, you must determine who "owns" the methodology, where it lives in the organization, and how it can be applied for greatest leverage.

Determining Who "Owns" the Change Process Model

Somewhere in the organization—in one person, several, or most—mastery of the change methodology must exist. Its use can then be tailored, promoted, and applied throughout the organization as the need arises. There are a number of options for where in the organization change expertise can live.

One strategy is to house this expertise in internal OD or change management consultants and trainers, if the organization has them. If it does not, the leaders may want to hire an adequate number of professionals who have the appropriate levels of expertise, including proficient or master practitioners.

These professionals use the Change Process Model to guide their consultations with change leaders on change strategy development and change process facilitation. With visible executive sponsorship, these consultants can be responsible for designing how to build change leadership capacity throughout the organization. The consultants—and their executive and management development counterparts—can be deployed on all major change efforts, supporting the line change leaders of each. This strategy works only if the leaders of the organization actively use OD and change facilitation expertise on major initiatives and if these consultants are competent and positioned to add real value.

While in-house consultants can own the change process expertise, line leaders must be actively involved, for reasons previously established. We believe that in today's fast-paced, ever-changing world, familiarity with the organization's change methodology is inevitably the job of every line leader in the organization. It is the line leaders who are in the position to champion the organization's collective transformation effectively. Therefore, leaders ought to have at least a strategic understanding of the Change Process Model. In-house consultants can assist, accelerate, and enable effective change, but line leaders must ultimately be accountable for it.

Organizations that have neither the line expertise nor sufficient in-house OD staff often contract for change help with external consultants. This can also be done when there are only novice or basic internal consultants who may need more development and support or when line leaders have little experience with leading successful transformation. If your organization has internal resources, make sure to partner them with the external consultants. This is the only way both to build in-house competency and to ensure that the methods used by the external consultants are tailored to the needs of the organization.

When hiring external consultants, test their willingness to work in partnership with your in-house consultants as well as their willingness to teach their methodology as they use it. If you intend to build internal change leadership capacity, you should only hire external consultants who will share or license their methodology to your organization. Make this expectation for knowledge transfer explicit during the selection process. You will receive greater return on your investment by simultaneously building internal expertise as you receive the consulting support needed on your current transformation.

The responsibility for thinking through how to apply and tailor any change model must be kept within the organization. Change leaders at all levels of the organization must step up to becoming the key strategists for the transformation of the organization from the beginning of the process. Ideally, they will work in active partnership with the organization's internal resources and, if they use them, their external consultants as well. This partnership is critical because line leaders often believe that they know much more about leading transformation than they really do. We have seen too many well-intended efforts fail because line leaders don't accept needed support. If the organization has selected a change model as the guidance system for all of its change initiatives, the executives must ensure that the model is understood, respected, and tailored to fit their changes.

We continue to explore how to position the Change Process Model to be of greatest value in organizations that are fast-paced, high-tech, or emergent growth companies. These organizations are most interested in speed, flexibility, and ease of use. Their leaders often are reluctant to invest adequate time up-front to learn the methodology as suggested in the operating system strategy above. Let's next explore one strategy we have used to infuse the Change Process Model without slowing down the organization's changes or overly burdening the change leaders.

Understanding the Just-in-Time Change Consulting Strategy

The just-in-time consulting strategy is an approach for using the Change Process Model to serve fast-paced organizations that would otherwise never reap its benefits, although they urgently need them. What follows is a composite of recommendations that can assist organizations to transform when their line leaders have little tolerance or time for learning what they need to succeed. We have not yet enacted this strategy in its entirety in any one organization—only in pieces. We have used our learnings from these experiences to craft this overall approach.

The just-in-time change consulting strategy can be used when fast-track companies recognize that they: (1) need a consistent approach to change; (2) need better change leadership; (3) are undergoing primarily transformational change; and (4) don't have the time or the interest to stop, learn, and master a methodology as thorough as the nine-phase model. Rather than attempt to teach all the subtleties of the Change Process Model to an already pressured organization, we use this approach to go deep with the few. Its intent is to create a small cadre of proficient change consultants who can offer competent advice to line leaders only as needed or wanted.

Often, organizations that most desperately need just-in-time consulting do not understand the complexities of transformation and unknowingly make critical assumptions about how to lead it that end up being costly to their results and people. The just-in-time change consulting strategy can help raise their awareness in relatively painless ways. Here are the dynamics and various steps that make it work.

To begin this strategy, the leaders must first recognize that their old mindsets and assumptions about change are a part of the problem. There is no way around this mindset issue. They must agree to address their mindsets about how they view transformation and how they have reacted to the dilemmas it presents. This strategy of raising leaders' awareness then requires one or both of the following: (1) Initial change education for executives about the Change Process Model and human dynamics of conscious transformation and (2) a breakthrough training experience to drive home the requirement that leaders must walk the talk of the transformation from its inception, in both their thinking and their behavior.

If these two initial interventions are successful, the leaders will come away with new perceptions about the changes that are happening in the organization. They will have been introduced to the strategic level of the Change Process Model and be in active dialogue about how it should be used. These two initial executive-level sessions set the stage for just-in-time change consulting.

If the organization doesn't already have an in-house OD or change management function, the executives would next establish one, staffed with a majority of proficient and master-level practitioners who have tangible experience in the people, process, and perhaps even the needed content elements of their changes. We highlight the selection of at least a majority of proficient practitioners because novices and basic-level consultants will realistically spend more time learning than delivering sound change advice. They can, however, be mentored by the proficient practitioners as they work.

This OD function becomes the organization's primary "change agent" resource team. These consultants would be in charge of mastering, tailoring, and owning the change methodology that will best serve the changes the organization faces. External consultants can support the team's learning process and work, but customizing and mastering the methodology is the internal team's primary responsibility. With full ownership of the customized change process, the consultants can better support the needs of line leaders and educate the rest of the organization.

Before their development process gets underway, this consulting group would identify a select number of line leaders who have the *innate* ability to understand complex organizational system dynamics, conscious process thinking and design, political realities, and people dynamics. The change agents would partner with these line leaders and, together, learn as much of the methodology as possible. This would be done in a combination of classroom and on-the-job consulting on active change initiatives. This partnership is critical. Organization development consultants can be used to build a strong team of this combined group of people.

Together the consultants and line people would become the formal and informal resource pool of change agents available to the entire organization. As in organizations that have created formal departments devoted to quality or knowledge management, these people would become the masters of change strategy, design, and facilitation. They would be charged with teaching and consulting to any leader in the organization needing assistance in any phase of their change efforts.

The key to this group's success with active change leaders is *just-in-time advice*. The consultants would be the keepers of the entire methodology and only use what is needed with their clients as they recognize challenging issues during the course of their change efforts. For instance, if change leaders want to create clear change leadership roles, the consultants would assist with this particular work. If the client is ready to do an impact analysis, the consultants support that effort. The clients never have to know that they are in Task I.A.2 or Phase V. They only need to receive the help they require in the moment.

The change agents would also attend to the personal development and mindset work essential to making the organization's transformation conscious. They could facilitate this personal work with their clients themselves, if they have the experience, organizational trust, and capability, or they could bring in external expertise to assist at the right time in their clients' efforts. Rather than doing this work at the organization-wide scale, it would be brought into the individual initiatives when needed.

It is important that the consultants stay close enough to their clients' change efforts to assess what work is needed when, because the client will not always know. This requires clear contracting and partnering agreements between the consultants and the leaders they serve.

In addition to supporting individual client work, this group might also work with the executives on organization-wide change issues, such as:

- Facilitating the executives to build an enterprise-wide change strategy for transformation, including both cultural and technical components of the change;

- Integrating the multitude of initiatives that may be ongoing in the organization;

- Coordinating the many external consultants who may be engaged throughout the organization;

- Keeping an active eye on the capacity of the workforce for handling the transformation—emotionally, culturally, and physically—and coaching the executives to alter their change process and pace, if that is required;

- Designing large group interventions when major segments of the organization, or the organization as a whole, must address change issues through widespread participation; or

- Continually evolving the organization's Change Process Model and building organization-wide best change practices.

The just-in-time change consulting strategy offers the organization a choice about whom to expose to the Change Process Model and to what extent. Some organizations that want to embed the Change Process Model as their change operating system would choose to involve and expose more people to it throughout the organization. In addition to providing just-in-time consulting support to project teams, these organizations would integrate modules of the Change Process Model into their existing executive, management, and supervisory training. They could create a Best Practices for Change forum and learning groups throughout the organization to focus on conscious transformational leadership. In all cases, eventually a critical mass of leaders with competent change leadership skills would be developed through the *real-time* support and exposure they would receive from their change agents.

The conditions required to support the just-in-time change consulting strategy include:

- Executive understanding and commitment to the strategy and the change process model being proposed;

- Ensuring enough capable in-house change agents (representing both staff and line);

- Sufficient resources and time to support the change agents' continued development;

- Visibly positioning and sponsoring the change agents as dedicated, available, and competent to assist with major change efforts; and

- Ensuring that external consultants understand that *your* change process methodology, *not theirs,* is the operating system to be used and being sure that they are willing to have your in-house resources partner with them to create the strategy for how their work will be carried out.

▶ CASE IN POINT

We worked with one global manufacturing organization to develop in-house change leadership capacity worldwide. We were able to use some aspects of the just-in-time strategy, but not all of what we have just described. The company was not undergoing an enterprise-wide transformation, but many of its businesses were engaged in transformational change. Our general strategy was to educate a select group of change consultants from around the world in the Change Process Model and transformational change leadership approaches and to coach them as they offered just-in-time support to their line clients. During start-up, the clients were also introduced to the methodology. Overall, the experience was seen as valuable, and it also produced some very important learnings.

During the development process, some of the consultants were open to attending to their own personal and mindset change; others were not. Those who engaged in their own personal work were, by and large, most adaptable and effective with addressing this work with their line clients. Those who chose not to do the personal work struggled with how to get their clients to see that their leadership style and way of thinking about their change strategy was insufficient to deliver their desired results. Because these consultants were unsuccessful in conveying this foundational message to their clients, their advice about how to deal with change process dilemmas and people issues fell on deaf ears.

Another factor in the varied level of success was the wide range of capability and experience the consultants had with supporting large scale change efforts. The more proficient consultants were able to recognize the complexities of people and process issues and were able to provide focused, valuable advice to their clients. Those who were new to whole-systems dynamics were intimidated by the challenging requests coming from their clients. A flaw in the overall effort was that budget and time constraints prohibited the less experienced consultants from being mentored by or partnered with the more proficient consultants. Budget also placed limitations on our ability as external consultants to support these people over time.

From this experience, we learned that the just-in-time change consulting strategy has to be designed as a comprehensive approach, fully supported and funded by leadership. A piecemeal approach can add some value, but not nearly what is possible by setting it up for system-wide success from the beginning, complete with proficient consultants, mentoring novices, and a long-term development plan. ◄

Accelerating the Change Process

The conscious approach to leading transformation is the fastest accelerator of the process we know. We have designed the Change Process Model to create the greatest possibility for breakthroughs in people's mindsets, behavior, and abilities—early, fast, and frequently throughout the entire process.

Traditional "reactive" leaders have very different ideas of what it takes to speed up change, such as mandating a more urgent pace or skipping critical activities, neither of which work.

We recommend that leaders explore their assumptions about what causes change to go slowly in their organizations and what they think would accelerate it. Our own research has uncovered many causes of slowdown. The causes are largely reflections of the reactive approach to transformation, which we covered in depth in our companion book, *Beyond Change Management*. A few of the major drags on the transformation process include:

- Unclear case for change and competing outcomes;

- An inadequate process map for the actual change activities required;

- No clear governance for the change effort or governance that is superimposed over the existing management structure and, therefore, competes with the demands of running current operations;

- Leaders who do not walk their own talk, which causes employee distrust and resistance;

- Inadequate resources and unrealistic time pressures;

- Operational and human resource systems that are unable to accommodate the additional demands of the change;

- Resistance to personal development and becoming more conscious of the personal and organizational transformation dynamics; and

- Lack of recognition of the need to course correct the process continuously or the inability to do so.

So the acceleration question is: "How do you resolve these conditions if they exist or prevent them in the first place?" Our answer is by using the Change Process Model as a vehicle for *conscious* change leadership. Our recommendations for accelerating transformation include five strategies that you will recognize from our discussions of the model. They are all direct actions that result from taking a conscious approach to planning and leading the change. The five strategies are:

1. Create the conditions for success up front and course correct them throughout the process;

2. Design an integrated change strategy and process plan that maximizes parallel and concurrent actions;

3. Build alignment among the change leaders, all members of the project community, and the various change initiatives required by the transformation;

4. Build a critical mass of commitment through organization-wide participation; and

5. Provide personal transformation opportunities for both leaders and employees throughout the change effort.

One last point about the pace and timing of transformation: Inasmuch as we wish we had the power to make transformation happen faster than is humanly possible, and we continue to search for ways to speed it up, the truth—plain and simple—is that *transformation takes the time it takes*. Winter lasts as long as it does. A human baby takes nine months to develop, no matter how fast the mother wants the baby to be born. It is a sign of masterful change leadership to accept this reality and design change strategies that support the change to occur as fast as *is* humanly possible, and not to expect more.

Summary

The Change Process Model has abundant potential for providing value. We have described how it can be used to support and accelerate all of the organization's change efforts as an internalized change operating system. We offered various scenarios for who owns the change methodology in the organization and described the possibilities for making the methodology useful to change leaders in organizations that have little tolerance for transformation's complexities. We also addressed how consciously approaching the design of the transformation process speeds it up more than any other acceleration strategy.

With all of this in mind, we want to conclude this exploration into the Change Process Model by posing some questions to guide your thoughts and next actions for your own change leadership development process. Chapter 15 concludes this journey.

Continuing the Journey to Conscious Transformation

THE PROCESS OF TRANSFORMATION IS ONGOING, as is the pursuit of greater consciousness about how to lead and consult to it. Rather than conclude the journey here, we would like to offer you some things to think about to keep your thought process going. We invite you to ponder these questions and talk about them with like-minded colleagues.

- What are your reactions to the Change Process Model? What conclusions have you drawn about its use and value to you and the organizations you support?

- In reading through the Change Process Model as a roadmap for conscious transformation, in what way has your thinking about leading transformation changed?

- What are the most important insights you have had about how you have been leading or consulting to large systems change? How will each insight affect your practice and your way of being from this point on?

- If you could position and use the Change Process Model in any way at all in your organization, what would that be? What outcomes or effect would this strategy ideally accomplish?

- If you could change the model in any way, how would you alter it and why?

- Are you currently positioned to use a methodology such as this effectively? If not, what would have to be different in your situation to enable you to use it to its greatest advantage? Who else would you need to work with to accomplish this?

- What would you have to do to develop mastery as a conscious change leader or consultant? What obstacles or factors would you have to overcome to move your development process forward? What support would you require? How can you obtain that support?

- What natural strengths and ways of being do you have that support your effectiveness as a conscious leader or consultant? Are you using these assets in your work and life? What would have to happen for you to be able to bring them more fully into your normal way of working and living?

- What would support you to continue to think about and act on your responses to these questions after you close this book?

Some Thoughts for Change Consultants

Becoming masterful at consulting to large scale transformational change requires serious professional and personal growth for change consultants in OD and change management. As we personally evolve this body of work, we continue to grow ourselves; the work, in fact, "grows us."

We see several key leverage points for building consulting proficiency. Some of these may be relevant to you. Here is our overview, for your consideration:

- View yourself as a full-fledged partner with executives in charge of change. You cannot do the work of helping build change strategy for the full lifecycle of a transformation from the sidelines or behind the scenes. In our experience, until you embrace this fact, you will not be able to enter a client engagement properly positioned to do the work that is required.

- The OD profession has always been a thought leader for the concept and skills of process; now consultants must expand their own expertise to support transformational change. Evolve your definition of "process" to what our companion book describes as "the natural or intentional unfolding of continuous events, at all levels of reality, toward a desired outcome." See and work with process as the multi-dimensional, ever-changing dynamic process inherent in transformation and life. Learn to master and teach conscious process thinking, the operating principles of conscious transformation, and the competencies of process design and facilitation.

- If you are a consultant who has a content specialty, learn about how to apply it to organizations from a change *process* perspective. Learn a change process model and how to integrate the people and process components into your content contribution. You will provide a far more usable and powerful contribution to your clients.

- Learn how to become the bridge between dealing with the comfortable challenges of the "external" world (the environment, business strategy, organizational configurations) and the less familiar realms of the "internal" world (culture, mindset, emotions, and relationships). Position yourself to serve as a translator and integrator of these two worlds in creating integrated change strategy and facilitating transformational change.

- Commit to doing the personal work on your own mindset, style, and behavior to better serve your clients as a model and mirror of the personal development that transformational change requires of leaders.

- Further develop your skills in building integrated change strategy for transformational change, addressing enterprise-wide transformation in global organizations, and effecting real change in mindset and culture.

Some Thoughts for Leaders

Having consulted with leaders for over twenty-five years, mostly on designing and implementing transformational change strategy and cultural/personal transformation, we have experienced tremendous satisfaction when making a significant contribution to the success of their efforts and their development as change leaders. We have also had times of extreme frustration at not being able to get leaders' attention about what was required to make a profound difference in their work and organizations. Today we are in a balanced state about this, accepting that leaders are typically in one of three different places. Some leaders (growing in numbers!)

are traveling in the same boat of exploration with us, pioneering and testing break-throughs in how transformation can best be supported. Some are on the boat launch, with a toe, if not a foot, on the boat, intrigued by the possibilities of this "mysterious" yet compelling journey. And others, quite frankly, are firmly rooted on dry land, either not aware of the journey being made by their peers or not believing that it is necessary or possible. For those in the first two places, we offer these thoughts. Perhaps you can bring those on dry land to the water.

- Learn as much as you can about what transformation entails. Partner with conscious, process-oriented consultants, internal or external, who are committed to their own transformations and make this journey together.

- Learn to *use* your consultants in ways that enable them to support you, your personal work, and the organization as it transforms. Use them to assist you to observe the internal and external dynamics that occur during the process and to map the subtleties of the system dynamics that can make or break your transformation. Let them be your coaches to expand your conscious awareness of all that demands your attention as you lead the organization through its transformation.

- Do the personal work to become the change leader that your organization needs to succeed in its transformation. Look in the mirror at your fundamental assumptions and beliefs and how they impact your change leadership performance, relationships, and results.

- Explore the makeup of your mindset and re-create it to consciously serve the requirements of the present and future.

- Accept that the organization is made up of people—people who are devoting much of their lives to its success. The organization is a living, dynamic human system. All of its members want and deserve to be treated with respect, concern, and gratitude for their contribution to the organization's continuing viability. They want to be accepted, as you do, for having physical, emotional, mental, and spiritual dimensions that, whether or not they like it, are impacted by *your* leadership and the realities at play in the organization.

- Learn your version of the facilitative style of leading transformation. Whereas many leaders judge the facilitative style as too soft or "wimpy" for their image of a strong leader, we have come to recognize that it takes a great deal more courage and ability than command and control. Facilitating the organization's transformation acknowledges that transformation must be co-created by the entire organization, not just you. Letting go of control, having faith, and setting up the conditions for the whole system to re-create itself require strength of character and an evolved mindset.

- Instead of getting swept up in the tidal wave of "faster, faster, faster," we encourage you to discover the art of "right timing for leveraged action." In this book, we spoke of discovering the strategic leverage points in the organization's patterns of behavior that can catalyze profound change with efficient effort. We spoke of appropriate pacing of change activities. "Right timing for leveraged action" integrates these two strategies. Together, they enable the breakthrough in speed and performance that is possible in the transformation. You cannot control or mandate breakthrough; you can only facilitate the conditions for it to occur. Often, this is intuitive. When faced with urgency and complexity, before getting sucked in to the vortex of "do-mode," ask yourself where the leverage is that can deliver maximum gain for minimum effort and when is the right time to pull the lever. The answer you come up with may not match your original plan, yet it may be the very catalyst you need for transformational breakthrough. To access these catalysts, learn to *listen to your intuition*.

Summary

Our life's work is to help people and organizations transform and to be active models of conscious transformation as we have described it. In so doing, we place ourselves on a lifelong path of personal and professional development. We believe wholeheartedly that expanding conscious awareness is the direction of human evolution. In our worldview, learning about and mastering the process dynamics of all levels of our reality—beginning with ourselves—is the greatest leverage for leading the transformation of our organizations. All transformational leadership skills derive directly from this increased insight and capability.

Assisting organizations to transform and developing transformational change leaders give us the vehicles through which to bring the benefits of conscious awareness and mindset into the open. They must become legitimate, sought-after leadership and consulting requirements if our organizations are going to transform successfully. It has been our intent in writing this book to provide you with both a well-balanced experience of conceptual models and pragmatic guidance for leading transformation consciously. Our goal has been to offer potent, user-friendly tools and processes to increase your awareness and your transformational leadership capability.

The Change Process Model is the change leader's roadmap, the overarching guidance system through which conscious transformational leadership can be expressed and catalyzed in organizations. Through its use, we hope you will choose to be more than a leader. We hope you will choose to be a change leader and continue to explore and evolve this expanding role and work. Above all, we hope the roadmap has broadened your view of the territory of transformation, and we hope that it serves you and the people you serve well.

Appendix:
Phases, Activities, and Tasks of the Change Process Model

PHASE I: **PREPARE TO LEAD THE CHANGE**

      Activity I.A: **Start Up and Staff the Change Effort**

            Task I.A.1:   Obtain a Project Briefing

            Task I.A.2:   Clarify Required Change Leadership Roles and Staff the Change Effort

            Task I.A.3:   Create Optimal Working Relationships

            Task I.A.4:   Identify the Project Community

      Activity I.B: **Create the Case for Change and Determine Your Initial Desired Outcomes**

            Task I.B.1:   Identify Who Will Do This Work and the Process for How It Will Be Accomplished

            Task I.B.2:   Assess the Drivers of Change

Task I.B.3:   Assess the Organization's
                 System Dynamics to Identify
                 the Leverage Points for Change

Task I.B.4:   Perform an Initial Impact
                 Analysis

Task I.B.5:   Identify the Type, Scope, and
                 Targets of the Change

Task I.B.6:   Determine the Degree of
                 Urgency

Task I.B.7:   Determine Your Initial Desired
                 Outcomes and Compile the
                 Case for Change

**Activity I.C: Assess the Organization's Readiness and
                 Capacity to Succeed in the Change**

Task I.C.1:   Assess the Organization's
                 Readiness and Capacity to
                 Succeed in the Change

Task I.C.2:   Identify the Strategy for Building
                 Organizational Readiness and
                 Capacity for the Change

Activity I.D: Build Leaders' Capacity to Lead the Change

Task I.D.1:   Create an Overall Strategy for
                 Building Leadership's Capacity
                 to Lead the Change

Task I.D.2:   Initiate the Strategy for
                 Addressing Leadership Mindset,
                 Style, and Behavior

Task I.D.3:   Build Leader Commitment and
                 Alignment

Task I.D.4:   Initiate the Plan to Educate
                 the Executive and Change
                 Leadership Teams About Change

Task I.D.5:   Initiate the Process to Develop
                 the Executive and Change
                 Leadership Teams into Teams
                 Capable of Successfully Leading
                 the Change

Task I.D.6:   Initiate Development Plans
                 for Individual Executives and

	Change Leaders to Increase Their Ability to Lead and Walk the Talk of the Change
Activity I.E:	**Identify and Build the Infrastructure and Conditions to Support the Change Effort**

Task I.E.1: Develop and Initiate Strategies for Dealing with the Politics of Change

Task I.E.2: Clarify the Process and Style for Making All Major Change Decisions

Task I.E.3: Create Conditions for Success

Task I.E.4: Design and Initiate the Overall Communication Plan for the Change and Decide How to First Inform the Organization

Task I.E.5: Identify the Process for Creating Shared Vision Throughout the Organization

Task I.E.6: Design Information Generation Strategies

Task I.E.7: Design and Initiate the Course Correction Strategy and System

Task I.E.8: Design How to Minimize the Human Trauma of the Change, and Initiate Strategies for Helping People Through Their Emotional Reactions

Task I.E.9: Select and Initiate Temporary Change Support Structures, Systems, Policies, and Roles

Task I.E.10: Secure Commitment for Resources to Support the Change

Task I.E.11: Determine and Initiate Appropriate Measurements of the Change

Task I.E.12: Develop, Communicate, and Initiate Temporary Rewards to Support the Change Process and Outcomes

Activity I.F: **Clarify the Overall Change Strategy**

Task I.F.1:   Identify the Process for Building the Change Strategy

Task I.F.2:   Determine How to Lead the Change As One Unified Change Effort and How to Integrate Separate and Distinct Initiatives Within It

Task I.F.3:   Scan All Other Change Efforts Occurring or Being Planned in the Organization to Determine the Fit and Priority of this Effort

Task I.F.4:   Identify Bold Actions and Strategic Levers for Both the Content and People Changes

Task I.F.5:   Clarify Your Participation Strategies for How to Gain a Critical Mass of Commitment

Task I.F.6:   Identify the Critical Milestones and General Timeline for the Change and Complete the Change Strategy

PHASE II: **CREATE ORGANIZATIONAL VISION, COMMITMENT, AND CAPACITY**

Activity II.A: **Build Organizational Understanding of the Case for Change and the Change Strategy**

Task II.A.1:   Communicate the Case for Change and the Change Strategy

Activity II.B: **Create Shared Vision and Commitment**

Task II.B.1:   Roll Out the Visioning Process to Create Shared Vision and Commitment

Activity II.C: **Increase the Organization's Readiness and Capacity to Succeed in the Change**

Task II.C.1:   Increase the Organization's Level of Readiness to Change

Task II.C.2:   Initiate the Plan to Build the Organization's Change Knowledge and Skills

Task II.C.3: Initiate the Plan to Promote the Mindset and Behavioral Changes Required to Support the Transformation

Activity II.D: **Demonstrate that the Old Way of Operating Is Gone**

Task II.D.1: Demonstrate that the Old Way of Operating Is Gone

PHASE III: **ASSESS THE SITUATION TO DETERMINE DESIGN REQUIREMENTS**

Activity III.A: **Assess the Situation to Determine Design Requirements**

Task III.A.1: Assess Current Reality Within the Organization Against Your Vision for the Change

Task III.A.2: Benchmark Other Organizations for Best Practices

Task III.A.3: Clarify Customer Requirements

Task III.A.4: Write the Statement of Design Requirements

PHASE IV: **DESIGN THE DESIRED STATE**

Activity IV.A: **Design the Desired State**

Task IV.A.1: Create the Process and Structure to Design the Desired State

Task IV.A.2: Design the Desired State

Task IV.A.3: Pilot Test

Task IV.A.4: Communicate the Desired State

PHASE V: **ANALYZE THE IMPACT**

Activity V.A: **Analyze the Impact of the Desired State**

Task V.A.1: Create the Process for Conducting the Impact Analysis

Task V.A.2: Conduct the Impact Analysis of the Desired State

Task V.A.3: Assess the Magnitude of Impacts, Individually and Collectively, to Discover System-Wide Implications of the Desired State Design

Task V.A.4: Refine the Desired State as Necessary

Task V.A.5: Communicate the Summary Results of the Impact Analysis and the Newly Defined Desired State to the Targets of the Change, the Organization, and All Stakeholders

PHASE VI: **PLAN AND ORGANIZE FOR IMPLEMENTATION**

Activity VI.A: **Identify the Actions Required to Implement the Desired State and Develop the Implementation Master Plan**

Task VI.A.1: Create the Process for Identifying Actions Required to Implement the Desired State and for Developing the Implementation Master Plan

Task VI.A.2: Create Plans to Resolve the Individual Impacts of the Desired State

Task VI.A.3: Integrate Individual Impact Plans to Identify Actions for the Detailed Implementation Master Plan

Task VI.A.4: Design Strategies to Sustain the Energy for Change Throughout Implementation and Integrate Them into the Plan

Task VI.A.5: Determine the Pacing Strategy and Timeline and Apply Them to the Implementation Master Plan

Activity VI.B: **Prepare the Organization to Support Implementation**

Task VI.B.1: Refine and Establish the Conditions, Structures, Systems, Policies, and Resources Required to Support Implementation

Task VI.B.2: Initiate Strategies for Supporting People to Embrace the Desired

State and Manage Their Reactions to the Change

Task VI.B.3: Communicate the Implementation Master Plan to the Targets of the Change, the Organization, and All Stakeholders

PHASE VII: **IMPLEMENT THE CHANGE**

Activity VII.A: **Implement the Change**

Task VII.A.1: Roll Out the Implementation Master Plan

Task VII.A.2: Monitor and Course Correct the Implementation Process

Task VII.A.3: Monitor and Course Correct the Desired State

PHASE VIII: **CELEBRATE AND INTEGRATE THE NEW STATE**

Activity VIII.A: **Declare, Celebrate, and Reward the Achievement of the Desired State**

Task VIII.A.1: Declare, Celebrate, and Reward the Achievement of the Desired State

Activity VIII.B: **Support Integration and Mastery of the New State**

Task VIII.B.1: Support Individuals and Intact Work Units to Optimize Their Performance by Increasing Their Integration and Mastery of the New State

Task VIII.B.2: Support the Whole System to Optimize Its Performance by Increasing Its Integration and Mastery of the New State

PHASE IX: **LEARN AND COURSE CORRECT**

Activity IX.A: **Build a System to Refine and Continuously Improve the New State**

Task IX.A.1: Build a System to Refine and Continuously Improve the New State

Activity IX.B: **Learn from the Change Process and Establish Best Practices for Change**

　　　　　　　　Task IX.B.1:   Learn from the Change Process and Establish Best Practices for Change

Activity IX.C: **Dismantle the Temporary Change Support Structures, Management Systems, Policies, and Roles**

　　　　　　　　Task IX.C.1:   Dismantle the Temporary Change Support Structures, Management Systems, Policies, and Roles

Bibliography

Ackerman Anderson, L. (1986). Development, transition or transformation: The question of change in organizations. *OD Practitioner, 18*(4).

Ackerman Anderson, L., & Anderson, D. (1996). *Facilitating large systems change participant manual.* Durango, CO: Being First, Inc.

Ackerman Anderson, L., & Anderson, D. (2001). *Beyond change management: Advanced strategies for today's transformational leaders.* San Francisco: Jossey-Bass/Pfeiffer.

Adams, J. (1984). *Transforming work: A collection of organizational transformation readings.* Alexandria, VA: Miles River Press.

Adams, J. (1986). *Transforming leadership: From vision to results.* Alexandria, VA: Miles River Press.

Anderson, D. (1986). *Optimal performance manual.* Durango, CO: Being First, Inc.

Alban, B., & Bunker, B. (1997). *Large group interventions: Engaging the whole system for rapid change.* San Francisco: Jossey-Bass.

Anderson, D., & Ackerman Anderson, L. (2001). *Beyond change management: Advanced strategies for today's transformational leaders.* San Francisco: Jossey-Bass/ Pfeiffer.

Argyris, C. (1985). *Strategy, change, and defensive routines.* Marshfield, MA: Pitman.

Ashkenas, R., Ulrich, R., Jick, T., & Kerr, S. (1995). *The boundaryless organization: Breaking the chains of organizational structure.* San Francisco: Jossey-Bass.

Axelrod, R. (1992). *Terms of engagement: Changing the way we change our organizations.* San Francisco: Berrett-Koehler.

Beck, D., & Cohen, C. (1996). *Spiral dynamics: Mastering values, leadership, and change.* Cambridge, MA: Blackwell.

Beckhard, R. (1997). *Agent of change: My life, my practice.* San Francisco: Jossey-Bass.

Beckhard, R., & Harris, R. (1987). *Organizational transitions.* Reading, MA: Addison-Wesley.

Bennis, W. (1989). *Why leaders can't lead: The unconscious conspiracy continues.* San Francisco: Jossey-Bass.

Bennis, W. (1995). *On becoming a leader* (audio). New York: Simon & Schuster.

Bennis, W., & Nanus, B. (1985). *Leaders: The strategies for taking charge.* New York: Harper & Row.

Blanchard, K., & Hersey, P. (1982). *Management of organizational behavior: Utilizing human resources.* Upper Saddle River, NJ: Prentice Hall.

Blanchard, K., & O'Connor, M. (1997). *Managing by values.* San Francisco: Berrett-Koehler.

Block, P. (1999). *Flawless consulting: A guide to getting your expertise used* (2nd ed.). San Francisco: Jossey-Bass/Pfeiffer.

Bohm, D. (1980). *Wholeness and the implicate order.* New York: Routledge.

Bridges, W. (1980). *Transitions* (2nd ed.). New York: Perseus Publishing.

Bridges, W. (1991). *Managing transitions: Making the most of change.* Reading, MA: Addison-Wesley.

Bridges, W. (1994). *Jobshift: How to prosper in a workplace without jobs.* Reading, MA: Addison-Wesley.

Briggs, J., & Peat, D. (1989). *Turbulent mirror: An illustrated guide to chaos theory and the science of wholeness.* New York: Harper & Row.

Briggs, J., & Peat, F.D. (1999). *Seven life lessons of chaos: Spiritual wisdom from the science of change.* New York: HarperCollins.

Bunker, B., & Alban, B. (Eds.). (1992/December). Special issue: Large group interventions. *Applied Behavioral Science, (28)*4.

Capra, F. (1983). *The turning point: Science, society, and the rising culture.* New York: Bantam.

Capra, F. (1991). *The tao of physics: An exploration of the parallels between modern physics and eastern mysticism.* Boston, MA: Shambhala.

Capra, F. (1996). *The web of life.* New York: Anchor Press.

Case, J. (1998). *The open-book experience: Lessons from over 100 companies who successfully transformed themselves.* Reading, MA: Addison-Wesley.

Collins, J., & Porras, J. (1994). *Built to last: Successful habits of visionary companies.* New York: HarperCollins.

Conger, J., Spreitzer, G., & Lawler, E., III (1999). *The leader's change handbook: An essential guide to setting direction and taking action.* San Francisco: Jossey-Bass.

Conner, D. (1993). *Managing at the speed of change: How resilient managers succeed and prosper where others fail.* New York: Villard Books.

Conner, D. (1998). *Leading at the edge of chaos: How to create the nimble organization.* New York: John Wiley & Sons.

Csikszentmihalyi, M. (1990). *Flow: The psychology of optimal experience.* New York: Harper & Row.

De Chardin, P. (1962). *Human energy.* New York: Harcourt Brace Jovanovich.

Deal, T., & Kennedy, A. (1982). *Corporate cultures: The rites and rituals of corporate life.* Reading, MA: Addison-Wesley.

Drucker, P. (1999). *Management challenges for the 21st century.* New York: HarperCollins.

Dym, B. (1995). *Readiness and change in couple therapy.* New York: HarperCollins.

Ferguson, M., & Naisbitt, J. (1980). *The aquarian conspiracy.* Los Angeles: Jeremy P. Tarcher.

Forrester, J. (1961). *Industrial dynamics.* Cambridge, MA: MIT Press.

Francis, D., & Woodcock, M. (1990). *Unblocking organizational values.* Glenview, IL: Scott, Foresman.

Frenier, C. (1997). *Business and the feminine principle: The untapped resource.* Boston: Butterworth-Heinemann.

Galbraith, J., Lawler, E., & Associates. (1993). *Organizing for the future: The new logic for managing complex organizations.* San Francisco: Jossey-Bass.

Gleick, J. (1987). *Chaos: Making a new science.* New York: Penguin.

Gleick, J. (1999). *Faster: The acceleration of just about everything.* New York: Pantheon.

Goldstein, J. (1994). *The unshackled organization: Facing the challenge of unpredictability through spontaneous reorganization.* Portland, OR: Productivity Press.

Goleman, D. (1995). *Emotional intelligence: Why it can matter more than IQ.* New York: Bantam.

Greenleaf, R. (1977). *Servant leadership: A journey into the nature of legitimate power and greatness.* Mahwah, NJ: Paulist Press.

Grof, S. (1993). *The holotropic mind: The three levels of human consciousness and how they shape our lives.* New York: HarperCollins.

Gross, T. (1996). *The last word on power: Executive re-invention for leaders who must make the impossible happen.* New York: Doubleday.

Hagberg, J. (1984). *Real power: Stages of personal power in organizations.* Minneapolis, MN: Winston Press.

Hall, B. (1995). *Values shift: A guide to personal & organizational transformation.* Rockport, MA: Twin Lights Publishers.

Hammer, M., & Champy, J. (1993). *Reengineering the corporation: A manifesto for business revolution.* New York: HarperCollins.

Hammond, S. (1996). *The thin book of appreciative inquiry* (2nd ed.). Plano, TX: Thin Book Publishing.

Hammond, S., & Royal, C. (1998). *Lessons from the field: Applying appreciative inquiry.* Plano, TX: Practical Press.

Heisenberg, W. (1958). *Physics and philosophy.* New York: Harper Torchbooks.

Henricks, G., & Ludeman, K. (1996). *The corporate mystic: A guidebook for visionaries with their feet on the ground.* New York: Bantam.

Herbert, N. (1985). *Quantum reality: Beyond the new physics.* New York: Doubleday.

Herman, S. (1994). *The tao at work: On leading and following.* San Francisco: Jossey-Bass.

Hesselbein, F., Goldsmith, M., & Beckhard, R. (1996). *The leader of the future: New visions, strategies, and practices for the next era.* San Francisco: Jossey-Bass.

Huxley, A. (1956). *The doors of perception and heaven and hell.* New York: Harper Colophon.

Jacobs, R. (1994). *Real time strategic change: How to involve an entire organization in fast and far-reaching change.* San Francisco: Berrett-Koehler.

James, W. (1999). *The varieties of religious experience: A study in human nature.* New York: The Modern Library.

Jantsch, E. (1980). *The self-organizing universe.* New York: Pergamon Press.

Jaynes, J. (1990). *The origin of consciousness in the breakdown of the bicameral mind.* Boston, MA: Houghton Mifflin.

Johnson, B. (1996). *Polarity management: Identifying and managing unsolvable problems.* Amherst, MA: HRD Press.

Jones, J., & Bearley, W. (1996). *360-degree feedback: Strategies, tactics, and techniques for developing leaders.* Amherst, MA: HRD Press.

Jung, C. (1963). *Memories, dreams, reflections.* New York: Random House.

Jung, C. (1973). *Synchronicity: An acausal connecting principle.* Princeton, NJ: Princeton University Press.

Kanter, R. (1983). *The change masters: Innovation for productivity in the American corporation.* New York: Simon & Schuster.

Katzenbach, J., & Smith, D. (1993). *The wisdom of teams: Creating the high performance organization.* Boston, MA: Harvard Business School Press.

Klein, E., & Izzo, J. (1998). *Awakening corporate soul: Four paths to unleash the power of people at work.* Lions Bay, BC, Canada: Fairwinds Press.

Koestenbaum, P. (1991). *Leadership: The inner side of greatness.* San Francisco: Jossey-Bass.

Kotter, J. (1996). *Leading change.* Boston, MA: Harvard Business School Press.

Kouzes, J., & Posner, B. (1995). *The leadership challenge: How to keep getting extraordinary things done in organizations.* San Francisco: Jossey-Bass.

Kouzes, J., & Posner, B. (1999). *Encouraging the heart: A leader's guide to rewarding and recognizing others.* San Francisco: Jossey-Bass.

Kuhn, T. (1962). *The structure of scientific revolutions* (1st ed.). Chicago, IL: The University of Chicago Press.

Land, G., & Jarman, B. (1992). *Breakpoint and beyond: Mastering the future today.* San Francisco: HarperCollins.

Laszlo, E., Grof, S., & Russell, P. (1999). *The consciousness revolution.* Boston, MA: Element Books.

Lebow, R., & Simon, W. (1997). *Lasting change: The shared values process that makes companies great.* New York: John Wiley & Sons.

Liebau, P. (1985). *Thoughts on relationships.* London, Ontario, Canada: P.S.A. Ventures.

Lipnack, J., & Stamps, J. (1993). *The teamnet factor: Bringing the power of boundary crossing into the heart of your business.* Essex Junction, VT: Oliver Wright.

London, M. (1988). *Change agents: New roles and innovation strategies for human resource professionals.* San Francisco: Jossey-Bass.

Lovelock, J.E. (1987). *Gaia.* London, England: Oxford University Press.

Maslow, A. (1964). *Religions, values, and peak experiences.* New York: Penguin.

Maslow, A. (1999). *Toward a psychology of being* (3rd ed.). New York: John Wiley & Sons.

Maynard, H., & Mehrtens, S. (1993). *The fourth wave: Business in the 21st century.* San Francisco, Berrett-Koehler.

McFarland, L., Senn, L., & Childress, J. (1994). *21st century leadership: Dialogues with 100 top leaders.* Los Angeles: The Leadership Press.

Miles, R. (1997). *Leading corporate transformation: A blueprint for business renewal.* San Francisco: Jossey-Bass.

Mink, O., Mink, B., Downes, E., & Owen, K. (1994). *Open organizations: A model for effectiveness, renewal, and intelligent change.* San Francisco: Jossey-Bass.

Morton, C. (1984). *Managing operations in emerging companies.* Reading, MA: Addison-Wesley.

Nadler, D. (1998). *Champions of change: How CEO's and their companies are mastering the skills of radical change.* San Francisco: Jossey-Bass.

Nadler, D, Shaw, R., & Walton, A. (1995). *Discontinuous change: Leading organizational transformation.* San Francisco: Jossey-Bass.

Nadler, D., & Tushman, M.L. (1977). A diagnostic model for organizational behavior. In J.R. Hackman, E.E. Lawler, & L.W. Porter (Eds.), *Perspectives on behavior in organizations.* New York: McGraw-Hill.

Naisbitt, J., & Aburdene, P. (1985). *Re-inventing the corporation: Transforming your job and your company for the new information society.* New York: Warner Books.

Nevis, E., Lancourt, J., & Vassallo, H. (1996). *Intentional revolutions: A seven-point strategy for transforming organizations.* San Francisco: Jossey-Bass.

Oshry, B. (1992). *The possibilities of organization.* Boston, MA: Power & Systems.

Oshry, B. (1995). *Seeing systems: Unlocking the mysteries of organizational life.* San Francisco: Berrett-Koehler.

Pascarella, P., & Frohman, M. (1989). *The purpose-driven organization: Unleashing the power of direction and commitment.* San Francisco: Jossey-Bass.

Peat, D. (1987). *Synchronicity: The bridge between matter and mind.* New York: Bantam.

Penfield, W. (1975). *Mystery of the mind: A critical study of consciousness.* Princeton, NJ: Princeton University Press.

Peters, T., & Waterman, R.H. (1982). In search of excellence. New York: Harper & Row.

Pribram, K. (1971). *Languages of the brain: Experimental paradoxes and principles in neuropsychology.* New York: Brandon House.

The Price Waterhouse Change Integration Team. (1995). *Better change: Best practices for transforming your organization.* New York: Irwin.

Prigogine, I. (1997). *The end of certainty: Time, chaos, and the new laws of nature.* New York: The Free Press.

Prigogine, I., & Stenger, I. (1984). *Order out of chaos.* New York: Bantam.

Ralston, F. (1995). *Hidden dynamics: How emotions affect business performance & how you can harness their power for positive results.* New York: American Management Association.

Ray, M., & Rinzler, A. (1993). *The new paradigm in business: Emerging strategies for leadership and organizational change.* New York: Tarcher/Pergee.

Reder, A. (1995). *75 best business practices for socially responsible companies.* New York: Tarcher/Putnam.

Renesch, J. (Ed.) (1992). *New traditions in business: Spirit and leadership in the 21st century.* San Francisco: Berrett-Koehler.

Renesch, J. (1994). *Leadership in a new era: Visionary approaches to the biggest crisis of our time.* San Francisco: New Leaders Press.

Rogers, R., Hayden, J., Ferketish, B., with Matzen, R. (1985). *Organizational change that works: How to merge culture and business strategies for maximum results.* Pittsburgh, PA: Development Dimensions International.

Ross, G. (1994). *Toppling the pyramids: Redefining the way companies are run.* New York: Times Books.

Russell, P. (1995). *The global brain awakens: Our next evolutionary leap.* Palo Alto, CA: Global Brain, Inc.

Ryan, K., & Oestreich, D. (1991). *Driving fear out of the workplace: How to overcome the invisible barriers to quality, productivity, and innovation.* San Francisco: Jossey-Bass.

Schein, E. (1969). *Process consultation: Its role in organization development.* Reading, MA: Addison-Wesley.

Schein, E. (1999). *The corporate culture survival guide: Sense and nonsense about culture change.* San Francisco: Jossey-Bass.

Schwartz, P. (1996). *The art of the long view.* New York: Doubleday.

Senge, P. (1990). *The fifth discipline: The art and practice of the learning organization.* New York: Doubleday.

Senge, P., Kleiner, A., Roberts, C., Ross, R., & Smith, B. (1994). *The fifth discipline fieldbook.* New York: Doubleday.

Senge, P., Kleiner, A., Roberts, C., Roth, G., Ross, R., & Smith, B. (1999). *The dance of change: The challenges of sustaining momentum in learning organizations.* New York: Doubleday.

Sheldrake, R. (1995). *A new science of life: The hypothesis of morphic resonance.* Rochester, VT: Park Street Press.

Singer, J. (1994). *Boundaries of the soul: The practice of Jung's psychology.* New York: Doubleday.

Smith, H. (1992). *Forgotten truth: The common vision of the world's religions.* San Francisco: HarperCollins.

Spencer, S.A., & Adams, J.D. (1990). *Life changes: Growing through personal transitions.* San Luis Obispo, CA: Impact Publishing.

Stacey, R.(1992). *Managing the unknowable: Strategic boundaries between order and chaos in organizations.* San Francisco: Jossey-Bass.

Talbot, M. (1986). *Beyond the quantum.* New York: Bantam.

Tart, C. (1975). *States of consciousness.* New York: E.P. Dutton.

Tichy, N., with Cohen, E. (1997). *The leadership engine: How winning companies build leaders at every level.* New York: HarperCollins.

Waldrop, M. (1992). *Complexity: The emerging science at the edge of order and chaos.* New York: Touchstone.

Walsh, R., & Vaughan, F. (1993). *Paths beyond ego: The transpersonal vision.* New York: Penguin/Putnam.

Waterman, R. (1987). *The renewal factor: How the best get and keep the competitive edge.* New York: Bantam.

Watkins, J.M., & Mohr, B. (2001). *Appreciative inquiry: Change at the speed of imagination.* San Francisco: Jossey-Bass/Pfeiffer.

Weisbord, M.R. (1978). *Organizational diagnosis: A workbook of theory and practice.* Reading, MA: Addison-Wesley.

Weisbord, M., & Janoff, S. (1995). *Future search: An action guide to finding common ground for action in organizations.* San Francisco: Berrett-Koehler.

Weisinger, H. (1998). *Emotional intelligence at work: The untapped edge for success.* San Francisco: Jossey-Bass.

Wheatley, M. (1994). *Leadership and the new science: Learning about organization from an orderly universe.* San Francisco: Berrett-Koehler.

Wheatley, M., & Kellner-Rogers, M. (1995). *A simpler way.* San Francisco: Berrett-Koehler.

Wilber, K. (1977). *The spectrum of consciousness.* Wheaton, IL: Theosophical Publishing House.

Wilber, K. (1982). *The holographic paradigm and other paradoxes.* Boston, MA: Shambhala.

Wilber, K. (1996). *A brief history of everything.* Boston, MA: Shambhala.

Wilber, K. (1998). *The marriage of sense and soul.* New York: Random House.

Wilber, K. (1999). *One taste: The journals of Ken Wilber.* Boston, MA: Shambhala.

Williamson, M. (1992). *Return to love.* New York: HarperCollins.

Wilson, J. (1994). *Leadership trapeze: Strategies for leadership in team-based organizations.* San Francisco: Jossey-Bass.

Wolf, F. (1988). *Parallel universes: The search for other worlds.* New York: Touchstone.

Wolf, F. (1989). *Taking the quantum leap: The new physics for nonscientists.* New York: Harper & Row.

Young, A. (1976). *The reflexive universe.* Englewood Cliffs, NJ: Prentice Hall.

Zukav, G. (1979). *The dancing Wu Li masters.* New York: Bantam.

About the Authors

Photo credit Jonas Grushkin/Photogenesis

Linda S. Ackerman Anderson is a co-founder and principal in the consulting and training company, Being First, Inc. She specializes in facilitating large-system change in Fortune 500 businesses and the military, particularly enterprise-wide transformational change. She is currently creating a curriculum for developing women executives called "Women As Leaders of Change." Over the past twenty-five years, her work has focused on change strategy development for transformational changes. In the past ten years, she and her partners have established themselves as thought leaders on facilitating conscious transformation and changing organizational mindset and culture as drivers of transformational change.

Ms. Ackerman Anderson was a founding creator of the organization transformation field, and chaired the Second International Symposium on Organization Transformation in 1984. To help define this field, she has published several articles, including "Development, Transition or Transformation: Bringing Change Leadership into the 21st Century"; "The Flow State: A New View of Organizations and Leadership"; and "Flow State Leadership in Action: Managing Organizational Energy." She was one of the first to articulate the notion and use of organizational energy as a tool for transformation.

In 1981, Ms. Ackerman Anderson formed Linda S. Ackerman, Inc., then merged it in 1988 with the Optimal Performance Institute, headed by Dean Anderson, to form Being First, Inc. Prior to forming her first business, Ms. Ackerman Anderson spent four years working at Sun Company, Inc., and one of its subsidiaries, Sun Petroleum Products Company. During this time, she was both an organization development consultant and manager of human resources planning and development.

Ms. Ackerman Anderson's professional education includes Columbia University's Advanced Organization Development and Human Resources Management Program (1978–1979) and University Associates' Laboratory Education Internship Program (1977–1978). She has served on the faculty for the UA Intern Program and other UA conferences and many university professional development programs.

Ms. Ackerman Anderson received her master's degree in interdisciplinary arts from Columbia University's Teachers College and her bachelor's degree in art history and education from Boston University.

Photo credit Jonas Grushkin/Photogenesis

Dean Anderson is co-founder and principal in the consulting and training firm, Being First, Inc. Mr. Anderson consults to Fortune 500 companies in transformational change, assisting them to build change strategy and develop executives, consultants, and project managers into change leaders. His current passion is helping his clients create enterprise-wide personal and cultural breakthroughs to a conscious way of being, working and relating. In 1980, Mr. Anderson founded the Optimal Performance Institute, which was one of the first organizations in the country providing the pragmatics of self-mastery and personal change to organizational leaders.

Mr. Anderson created Being First's renown leadership breakthrough training, is the central developer of The Co-Creating System,™ and is co-author of Being First's comprehensive Change Tools. He authored the *Optimal Performance Manual* and "Making Personal Change Trainings Work in Organizations," developed the Co-Creative Partnering and Team Development Process, and produced the *Self Mastery Series* audiotape program.

Mr. Anderson has two degrees from Stanford University, a bachelor of arts in communications and a master's degree in education.

For further information, contact:

Being First, Inc.
1242 Oak Drive, DW2
Durango, CO 81301
USA
(970) 385-5100 voice
(970) 385-7751 fax
www.beingfirst.com
email:danderson@beingfirst.com
        lindasaa@beingfirst.com

About the Editors

William J. Rothwell, Ph.D. is professor of human resource development in the College of Education at The Pennsylvania State University, University Park. He is also president of Rothwell and Associates, a private consulting firm that specializes in a broad array of organization development, human resource development, performance consulting and human resource management services.

Dr. Rothwell has authored, co-authored, edited, or co-edited numerous publications, including *Practicing Organization Development* (with R. Sullivan and G. McLean, Jossey-Bass/Pfeiffer, 1995). Dr. Rothwell's latest publications include *The ASTD Reference Guide to Workplace Learning and Performance*, 3rd ed., 2 vols. (with H. Sredi, HRD Press, 2000); *The Competency Toolkit,* 2 vols. (with D. Dubois, HRD Press, 2000); *Human Performance Improvement: Building Practitioner Competence* (with C. Hohne and S. King, Gulf Publishing, 2000); *The Complete Guide to Training Delivery: A Competency-Based*

Approach (with S. King and M. King, Amacom, 2000); *Building In-House Leadership and Management Development Programs* (with H. Kazanas, Quorum Books, 1999); *The Action Learning Guidebook* (Jossey-Bass/Pfeiffer, 1999); and *Mastering the Instructional Design Process*, 2nd ed. (with H. Kazanas, Jossey-Bass/Pfeiffer, 1998).

Dr. Rothwell's consulting client list includes thirty-two companies from the *Fortune* 500.

Roland Sullivan has worked as an organization development (OD) pioneer with nearly eight hundred organizations in ten countries and virtually every major industry.

Mr. Sullivan specializes in the science and art of systematic and systemic change, executive team building, and facilitating Whole System Transformation Conferences—large interactive meetings with from three hundred to fifteen hundred people.

Mr. Sullivan has taught courses in OD at seven universities, and his writings on OD have been widely published. With Dr. Rothwell and Dr. McLean, he was co-editor of *Practicing OD: A Consultant's Guide* (Jossey-Bass/Pfeiffer, 1995).

For over two decades, Mr. Sullivan has served as chair of the OD Institute's Committee to Define Knowledge and Skills for Competence in OD and was a recent recipient of the Outstanding OD Consultant of the World award from the OD Institute.

Mr. Sullivan's current professional learning is available at *www.RolandSullivan.com*.

Kristine Quade is an independent consultant who combines her background as an attorney with a master's degree in organization development from Pepperdine University, and years of experience as both an internal and external OD consultant.

Ms. Quade draws from experiences in guiding teams from divergent areas within corporations and across many levels of executives and employees. She has facilitated leadership alignment, culture change, support system alignment, quality process improvements, organizational redesign, and the creation of clear strategic intent that results in significant bottom-line results. A believer in whole systems change, she has developed the expertise to facilitate groups ranging in size from eight to two thousand in the same room for a three-day change process.

Recognized as the 1996 Minnesota Organization Development Practitioner of the Year, Ms. Quade teaches in the master's programs at Pepperdine University and the University of Minnesota at Mankato and the master's and doctoral programs at the University of St. Thomas in Minneapolis. She is a frequent presenter at the Organization Development National Conference and also at the International OD Congress and the International Association of Facilitators.

Index

A

Abrupt approach to letting go of old ways, 142

Accelerating the change process, 258–259

Ackerman Anderson, L., 79

Actions for Implementation Master Plan, identifying, 184–188

Activities, of Change Process Model, 16

Activity levels of Change Process Model, 17

Adams, J., 90

Adams' Individual Transition Model, 193

Aligning organizational changes with new mindset, 65

Alignment, building leader, 65–66, 72

Alignment style of decision-making, 78

Analyzing impact performance, 45–46, 53

Anderson, D., 79

Anderson, L. *See* Ackerman Anderson, L.

Announcing/implementing desired state, 171

Applying Implementation Master Plan, case in point for, 190

Applying pacing strategy/timeline to Implementation Master Plan, 189–191, 197

Appreciative Inquiry approach, 91

Approaches: abrupt, 142; Appreciative Inquiry, 91; conscious leadership, 258–259; gradual approach, 142; Just-In-Time, 253–258; multi-directional versus top-down, 243–246; reactive leadership, 6, 258; transformation leadership, 6

Assessment: of change process, 227–228; cost, 176; current degree of commitment/ alignment to change process, 65–66; of drivers of change, 40–44; drivers of change worksheet, 41–42; of effectiveness of teams, 68–70; of impacts of desired state design, 176, 178; issues, 150; of leader's mindset, 60; of readiness of organizations for change, 55–59, 71; studies, 149; of system dynamics, 52–53; of team effectiveness, 68–70; Team

Effectiveness Assessment worksheet, 68–70; of time needed, 189–191; of your vision against current organizational reality, 148–152, 154

Assumptions of leaders: about leadership, 140; exploring, 258; mandating change, 75; regarding resources needed, 102–103

Attention of individuals, getting, 64–65, 117

Authoritarian style of decision-making, 78

Aversion to complexity, 240–241

Axelrod, R., 85

B

Balance between organizational/human requirements, 160

Barrier buster teams, 100

Basic practitioners, 238

Behavior: defining leaders', 60–61; organizational, 150; promoting changes to, 141, 144; reinforcing change in, 65; resistance, 202–203; returning to old, 203–204, 218–219; strategy for addressing leadership, 72

Behavior modeling: course correction, 88; by leaders, 33–34, 134, 203; of values, 151

Best practices: benchmarking other organizations for, 152, 154; for change, establishing, 226–228, 232

Beyond Change Management (Anderson & Ackerman Anderson), 3

Bold actions, 117

Breakthrough process of leadership, 62–63, 141

Breakthrough programs, 139

Bridges, W., 89–92

Briefing the workforce, 80

Briefings, obtaining project, 28–39

Building a system for refining new state, 224–225

Building change knowledge/skills, 139–140, 144

Building leadership capacity, 59–60

Building ownership of vision, 136–137

Business imperatives, 150

C

Capacity for successful change, 56–58, 59

Case for change, creating, 39–40, 52–54

Cases in point: applying Implementation Master Plan, 190; challenges of leadership, 229–230; Change Process Model as operating system, 248–251; communication strategy, 82–83; consulting strategies, 257–258; creating shared vision, 137; demonstrating end of old way of operating, 142; implementation of desired state, 207; integration of new state, 218; leadership breakthrough strategy, 62–63; letting go of past, 194–195; multiple project integration teams, 97–98; pilot testing design of desired state, 166–167; readiness for change, 56–57; resistance to integrating Implementation Master Plan, 185; rewards for achieving desired state, 213; rewards for motivating staff, 105–106

Categories affecting readiness for change, 57–58

Categorizing impact issues, 175–176

Celebrating the new state, 212–213

Challenges of leadership, 229–230

Change: compiling the case for, 49–50; determining type of, 46–48; going faster, 241–243; how people react to, 90–92; multi-directional versus top-down approach to, 243–246; in thinking/behavior, reinforcing/sustaining, 65; types of, 3–4, 47

"Change agents," 254

Change assessments, 148–149. *See also* Assessment

Change consultants/leaders. *See* Leaders

Change effort: failure of, 188; Phase I overview, 25–26, 27–28; Phase II overview, 129–130; Phase III overview, 147–148;

Phase IV overview, 159–160; Phase V overview, 171–172; Phase VI overview, 181–182; Phase VII overview, 201–202; Phase VIII overview, 211–212; Phase IX overview, 223–224; start-up/staffing, 28–39; summary of phases, 243–244

Change frameworks, vs. change process models, 11

Change leadership team, 30. *See also* Leadership

Change navigation centers, 99

Change process: accelerating the, 258–259; establishing best practices for, 232; learning from, 226–228; learning the methodology of, 237

Change process leaders. *See* Leaders

Change process leadership. *See* Leadership

Change Process Model: activity levels of, 17; determining who "owns" the, 251–253; developmental strategies for learning, 236–239; Just-In-Time approach to using, 253–258; making the most of, 247; as operating system, 248–251; overview of, 13–15; reactions to, 239–243; structure of, 15–18; summary of phases of, 243–244; as thinking discipline, 76, 236; using as operating system, 248–251. *See also* Models

Change process models vs. change frameworks, 11

Change Process Operating System, determining value of, 250

Change process perspective, 263

Change-related activity, 8

Change strategy: determining how to lead/integrate change, 115–116, 124–125; elements of, 4–5; gaining commitment, 118–120, 125; identifying bold actions for, 117, 125; identifying milestones/timelines, 120–124, 126; identifying process for, 114–115, 124; identifying strategic levers for, 118; scanning other change efforts, 116, 125; template for building, 121

Change Team Network Structure, 94

Change trauma, 91

Chaos, working with, 85

"Chat rooms," 99

Checklists, building your course correction system, 89

Clarifying customer requirements, 152–153, 154

Coaching of leaders, 70

Collective intention, creating, 129–130

Collective ownership of vision, 136–137

Commitment, 65–66, 72, 134–137

Communication: addressing political dynamics of change, 76–77; of case for change, 130–134; of change strategy to organization, 124; for creating collective intention, 129–130; designing plan for, 107–108; of desired state, 167–168, 169; effective, 132; of Implementation Master Plan to targets of change, 195–196, 197; initiating plan for, 80–84; levels of, 81, 136; modeling course correction behavior, 88; of policies for people support, 192–193; in project community, 36; of results of impact analysis, 177, 178; of roles/responsibilities, 96

Communication strategy, case in point for, 82–83

Compiling the case for change, 49–50, 53

Complexity, aversion to, 240–241

Conditions for Just-In-Time strategy, 256–257

Conditions for success, 78–80

Conducting impact analysis, 173–176, 175–176, 177–178

Confusion caused by change effort, 116

Confusion of roles, 32

Conscious leadership approach, 258–259

Conscious process thinking, 8

Conscious transformation: change process models vs. change frameworks, 11; defining mindset/style/behavior, 60–61; dimensions of, 7; methods of leading, 115–116; principles of, 10. *See also* Change Process Model

Consensus style of decision-making, 78

Constraints, organizational, 149

Consultants: building proficiency as change, 262–263; roles of, 34. *See also* Leaders

Consulting services, 161–163

Consulting strategies, 253–258, 257–258

Consultive input style of decision-making, 78

Content component of change strategy, 4–5

Continuous improvement, 225

Controlling style of leadership, 8

Cost assessment, 176

Counseling for employees, 193

Course correcting, of desired state design, 176–177

Course correcting the Implementation Master Plan, 205–206, 208

Course Correction Model, 87

Creating conditions for success, 78–80

Creating process for analyzing desired state, 173–174

Creating process/structure for desired state design, 160–168

Creating shared vision, 134–137

Creating unified initiatives, 115–116

Creating working relationships, 33–34, 51

Critical mass of support, 77

Cultural imperatives, 151

Culture scanning groups, 99

Current state. *See* New state

Customer requirements, clarifying, 152–153, 154

D

Decision making: about timing, 190; clarifying style of, 77–78, 107

Definitions: integration, 214; leadership styles, 60–61; mastery, 214; organization, 14; process, 8, 263; right people, 33; types of change, 3–4

Degree of urgency, determining, 48–49, 49–50, 53

Demonstrating end of old way of operating, 141–143, 145

Design levels applied to reorganization, 164–166

Design of future state vs. vision of transformation, 159–160

Design of impact analysis process, 174

Design requirements: benefits of clarifying, 148; "decision rights" for, 33; determining, 148–153, 154

Designing strategies. *See* Strategies

Desired outcomes: assessing drivers of change, 40–44; assessing system dynamics of organization, 44–45; and compiling case for change, 49–50; degree of urgency, determining, 48–49; elements of, 39–40; identifying staff/process, 40; identifying type/scope/targets of change, 47; performing initial impact analysis, 45–46

Desired state: analyzing, 173–176; designing, 160–169; mistakes of announcing, 171; monitoring/course correcting topics during implementation of, 206–208; refining, 176–177, 231. *See also* Implementation Master Plan; New state

Determining pacing strategy/timeline for Implementation Master Plan, 189–191, 197

Developing executive/leadership teams, 67–70, 73

Developing implementation plan. *See* Implementation Master Plan

Development plans, initiating, 73

Developmental change, 3–4

Developmental strategies for learning Change Process Model, 236–239

Dimensions of conscious transformation, 7

Dimensions of focus for leaders, 6

Discussions about change process, 132

Downstream stage of transformation, 10, 201

Drivers of change, assessing, 40–44

Drivers of Change model, 5–6

Dynamics, human, 131, 218–219
Dynamics of change: political, 76–77; reactions, 131. *See also* System dynamics

E

Education, of teams about change, 72
Emerging Mindset vs. Industrial Mindset, 8, 9
Emotional aspects of change: attending to, 89–92, 109, 139, 184; creating rituals, 194–195; dynamics of, 131; participation of employees, 118–120; strategies for minimizing, 192–194; supporting people's reactions, 203–204; well-being of organization, 211–212
Emotional domain of human experience, 6
Employees: assessing capacity of to engage in transformation, 58; counseling for, 193; creating collective intention in, 129–130; participation of, 118–120; support for, 192; training of, 139, 140; understanding of change effort by, 116. *See also* Emotional aspects of change
Energy, sustaining, 188–189
Establishing conditions required to support Implementation Master Plan, 191–192, 197
Executive team: developing, 73; educating, 72; engaging, 60; role of, 30, 70
External consulting services, 140, 161–163, 252
External vs. internal leadership, 251–253

F

Facilitative style of leadership, 9–10, 163
Failure of change effort, 188, 239
Fifth Discipline, The (Senge), 45
Fifth Discipline Fieldbook, The (Senge, Kleiner, Roberts, Ross, Smith), 45
Fit of change effort, determining, 116
Five Levels of Communication, 81
Flexibility, in adherence to measures, 104

Flow chart of Implementation Master Plan, 186–187
Focus: areas of for generating impact issues, 172; dimensions of, 6; of leaders, 59; narrow, 161–162
Frameworks vs. change process models, 11
Fullstream process, Change Process Model as, 15–18
Fullstream Transformation Model, 10–11
Future Search: An Action Guide to Finding Common Ground for Action in Organizations (Weisbord & Janoff), 85

G

Going faster, 241–243
Gradual approach to letting go of old ways, 142
Group leaders, 184
Group work, 255–256

H

Human dynamics, 131, 218–219
Human experience, domains of, 6

I

Ideas, generating, 152
Identifying actions for Implementation Master Plan, 182–183, 184–188
Identifying best practices, 226–228
Impact analysis: creating process for conducting, 173–177; gathering of data, ongoing, 177; performing initial, 45–46, 53. *See also* Assessment
Impact assessment of desired state design, 176. *See also* Assessment
Impact directions among drivers of change, 6
Impact group leaders, 182–183
Impact resolution plan, 185
Implementation Master Plan: communicating to targets of change, 195–196, 197; design strategies for sustaining energy,

186–197, 188–189; determining pacing strategy/timeline for, 189–191, 197; establishing conditions required to support, 191–192, 197; identifying actions required for, 182–183; initiating strategies for supporting people in, 192–194; integrating individual, 184–188; monitoring/course correcting, 205, 208; resolving individual impacts of desired state, 184; rolling out the, 202–207, 208

Implementation of desired state, 207

Implications of desired state, 176, 178

Improving new state, 224–225, 225

Individual client work, 255–256

Individual Transition Model, 193

Industrial Mindset vs. Emerging Mindset, 8, 9

Information: collection of, 176; importance of gathering, 148–149; open-mindedness to new, 85–86; "outside the box," 100

Information generation networks, 100, 108

Information generation strategies, designing, 85–86

Informed guesses, 120

Informing the organization of change, 107–108

Infrastructure and conditions supporting change effort: clarifying process/style for decision making, 77–78, 107; conditions for success, creating, 78–80; course correction strategy/system, 86–89, 109; creating conditions for success, 107; creating shared vision, 84–85, 108; designing/initiating communication plan for change, 80–84, 107–108; determining/initiating measurements of change, 103–104, 110; emotional aspects, minimizing, 89–92, 109; information generation strategies, designing, 85–86, 108; initiating support structures, 109; initiating temporary rewards, 105–106, 110; initiating temporary support structures, 92–101; politics of change in, 76–77; securing resources to support change, 102–103, 110

Initial Impact Analysis Audit, 46

Initiating process of developing teams, 67–70

Initiating strategies for supporting people with Implementation Master Plan, 192–194

Initiatives, integrating, 115–116

Integration: definition of, 214; of design efforts across organization, 163, 196–197; ideal state of, 214–215; of individuals into Implementation Master Plan, 184–188; of initiatives in change effort, 115–116; of new state, 215–217, 217–219, 220; of organizational changes with new mindset, 65

Intention, creating collective, 129–130

Interactive impacts, 172

Interim business management structure, 94–96

Internal vs. external leadership, 251–253

Interpretation of purposes of phases of Change Process Model, 243–244

Intuition, 265

J

Jacobs, R., 85

Janoff, S., 85

Job requirements, 150

Just-in-Time change consulting strategy, 253–258

K

Kickoff communication, planning your, 83–84, 131–132

Kleiner, A., 45

Knowledge, increasing organization's change, 144

L

Leaders: addressing mindset/style/behavior, 60–65; assessing capacity of, 57–58; assessing mindset of, 60; assumptions of, 75, 102–103; building

commitment/alignment for, 65–66;
building proficiency as, 262–263; creating strategy for building capacity of, 60;
developing plans for increasing capacity of, 70, 73; group, 184; impact group,
182–183; initiating education plan for
executives/teams, 66–67; modeling
behavior, 33–34, 88; reason for emphasizing roles of, 243–245; role of, 31–32;
self-exploration for, 263–265; stages of
growth of, 236–239; training/coaching
of, 70; willingness to transform themselves, 57–58
Leadership: behavior, strategy for addressing, 72; considerations for, 263–265;
defining styles of, 60–61; internal vs.
external, 251–253; learning your style
of, 264–265; preparing for the change,
27–28; reactive approach to, 258; roles
of, 29–33; strategy for addressing style/
mindset/behavior, 72; tasks of, 86–89;
of transformational change, 5–6; types
of styles, 8–10; unconscious, 245
Leadership breakthrough process, 62–63
Leading conscious transformation. *See*
Leadership
Learning from change process, 226–228
Learning organization movement, 87
Letting go of past: case in point for, 194–195;
strategies for, 91, 141–143, 193–194
Levels: of communication, 81, 136; of design
applied to reorganization, 164–166; of
development, 236; of expertise/mastery,
237–239; of organizational reality, 6; of
wake-up calls for change, 27
Levels of Design Model, 165
Leverage points for change, identifying,
44–45, 52–53

Ⓜ

Majority vote style of decision-making, 78
Management styles, decision-making, 78
Management systems, dismantling tempo-
rary, 96, 228–231

Maps, Project Community, 35
Master practitioners, 238–239
Mastering methodologies, 254
Mastery: of change education topics, 66–67;
definition of, 214; levels of, 237–239;
of new state, 215–217, 217–219, 220;
professional/personal growth for,
262–263
Measurements of change, 103–104
Mechanisms to improve new state, 225
Meetings about change process, 132
Mental domain of human experience, 6
Methodologies: attributes of Change
Process Model, 247; change process,
12–13; mastering, 254
Midstream stage of transformation, 10, 159
Milestones, identifying, 120–124
Mindset: aligning/integrating changes
with new, 65; assessing leader's, 60–61;
of customers, 153; exploring your own,
264; importance of, 245–246; of leaders,
effects of on change, 26–27; mistakes of,
161–162; organizational, 150; process
for changing organizational, 64–65; pro-
moting change of, 144; strategy for
addressing leadership, 72
Mission, 150
Mistakes: of design process, 161–162; fear
of making, 237–238; underestimated
disruption of change, 171
Modeling behavior. *See* Behavior modeling
Models: Course Correction, 87; Design
Model, 165; Drivers of Change, 5–6;
Fullstream Transformation, 10–11; Individual Transition, 193; Levels of Design,
165; Seven Stages of Transition, 90, 91;
Transition, 90. *See also* Change Process
Model
Mohr, B., 91
Momentum, building organizational, 65
Monitoring: change process topics, 205–206;
during Implementation Master Plan,
208
Monitoring/course correcting during imple-
mentation of desired state, 206–208

Morale, 192–194. *See also* Emotional aspects of change; Employees

Motivation: for changing leaders' mindsets, 64; rewards for maintaining, 105–106

Multi-directional approach to change, 243–246

Multiple project integration teams, 97–99

N

Navigation centers, 99

"Nerve center," 99

New state: attention to ending phase of, 223–224; declaring/celebrating, 212–213, 219; optimizing performance of system, 217–219; refining/improving, 224–225; support of individuals/work units in mastery of, 214–215; supporting integration/mastery of, 213–219. *See also* Desired state

Novice practitioners, 237–238

O

Open-mindedness, 85–86

Operating system: Change Process Model as, 248–251; designing an, 163. *See also* Change Process Model

Organic operation of change process, 36

Organization, definition of, 14

Organization development (OD): building consulting proficiency, 262–263; consultants, 253–254; history of field of, 1–3; practitioners, 162, 216, 236–239

Organization of start-up of change effort, 28–39

Organizational constraints, 149

Organizational mindset, process for changing, 64–65

Organizational reality, levels of, 6

Organizational studies, 149

Organizational understanding, communicating case for change, 130–134, 143

Organizations: assessing current reality of, 154; assessing readiness of for change, 55–59; building change knowledge/skills of, 144; system dynamics of, 52–53; transformation of, 5–6

Outside consulting services, 140, 161–163, 162–163, 252

"Outside the box" information, 100

"Ownership" of Change Process Model, 251–253

Ownership of the vision, building, 136–137

P

Pacing strategy, 190

Participation: clarification of strategies for, 118–120; creating collective, 129–130; emotional aspects of, 118–120; gaining commitment to, 118–120; types of, 119

Partnerships: between content consultants and organization development practitioners, 162; project/process, 33

People component of change, 4–5, 151, 160

People's reactions, attending to, 203. *See also* Emotional aspects of change

Performance, optimizing individuals', 215–217, 220

Personal transformation, 6–8, 138–139, 263

Phase I overview, 25–26, 27–28

Phase II overview, 129–130

Phase III overview, 147–148

Phase IV overview, 159–160

Phase V overview, 171–172

Phase VI overview, 181–182

Phase VII overview, 201–202

Phase VIII overview, 211–212

Phase IX overview, 223–224

Phases of Change Process Model, overview of, 14, 15–16

Physical domain of human experience, 6

Pilot testing design of desired state, 166–167, 168–169

Planning for change, 10–11

Policies: during change, 92–101, 109; communication of people support, 192–193; dismantling temporary, 96, 228–231; organization's people support, 192;

temporary management systems and, 100–101

Politics of change, 76–77, 151

Positioning the transformation, 133–134

Practitioners of change leadership, 236–239

Principles, of conscious transformation, 10, 115

Priorities: setting clear, 33; during transitions, 94–95

Priority of change effort, determining, 116

Process: beginnings of change, 26–27; for building change strategy, 114–117; for changing organizational mindset, 64–65; of creating desired state, 168; creating shared vision, 84–85; definition of, 8; designing impact analysis, 174, 177–178; evolving your definition of, 263; identifying for accomplishing project, 52; leadership breakthrough, 62–63

Process orientation, 8

Proficiency as change consultant, 262–263

Proficient practitioners, 238

Project briefings, obtaining, 28, 50

Project community, identifying, 34–39, 52

Project Community Map, 35

Project teams, 31, 96. *See also* Teams

R

Reactions to Change Process Model: areas influencing, 235–236; attending to people's, 89–92, 203; aversion to complexity, 240–241; dynamics of, 131; go faster, 241–242; structure and security, 240. *See also* Emotional aspects of change

Reactive approach to leadership, 6, 258

Readiness for change: assessing, 56–58, 71; case in point for, 56–57; identifying strategy for building, 59; increasing capacity for, 137–141, 144; promoting required mindset/behavioral changes, 141

Real Time Strategic Change: How to Involved an Entire Organization in Fast and Far-Reaching Change (Jacobs), 85

Reality, assessing organization's current, 154

Refining desired state design, 176–177, 178, 231

Relationships: creating working, 33–34, 51; identifying lower functioning, 36

Resistance, dealing with, 77, 202–203

Resistance to integrating Implementation Master Plan, 185

Resolving impact issues, 181, 183, 184

Resolving individual impacts of desired state, 184

Resources, ensuring sufficient, 102–103

Responsibilities: communication of, 96; giving to key players, 130; of taking on change leadership, 29

Results of impact analysis, communicating, 178

Rewards: for achieving desired state, 213; for motivating staff, 105–106; for supporting change process/outcomes, 105–106

Right people, 33

Rigidity, in adherence to measures, 104

Risks of celebrating new state, 213

Rituals, creating, 194–195

Roberts, C., 45

Roles: during change, 92–101; of change consultants, 31–32; change leadership team, 30; clarification of, 51, 215–217; clarifying leadership, 29–33; dismantling temporary, 96, 228–231; ending special, 229; executive team, 30, 70; leadership, 30–31; project teams, 31; sponsor, 29; team leadership, 30; team project, 31; during temporary change, 109

Rolling out Implementation Master Plan, 202–207, 208

Ross, R., 45

S

Samples: change strategy highlights, 122–123; flow chart of Implementation

Master Plan, 186–187; Project Community Map, 35; template for building change strategy, 121; Temporary Change Structure/Change team Network Structure, 94; temporary management systems, 100–101; temporary policies, 101
Scope of change, 5–6, 47–48, 53, 164
Scope of organization, 190
Security and structure, 240
Self-exploration, 141, 261–262, 263–265
Self-organizing style of leadership, 8–9
Senge, P., 45
Seven Stages of Transition Model, 90, 91
Shared vision, creating, 84–85, 108, 134–137
Signals for change, recognizing wake-up calls, 26–27
Skills, building change, 139–140, 144
Slowdowns, causes of, 258–259
Smith, B., 45
Special project teams, 96
Speed of change, 241–243
Spiritual domain of human experience, 6
Sponsor role, 29
Stability in organization, assessing, 58
Staffing: of change effort, 28–33; choosing the right people, 224–225; identifying, 52; for Implementation Master Plan, 182–183; of special project teams, 96; start up, 50–52
Stages of growth for change practitioners, 236–239
Stages of learning change process methodology, 237
Stakeholder maps, 34
Stakeholders, 177
Start up effort, 50–52, 117–118
Start-up staffing, 28–39
Statements, of design requirements, 153, 154
Steps: for accomplishing integration, 216; for changing organizational mindset, 64–65
Strategic levers, 118
Strategies: for accelerating transformation, 259; for addressing leadership behavior/mindset, 72; applying pacing/timeline

to Implementation Master Plan, 189–191, 197; building change, 4–5, 114–117; for building readiness for change, 59, 139; clarifying change, 118–120, 124–125; communication, 36, 82–83; consulting, 257–258; content component of change, 4–5; course correction system, 86–89, 109; creating overall for leadership capacity, 60–65, 71–72; for dealing with politics of change, 106–107; designing information generation, 85–86; designing measurement, 104–105; developmental, for learning Change Process Model, 236–239; dismantling temporary, 96, 228–231; fostering commitment/alignment to change process, 66; identifying, 59, 71; identifying milestones/timelines, 120–124, 126; identifying process for, 114–115, 124; identifying strategic levers for, 118; inhumane/shortsighted, 91; integration and mastery, 215–216; interim business management, 94–96; Just-in-Time change consulting, 253–258; leadership, 72; leadership breakthrough, 62–63; for learning Change Process Model, 236–239; for letting go of past, 193–194, 193–195; measurement, 104–105; for minimizing emotional trauma, 89–92; multiple project integration teams, 97–99; "ownership" of Change Process Model, 251–253; pacing/timing, 189–191; participation, 118–120; scanning other change efforts, 116, 125; for sustaining energy, 186–197, 188–189; template for building change, 121; that don't work, 92. *See also* Implementation Master Plan
Structure: of desired state, 168; dismantling temporary, 96, 228–231; and security, 240
Structure of Change Process Model, 15–18
Styles of leadership. *See* Leadership
Success: creating conditions for, 78–80, 107, 137–141; enablers of, 245; ensuring continued, 224–225

Summary of phases of Change Process Model, 243–244
Summary of results of impact analysis, 178
Support structures, initiating, 34, 109
Support systems, 92–101
Supporting the workforce, 105–106, 192–193
System dynamics: assessing, 44–45, 52–53; during change, 92–101; initiating temporary, 109; of organizations, 52–53
System for refining new state, 224–225
System-wide implications of desired state design, 176, 178
Systems thinking, 44

T

Targets of change: communicating Implementation Master Plan to, 195–196, 197; identifying, 47–48, 53
Tasks, required, 150
Team leadership, role of, 30. *See also* Leadership
Team project, role of, 31
Teams: assessing effectiveness of, 68–70; barrier buster, 100; design, 160; developing executive/leadership, 73; educating about change, 72; importance of unification of, 65; initiating process of developing, 67–70; multiple project integration, 97–99; roles of, 184; samples of temporary structures for, 94; special project, 96
Technological needs, 151
Temporary change support structures, 92–101, 96, 228–231
Temporary management systems/policies, 100–101
Tension, 32
Thinking, reinforcing change in, 65
Thinking discipline, Change Process Model as, 12, 76, 236
Thought process, questions for continuing your own, 261–262
Timeline for Implementation Master Plan, 189–191

Timelines, identifying general, 120–124
Timing, 265
Tools, for performing impact analysis, 172
Top-down versus multi-directional approach to change, 243–246
Topics constituting tasks of leaders, 66–67
Topics to monitor during Implementation Master Plan, 206–207, 208
Training of employees, 139, 140
Training of leaders, 70
Transformation: leadership approaches to, 6; occurrence of, 4; personal, 6–8; positioning the, 133–134; vision for your, 135–136
Transformational change, 3–4, 6–7, 12–13. *See also* Change; Change Process Model
Transition Model, 90
Transitional change, 3–4
Trauma, reducing change, 91. *See also* Emotional aspects of change
Types of change: definitions of, 3–4; determining, 47–48; identifying, 53
Types of participation, 119

U

Unconscious leadership, 245
Unified change effort, creating a, 115–116
Upstream stage of transformation, 10, 153
Urgency, determining degree of, 48–49, 53

V

Value of Change Process Operating System, 250, 251
Values-based vision, 137
Values to model, 151
Vision: assessing yours against current organizational reality, 148–152, 154; creating a shared, 84–85; determining content of, 135, 150
Vision of transformation vs. design of future state, 159–160
Vision statements, 136
Visioning process: building ownership of the, 143–144; rolling out the, 134–135

W

Wake-up calls, recognizing, 26–27

Walking your talk, 203–204

Watkins, J. M., 91

Weisbord, M., 85

Work units, 215–217

Workforce, suggestions for supporting, 192–193

Working relationships, creating, 33–34, 51

Worksheets: assessing drivers of change, 41–42; determining design requirements, 149–151; determining drivers of change, 35, 43; impact analysis audit, 46; Team Effectiveness Assessment, 68–70

Worldview. *See* Mindset

Writing statement of design requirements, 153, 154

Wrong people in roles, 33